PENGUIN BOOKS
DOUBLY DEVIANT, DOUBLY DAMNED

Ann Lloyd was born in Wigan, Lancashire, and educated at Notre Dame Convent there and at Sheffield University, where she gained a degree in English, Philosophy and Economics.

She has been a journalist for twenty-five years, specializing in health and women's issues. During the 1970s she spent eight years in New Zealand and since returning to England has written for such papers as the *Guardian*, the *Independent* and *The Times*, as well as for the medical press. She has been Technical Editor of the *Journal of Medical Ethics* since 1982 and is Assistant Editor of *The Principles of Health Care Ethics* (published in 1994). As well as continuing to write about women's issues, she is also helping to edit an updated edition of the *Dictionary of Medical Ethics*.

Ann Lloyd has also written several radio and television plays and hopes that the idea for her next radio play will lead to her first production.

ANN LLOYD

Doubly Deviant, Doubly Damned

Society's Treatment of Violent Women

PENGUIN BOOKS

PENGUIN BOOKS

Published by the Penguin Group
Penguin Books Ltd, 27 Wrights Lane, London W8 5TZ, England
Penguin Books USA Inc., 375 Hudson Street, New York, New York 10014, USA
Penguin Books Australia Ltd, Ringwood, Victoria, Australia
Penguin Books Canada Ltd, 10 Alcorn Avenue, Toronto, Ontario, Canada M4V 3B2
Penguin Books (NZ) Ltd, 182–190 Wairau Road, Auckland 10, New Zealand

Penguin Books Ltd, Registered Offices: Harmondsworth, Middlesex, England

First published in 1995
10 9 8 7 6 5 4 3 2 1

Filmset in 10.5/12 pt Monophoto Bembo
Printed in England by Clays Ltd, St Ives plc

This book is for Madeleine and Margaret

Before everything I am a human being

NORA IN *A Doll's House* BY HENRIK IBSEN

Contents

Preface

In March 1991 I wrote a story for the *Guardian*'s women's page that was based both on the book by Joyce Johnson, *What Lucy Knew*, and the conference organized by the section of Forensic Psychiatry at St George's Medical School, London, entitled Perspectives on Female Violence.

Sighing over the seemingly insoluble problem of the violence done *to* women, I sent off a copy of the conference's programme, with an accompanying note, to Louise Chunn, who was then the editor of the women's page. Only when Louise rang me to say she was interested in a story about female violence did I realize that we were talking about women who committed violent acts, *not* women who had violence done to them. I had been so conditioned by my unconscious assumption that women are never violent that I had completely failed to comprehend the conference's title. Fortunately, Louise had not.

I am grateful for her understanding, and for the clear and thoughtful brief she gave me for the story that was the seed for this book.

A.L. 1995

Foreword

A judge, recently retired from the Old Bailey, maintained that I was responsible for the rise in female crime. He took pains to explain that, of course, he did not mean me specifically. If women were going to demand equality, he claimed, and were moving into the traditional fields of male endeavour then we should not be surprised to find women committing more crime, especially violent offences. It was the obvious corollary of equal opportunities and 'women's lib' – a captain of industry today, a head of the criminal underworld tomorrow!

The reality is quite different, as Ann Lloyd so potently describes in this book. The profile of female crime has changed little in the past two decades despite the real changes there have been in women's lives. Very few women are involved in professional crime; although more women are now involved in drug offences – importing and selling narcotics as well as using them – they are rarely the prime movers in such organized offending. Increases in female crime correspond with more crime reporting and better record-keeping rather than a wash of deviant female behaviour. Women commit crime largely because of social deprivation and most of the women in our prisons should not even be there.

Media coverage would have us believe that battered women are now taking revenge on mankind and no husband is safe in his bed, but even here the statistics are showing little significant change.

However, there is a small minority of women who do commit violent crime and this book seeks to examine what brings women to that point, questioning many of the assumptions that are made about women who break the rules.

Over the course of my own professional life I have represented many women whose charges have ranged from the most insignifi-cant to the most heinous. At the serious end of the scale they have stabbed, poisoned, shot, garrotted, bludgeoned, burned and bombed, proving that women, too, can commit terrible crimes. However, apart from those involved in politically motivated offences, nearly all those women had killed someone within their domestic world: their children, their menfolk, their lovers (male or female), relatives, friends, neighbours, people (old or young) for whom they were caretakers. They rarely kill stran-gers, are hardly ever serial killers and never stalk their prey.

It became very clear to me over the years that there was a great deal of mythology in the courts about women and crime. There was a generalized belief that the judges were soft on women and they got away with murder. Yet this was not wholly borne out by my experience. If women got a better deal than men it was because they did not commit as serious crimes, and, even when they did, there would often be less aggravating features present.

I remember Ann Lloyd telephoning me, rather concerned that some Home Office statistics were being paraded to show that women were treated at times more favourably than men. But, as studies have now shown, simple number-punching can be very misleading. Robbery is the unlawful taking of another's property by force. It can include anything from the snatching of a shoulder bag by means of a push and pull to a bank raid involving the threat of a knife or the use of a firearm – but both would appear as robbery on a sheaf of statistics. No judge would treat these examples as equally serious and the sentences would reflect the difference in the nature of the crime rather than the gender of the offender. Needless to say, women rarely commit armed robbery.

Judges and juries do sometimes take a sympathetic view of a female offender. The interesting question is, what makes the difference? Which women receive courtroom approval? Some would have you believe that if a woman has a good pair of legs and a snub nose she does not need a defence lawyer. But a better gauge might be Mr Justice Caulfield's 'fragrancy' test as applied by him to that crucial witness in the Jeffrey Archer libel trial. If a woman fulfils society's expectations of the good wife and mother, she is much more likely to secure the judicial imprimatur. It is 'inappropriate' women, who are not passive and conformist but wanton, combative, independent and unconventional, who end up in prison. Sara Thornton is a woman who challenged the stereotype of the cowed, battered woman and is now reaping the consequences.

When judges were first challenged about gender bias they refused to recognize that there was a problem. Indeed, some women did too. They could not see that change had overtaken our political and social institutions and refused to accept that steps needed to be taken to introduce women's experience into the law at every level. The fiction that the law is neutral is one that is hard to shift.

Law does not spring out of a vacuum. Our legal system is based on the common law, which is a body of legal knowledge built up over the centuries by a process of accretion. It is based on the decisions of senior judges in given cases and, until very recently, there were no women involved in that process. It is, therefore, not surprising that a female perspective is missing from our substantive body of law.

Our other sources of law are statutes passed in that haven of male wit and wisdom, the Houses of Parliament, not renowned for their embrace of things female, save in extramural activities. In some instances, that absence of a woman's experience is clearly of no consequence but the recent debate about the law of provocation and its failure in relation to battered women has highlighted one of the serious lacunae. The whole approach to sexual offences is yet another area riven with injustice.

It is important that we understand what drives women to violent behaviour, and the response of the law thereafter. Displays of aggression are seen as the natural downside of traditional male behaviour but are utterly taboo for the fair sex. Ann Lloyd documents many of the problems for women in our criminal justice system and highlights the ways in which it has failed them because there is so little appreciation of the realities of their lives. Nowadays, women are not going to settle for a legal system that does not listen to them or take account of their experience. Women have gone past the stage where they did the adjusting; now it is time for the institutions to change.

It is essential that we are well informed in our quest for justice, which is why this book is a welcome addition to recent works on female offending. Creating a legal framework which is truly equitable requires a proper understanding of life beyond the courtroom door. The symbol of justice may be female, but why should we settle for symbols?

Helena Kennedy QC

Acknowledgements

The author and publishers wish to thank the following who have kindly given permission for use of copyright materials:

Reprinted with the permission of Macmillan from *Women and Crime* by Frances Heidensohn. Copyright 1985 by Macmillan, Inc.;

Reprinted with the permission of The Free Press, a Division of Macmillan, Inc. from *When Battered Women Kill* by Angela Browne. Copyright 1987 by The Free Press;

Extracts from *Justice Unbalanced* (1987) by Hilary Allen, reprinted with permission of Open University Press;

Extracts from *Women, Crime and Criminal Justice* (1987) by A. Morris, reprinted with permission of Blackwell Publishers;

Extracts from *Women on Trial* (1984) by S.M. Edwards, reprinted with permission of Manchester University Press;

Extracts from *Eve Was Framed* (1992) by Helena Kennedy, reprinted with permission of Chatto & Windus;

Extracts from *The Dynamics of Aggression in Women's Prisons in England* (1986) by A. Mandaraka-Sheppard, reprinted with permission of Avebury, Ashgate Publishing Limited;

Extract from *Headrot Holiday* (1992) by Sarah Daniels, reprinted with permission of Methuen Drama, Reed Consumer Books;

Extracts from *Moving Targets* (1993) edited by Helen Birch, reprinted with permission of Virago Press Ltd;

Extracts from the *Daily Telegraph*, the *Guardian*, the *Observer*, the *Sunday Times* and the *Yorkshire Post*.

Every effort has been made to trace all the copyright holders but if any has been inadvertently overlooked, the author and publishers will be pleased to make the necessary arrangement at the first opportunity.

ACKNOWLEDGEMENTS

With very special thanks to Terri Simpson, Pauline Brown, June Clarke, Jackie Child and Miriam Smith.

I want to say a heartfelt thank you to Moira Potier and Gwen Adshead, whose help and encouragement were invaluable.

The work of groups such as Women in Special Hospitals (WISH) and Women in Prison (WIP), and those women they are seeking to help, are at the heart of this book. Without the inspiration of WISH and WIP, the women I met through them and their constant, willing co-operation, this book wouldn't have been written. I want to thank all of them, but especially Prue Stevenson and Jennifer McCabe of WISH and Chris Tchaikovsky of WIP, all of whom were marvellously supportive and gave generously of their time.

Many thanks, too, to Justice for Women, Rights of Women and Southall Black Sisters for all their help, and also to the National Association for the Care and Resettlement of Offenders and the Howard League for Penal Reform. Thanks are also due to: Hilary Allen, Kim Andrews, Marian Barnes, Penny Barrett, Mervyn Barrett, Martin Butwell, Wendy Chan, Anita Dockley, Bridget Dolan, Mary Eaton, Virginia Eatough, Kim and David Etherington, Loraine Gelsthorpe, Chandra Ghosh, Jacqueline Gilliatt, Frances Heidensohn, Jeremy Horder, Julie Humphries, Lucy Johnstone, Sue Lees, Tony Maden, Alexandra Mandaraka-Sheppard, June Martin, Jill Matthews, Jane Mayers, Russell Miller, Allison Morris, Jennifer Munka, Bronwyn Naylor, Paula Nicolson, Katherine O'Donovan, Lorraine Radford, Clare Short, Sara Thornton, Jane Ussher, Philip H. White, Ania Wilczynski, and Paul Wolf-Light.

Thanks to the staff at: the Fawcett Library, London; the Institute of Criminology, Cambridge, and Richmond reference library.

And a final thank you to Ed, for understanding straight away that THE BOOK was 'just one of those things you've got to do'.

Introduction

A major theme of this book is the challenge to women's moral agency as adult human beings which is posed by 'understanding' and explaining their behaviour, violent and non-violent, in terms of their biology and what is seen as their inherent mental and emotional instability. This leads to excusing their violent behaviour on hormonal and/or psychiatric grounds.

Leniency was extended through her psychiatric diagnosis to Hedda Nussbaum, the American who, together with her lover, was charged with murdering their daughter. Her injuries evoked sympathy, and the psychiatric approach offered avoidance of responsibility and blame: she hadn't been responsible.

Raging hormones and moods governed by the moon, i.e. a woman's reproductive cycle, have been held responsible for women's violent outbursts. In court, women who have committed crimes, particularly violent crimes, are twice as likely as men to be dealt with psychiatrically: because they have stepped so far outside their approved social role, they are perceived to be 'mad'.

The seemingly easy acceptance by the courts of Pre-Menstrual Syndrome to excuse women's violence is deeply worrying. Sometimes a woman suffering from PMS may commit a violent act – but what about all the other factors involved, not least her own responsibility for her own actions? If you say that the PMS made her do it, that because of it she was no longer in control, you're putting at grave risk the moral autonomy of all women.

It's been estimated that as many as 90 per cent suffer from something like PMS at some time. The logical conclusion would be to deny women the right to drive cars, make important decisions – run their own lives? – at certain times of the month because you never know when they're suddenly going to go loopy *just because of their inherently unstable, reproductive biology*.

It's not the occasional woman claiming severe PMS as one of a cluster of mitigating factors that bothers me – toothache can make you short-tempered as well – but the ease with which it's been accepted as an excusatory factor and the implications this has for all women.

It is women's reproductive biology which defines them as other than men. If women constituted the ruling powers that be in our society there'd probably be no hormonal theory of women's behaviour, only an easily accepted and widely acknowledged explanation of male behaviour based on fluctuating levels of testosterone, and psychic wounds caused by not having vaginas and depth and internal power, only penises and scrotal sacs.

Those doing the defining, by that very act, are never defined as 'other', but are the norm. Those different from the norm – in this case, women – are thus off-centre, deviant. Man is the norm, the objective standard by which others are measured. Men are perceived to be independent, rational, autonomous and responsible. The 'distaff' side, the other, the female is therefore dependent, emotional, not entirely adult and irresponsible. She is defined in reference to men.

Language reflects this idea of men equalling the norm: for centuries 'man' has meant both men and women, and 'he' has been understood to stand not only for males but, when talking about all mankind, for females too. Language, and the problems associated with its androcentric base, is one of the running themes of the book, impossible to get away from. The use of 'he' to refer to all of us in general and of 'mankind' to mean women and men is not a trivial semantic point.

Imagine, for instance, that you lived on a planet where there were two types of beings, purple cubes and orange spheres, and when you wanted to refer to all the cubes and spheres collectively you used the term 'purple cubes'. How would that leave you feeling if you were an orange sphere? Less important than a purple cube? Insignificant? Overshadowed? And who do you think would have made the decision to use the third person singular of purple cube when referring to all inhabitants? Right, it would not have been an orange sphere. Now you know where the power lies on that planet.

This androcentrism, which makes men the norm, has profound implications for all women, and when it comes to the male-made law we shall see some of the implications for women who are violent.

Women who are violent are not qualitatively different from other women. They are not abnormal, unnatural evil monsters, witchlike and cunning, deadlier than the male. These descriptions are mythical, arising from the stereotypes which themselves are a result of a male-centred, 'other' understanding of creatures governed by their strange biology.

Of course there are women who commit violent crimes that shock us so much we consign them to the 'evil monster' category, Myra Hindley being the obvious example, just as there are men like Dennis Nilsen whose crimes make us cringe with revulsion. Still, the revulsion, the stigma, the vilification are all greater when it's a woman . . .

Another issue that is central to the reanalysis of the perception of violent women is the use of statistics and how it crops up in connection with the law's treatment of women. If, for instance, you wanted to understand how the law treats those who kill spouses and looked just at the statistics on domestic homicides, you'd conclude that women get off lightly and and would puzzle over why so many women are campaigning on their behalf to get the law changed.

However, you can't understand how the law treats domestic homicide in terms just of statistics, something the Home Office itself accepts. The statistics are misleading without the context: they have nothing to say about the circumstances of the crimes they allude to, which in turn prevents us from saying anything confidently about the justice or injustice of the treatment of the particular male and female defendants in those cases. This caveat should be borne in mind whenever disputes involving statistics are described. There's always far more going on, and reality always far more complex, than can be conveyed by statistics.

A further point about context. All that has been said so far – about an understanding of the world which is infused with gender bias without being aware of it, of women being 'understood' in reference to men, in terms of stereotypes based on that referential position and in terms of their 'other' biology – informs everything that happens prior to arrest and right through to treatment in, and discharge from, prison or Special Hospital.

The reality behind the rows of neat statistics is gendered, messy, complex and coloured and shaped by all kinds of factors that cannot be reflected in numbers. What the conviction and sentence figures for all crimes represent is the culmination of a long process that begins with somebody deciding what is a crime and what isn't.

I'm grateful to Dr Loraine Gelsthorpe, Lecturer in Criminology at the Institute of Criminology, Cambridge University, and Fellow of Pembroke College, for raising the following two general points. Firstly, she said, how you record rates makes a big difference. Research has shown that two neighbouring police forces which apparently had very different crime rates were merely recording them differently. The figures looked very odd – were all the criminals in jurisdiction A and all the law-abiding citizens in jurisdiction B? No, reality wasn't changed by different recording practices: it just looked as if it was.

Secondly, Dr Gelsthorpe posed the question: 'When is a crime not a crime?' She suggested we look at how an incident, perhaps a drunken brawl, a bit of a punch-up at a rugby do at the university, would be handled by the college authorities.

Now, suppose the same sort of drunken brawl, another bit of a punch-up, happened in the town amongst a group of local youths? There was a good chance the police would be called in and there was a good chance somebody might end up with a criminal record. The incidents might take place only a couple of hundred yards apart but in the first case, no crime; in the second, crime.

All sorts of prejudices and assumptions need to be borne in mind, as well as the gender stereotypes with which they interact, when considering who commits crime and how they are treated once they come into contact with the criminal justice system. And, just to test the strength of gender assumptions – in the scenario imagined above, substitute female for male and see how you feel. Nearly impossible to imagine the female Cambridge undergraduate in a brawl, isn't it? But picture a local girl in a fight in a pub. Not quite so difficult? But is it a more or less repulsive picture than the local youths scrapping?

We are all influenced by assumptions about what is appropriate behaviour for women and men, whether or not we are aware of it. The strength of these largely unconscious attitudes and assumptions is shown up by the way we react to violent women who, if they do not conform in all other respects to approved societal stereotypes for women, are at very great risk of being treated harshly.

One final note about another manifestation of the androcentric, semantic problem: the use of the word 'violent'. It has been tainted by its association with male violence. When I talk about a violent man, I mean one whose behaviour, interactions with others and life are characterized by a willingness to resort to physical aggression. It's always there, the likelihood of an explosion, looming. He may shout when others talk, lash out when others shout, attack when others swear. It describes an ever-present tendency; it describes the way he lives his life.

So, when you take this tainted adjective and put it in front of the word 'woman' it carries all that baggage with it. But most of the violent women I have met have been violent only once; the others, like Terri Simpson in Chapter 1, have been violent in response to tough circumstances as a way of survival. Typically, the very few women who are violent are less violent than men, much less frequently, and not in that characteristic, threatening, daily way. This needs to be borne in mind whenever the phrase 'violent woman' or 'violent women' appears in the book. The alternative is always to use the clumsy and cumbersome 'women who commit a violent act or acts'. It is yet another language problem.

Chapter 2 looks at the causes of aggression and asks why men are more aggressive than women, something which is undoubtedly true. It assesses, and rejects, the perennial and seemingly ever-popular arguments of those who seek to reduce the understanding of humanity to biology in the form of instincts, hormones or genes.

The argument for the force of culture on moulding human beings' behaviour is also considered. The conclusion reached is that male aggression is no more biologically determined than its supposed counterpart, female passivity. There is no single explanation for human behaviour or passivity or aggression: a complex interplay of cultural and biological factors, in which we ourselves are influential actors, helps to make us who we individually are. The important point is that we can change our behaviour, as individuals and as societies. If we didn't tolerate – or even encourage – greater male aggression we'd have much less of it. All of us have the potential for aggression, compliance and assertiveness. If we accept male violence as inevitable, then it will be – it becomes a self-fulfilling prophecy.

Chapter 3 considers the history of the explanations of women's crimes being rooted in women being understood as 'other',[1] and in terms of their biology and their conformity to the stereotypes arising from women being explained in reference to men, primarily in sexual terms. It also looks at the implications of the fact that there are so few women who are violent, which makes them appear freakish and 'truly' wicked to have deviated so far from the norm of good womanhood.

The kinds of crimes that women commit, especially violent crimes, and how they are treated by the courts, are discussed in Chapter 4. We shall see both how the argument that women are treated with chivalry by the courts doesn't hold up under closer examination of the statistics, and how women's ability or failure to measure up to the stereotypes affects their treatment. While it will become clear that some individual women gain from being 'psychiatrized' and others who have harmed their children profit by virtue of being mothers, such benefits are not handed out to those women who are perceived by the courts to fall short of proper standards of womanhood and/or not being good mothers.

Chapter 5 focuses on the experiences of battered women who have killed their abusers and their subsequent treatment by the courts. The first part examines the different patterns of spouse killing: when the man kills and when – much more rarely – the battered woman kills her abuser. The law in this area is shown to be historically male-made, grounded in male experience, fitted to a male view of the world which claims to be objective and which knows nothing of the realities and experiences of women's lives. The experiences of battered women fall outside the scope of the law.

Then there is a detailed examination of the statistics which have been offered on more than one occasion in the press as proof that battered women who kill are treated leniently by the courts. However, once you are aware of the conflation of battering scenario killings and the category 'domestic homicide', plus the contexts of most of the killings and what is not shown by the figures, such claims of leniency lose force.

The chapter goes on to discuss the different legal defences used by battered women who have killed and the complications and problems they have experienced. It concludes by considering what we can learn from developments in the United States, and by reviewing suggested changes to the law aimed at gaining more justice for battered women who have killed.

The subject of Chapter 6 is women in prison: the kind of women who go to prison and the nature of their crimes. Their experiences of prison are described, highlighting the major ways women suffer more than men.

The problem of women's greater aggression in prison and being harder to handle than men is also addressed. The explanation is fundamentally to do with being women: as mothers they have previously been closer to and more responsible for their children than most paternal offenders. But unlike many men who have wives on the outside to look after the children and keep the home going in their absence, many of these women, being divorced, separated or single, don't have a partner at home to do this. Women suffer much more stress than men while in prison, worrying about the welfare of their children and the breakup of their families.

That is one of the two reasons for their greater explosiveness, troublesomeness and aggression in prison. The other is that they are subject to far more petty rules and regulations and much closer supervision than the men. Higher standards are expected of women already under more emotional pressure than men because of anxiety about uncertainties to do with their children and their homes outside.

Chapter 7 focuses on women-offender patients, i.e. those who come via the criminal justice system and form the majority of women in the Special Hospitals. The kind of women who go there – and how much more likely it is for them to be sent there, proportionally, than men – is examined, as is the campaigners' anxiety about the (mis)use of the label of psychopath which is attached to many of these women and often results in their transfer to a Special.

The women's experiences of life in the Specials are related, as far as possible, in their own words. Mostly they feel frightened, powerless, degraded and infantilized. Few ex-patients feel they received any help there. They regard drugs as a means of control, and ECT and seclusion as punishment. In recent years, happily, there has been a decreasing use of seclusion. One woman describes the distressing experience of having to conform to acceptable feminine behaviour to 'prove' she was normal, i.e. to prove she was getting better.

The biggest fear for the women is to do with the indeterminate nature of what they see as their sentence. How do they know they'll ever get out? This fear is compounded by another anxiety: if, as seems the case as far as they can see, they are receiving no treatment, how will *they* know when the women are better? How will *they* know when they can be safely released?

Chapter 8 deals with the distressing and complex problem of women who turn their violence in upon themselves. The phenomenon of self-harming is much more common with women than with men and a devastatingly common problem with women in Special Hospitals. One study found that of forty women diagnosed as psychopathic all either were, or had been, self-harmers.

In the concluding chapter I offer some possible ways forward to ensure better understanding of, and better treatment for, the very few women in our society who commit violent crimes.

Tale of Two Women

TERRI SIMPSON

'I was born in Airdrie, Scotland, in 1961. I'm a Cancer. That means I've a soft centre but hard on the outside, I've a hard shell. Physically someone could beat me up and it wouldn't bother me, but they could say something and it would tear me to bits.

'My Dad, my real Dad, was in the merchant navy so he was always away. There were four of us, four kids. My Mum left him. She told us he'd tried to hang himself with his tie from the banister so she took us to live with her mother. They didn't get on. I was about three or four then.

'Eventually Mum got her own place and got involved with a man who became my stepfather. He started beating up on me. He singled me out; he didn't hit my brother and sisters. He used to beat up my Mum too. I remember she used to be there, crying on the stairs and I'd be there beside her, crying as well. In her frustration she used to turn round at me and say: "It's all your fault, you little bastard", and she'd wallop me. Mum used to put that foundation cream from Avon on me to cover up the bruises.

'I used to nick coppers from my Mum's purse but I always got caught. My elder sister used to nick as well but she never got caught; I always got the blame so I never got on with my elder sister. My Mum nearly killed me once with a poker but I managed to kick out at her and it landed on a lamp standard instead. I think that frightened her.

'I ran away once and refused to go back for a week. The neighbours used to get the NSPCC round. But not a lot happened when they came round. Right in front of my stepfather they asked me – and I'm five or six years old and terrified – they asked me if I liked him. I mean I'm not going to say anything, am I?

'Eventually my Mum put me in voluntary care. I don't know why she did it but maybe she was frightened of what both of them might do to me. At that time we were living in Norfolk and my real Dad used to come down and visit from Scotland; the idea was that I'd go and live up there with him and his family when I was a bit older. I worshipped my Dad.

'When I was in care I went up there. I went up there when I was twelve. And he raped me. My real father raped me. So, you know, all my worshipping totally disappeared. I was totally disillusioned. I hated him.

'In those days no one believed me so I had to deal with that on my own. It wasn't until my lifestyle as a junkie that I would have anything to do with blokes. I was quite frightened of them. But then I realized they weren't all the same because some of the people who saved my life when I was living on the streets were blokes.

'I was seven when I went into care and couldn't go home for holidays because within a couple of days the beating would start again. My experiences of being in care are of rewards and punishments but mainly strictness and punishment and no affection. In my first home we all had little numbers. I remember my wellies fell off the shelf once and I got what we called the "beat-about". They used to take you into the dining-room and beat you with this plastic baseball bat. Your bottom lip used to quiver but you'd never cry, you wouldn't cry.

'I also became disruptive at school because I was a bit slow at reading and writing. I was naturally left-handed but used to get slapped for it. And if you had problems at school and were in care you were treated differently. Most kids who were caught smoking would have a letter sent home to their parents, but kids in care would be expelled. They saw you as trouble anyway because you were from a kids' home. It's very hard to understand that when you're little: you're made to feel you're a horrible, evil person because of the way you are treated.

'Society automatically saw you as having done something

wrong to get into a kids' home. I think I brought myself up with the feeling that my Mum didn't like me, that my family didn't like me, so I must be a horrible person and that's what I thought about myself for years.

'And in the care system there's no time for anyone who's hard to handle, who gets caught smoking, is disruptive in school, fights with the other kids, runs off; they just move you on. I went to the same assessment centre eight times.

'So, on top of feeling like you were a little shit, you had all these messages coming at you, confirming. I'd never been in trouble with the police, not until I was fifteen when I got done for shoplifting. My only contact with the police was through running off. They'd bring you back. I used to run away to London. Not because of the bright lights but because it was such a big place it took them ages to find you.

'Some of the kids' homes were so big and all different age groups – you either learned how to stand up for yourself or you became a mug for the rest of your life. Because kids bully each other, bigger kids pick on you and that's where I began even more so to toughen up – to survive it, really. You had to learn to stand up for yourself no matter how young you were. The weaker ones didn't get very far.

'I had no contact with my family. My stepbrother Kevin, he went into care, and he was at the same assessment centre as I was for about a month. And my mother came to visit him and when she came to visit him they had to put me in a holding room with two members of staff because my Mum didn't want to see me. So there I was with two members of staff because my Mum was coming to pick up my stepbrother to take him out for the day. And I'd be there all day until she delivered him back.

'I think it was because my Mum was embarrassed, didn't know what to do. I don't really blame her anymore, not that much. It wasn't nice at that age but I'm older now and I can maybe understand a lot more than I did then. OK, I didn't help myself, I know that, but I think in the beginning I was a victim of circumstances.

'When I was fourteen I went to an older couple for Christmas. They had kids of their own but they were foster parents as well.

And they wanted to foster me. They tried for about a year. From the word go I got on really well with them. The plan was I would go to school there. They let me do basically what I wanted to do as long as I was straight with them.

'But Social Services wouldn't agree to them fostering me. They said I was too old. But I believed it was because this elderly couple had succeeded where the care system failed and that was embarrassing for Social Services.

'They laid down the law, were straight with me; they trusted me and I responded to that. They gave me responsibility and that worked. So my only chance of having stability and family life was denied. The authorities always, always knew what was best for me: no one ever asked me. I used to hate that.

'No one ever asked me why I was behaving the way I was – not in care, in prison, nowhere. No one ever asked me that. None of that kind of time was spent with you. So it became more and more of a problem because I had nowhere to direct it and I became quite, like, aggressive and violent. It was a cry for help. That was the only way you could get some kind of attention, even though you never got the right kind of attention, you never got what you were crying out for which was: "Listen to me, I'm not a happy person." You never got anyone helping you with that. They wouldn't listen.

'It became like a habit, I suppose. I learned to talk with my fists but nothing else. I hadn't learned any other way. The concept of surviving was to be tough. And the only way you could be tough was to be violent really, aggressive, beating up on each other. There were loads of kids who were quite violent, girls and boys. There were always your little gangs, you know. There always seemed to be fights.

'Eventually I got involved in drugs; I was thirteen when I started smoking pot; by fifteen I was, sort of, fixing. It came in with people who'd run off; they'd bring it back. Then eventually you'd run off and get it.

'The drugs for me were like a two-finger job: you say I'm not supposed to do this so I'm going to do it. It became a battle with the system. You weren't getting any help from them – eventually you became a rebel in all aspects. But then when you took the drugs you felt good, like you were on top. You were relaxed and all laid back and nothing bothered you. It was like going on holiday.

'We did everything with kids from other homes; we only really mixed with each other. So that was why, when I was sixteen, and they said right that's it, you got two weeks to go, to get out – because I was in voluntary care – I didn't know anybody outside an institution, I hadn't even been to a disco without the rest of the kids' home. I couldn't go home – home was just totally gone by then. I was shoved from pillar to post and became quite aggressive and violent, smashing windows with my fist and being disruptive like that and getting into fights.

'Sixteen years of age and they said I'd got to go – where, I didn't know. They weren't going to help me. They didn't tell me anything. We were right in the country. Norwich was three or four miles away. So I didn't know where I was going to go, I didn't know how to sign on or where I was going to get any money from, I was going to be totally on my own. I just – I didn't know what I was going to do. So I set fire to the place, the home, I was just so terrified.

'I don't know why I chose fire. I suppose it was like another cry for help really: what the hell am I going to do? So I got arrested and remanded in custody. As far as I'm concerned, I mean I know it was a silly thing to do to set fire to the place but I didn't know what else to do.

'There was no one I could go to and ask for help about what I should do. In care since I was seven and I'd been taught nothing apart from, really, aggression. All I'd learned in that environment was how to survive – and that was in an aggressive way: survival of the fittest.

'I used to be so wild and angry, I can remember running round the kids' home after a member of staff, with a kitchen knife. I mean believe it or not, him and his wife, they agreed to be seen as my next of kin; you wouldn't believe I was chasing after him with a knife. That was all, like, anger and frustration. I used to lose my temper sometimes. We used to "play-fight" and all of a sudden I'd lose control and I'd start actually strangling someone. I remember doing that a few times — it used to frighten the life out of me. I'd realize what had happened: just for a split second I'd lost control. I was capable of killing, very much so, but for some reason I'd snap out of it. And then it would totally freak me out but that was a lot — there was just so much anger and hurt inside of me from when I was in care and when I was at home.

'Nobody ever asked me if I needed any help. Everybody else knew what was best for me. I feel that if somebody had spent some time with me as a kid, helped me to find my feet, I most probably would have settled down. But they didn't: my behaviour was disruptive so they just moved me on. They put me in a mental home for three days, at one point, when I was fifteen, but they turned round and said, "Get her out of here, she's not crazy." Then my behaviour was so disruptive — by disruptive I mean I used to fight with other kids, like kids do, but it was never dangerous. I never stabbed them or anything, it was just like a fight. I was always running off, always playing up at school and talking back to the teachers.

'But I'd never, like, really hurt anybody in a way that gets you sent to prison. I think I was just defiant more than anything else and on top of that, I became aggressive. I was seen as violent because I used to fight a lot and run away. Out of control, basically, as they say. Lots of the girls I knew in homes got into prostitution and drugs when they left. An awful lot of us ended up on some sort of rocky road. You saw the older ones, the sixteen and seventeen year olds being brought back to the home because they'd been picked up in London and done for prostitution or something.

'The attitude of the police towards kids in the homes was just as bad; they saw you as troublemakers, what with you running off and them always having to find you. But there was no kind of understanding or sort of sympathy there. Because you're in a kids' home, an institution, automatically it's assumed you're there because you've done something wrong. People's attitudes — even towards kids of four and five years old — were that they must have done something terrible to be there. There was no understanding that maybe they're there because their parents had died and there was no one to look after them.

'And the things that go on with staff – they can't be bothered and they're messing around with younger kids, you know what I mean, abusing them. And they're allowed to do it. Well, now a lot of it's coming to light but it used to go on all the time. It was one of those other things in the olden days that people didn't recognize – they'd close their eyes to it. You couldn't complain about a member of staff because it would get you nowhere.

'Anyway, they remanded me in Holloway after I set the fire. I got committed to Crown Court at Norwich and I got a borstal sentence which I served in Holloway. My behaviour in Holloway was . . . I was always in trouble, beating up on the screws and on report all the time. My behaviour still didn't improve very much so I ended up doing eighteen months, all in Holloway.

'I was on C5Y and C5X, that was the psychiatric wing at the time. My aggression was directed towards authority – the police, the screws, the probation, social workers. I've never ever been done for hurting a member of the public because I never have done, it's always been to do with the police and authority of some sort. I was getting punished all the time because of my behaviour, losing remission, CC (cellular confinement – solitary confinement); eventually I refused to come out of my room and then they couldn't punish me anymore. They used to come in and say: "If you don't come out we're sending you to Rampton on Thursday." I'd say: "Go on then." Then they moved me downstairs to C1 where they locked me out of my room, instead of locking me in it. I just used to play 'em up all the time and eventually they would lock me in my room. By playing up I mean I used to ring the bells and be defiant, wallop one of 'em, be really mouthy all the time, refuse to do this, refuse to do that, be on report all the time, running around the grounds when we went on exercise, anything you could think of that would just give them a hard time. Make them work for their living, that was my motto.

'At the same time I still didn't have any stability or anyone to trust. Or if you did trust someone that trust would soon diminish, it would, you know, soon backfire. It was very much like being in kids' home still: no one ever had time for you, you were just punished. I was brought up on punishment and reward, but the rewards didn't – well, there weren't any really, but more than anything you learned about punishment. There was also this lack of trust, lack of responsibility, you never had any of that so you were never really able to develop beyond a kind of mistrust. I set fire to my cell in Holloway.

'And then after eighteen months they sent me to a Richmond Fellowship house in Bristol. I was on borstal licence but that didn't last because I couldn't stand it. They run on group meetings and that, but it was never group therapy, it was always, like, so and so hadn't done their share of cleaning. And when it came to any kind of issues they were just totally overlooked.

'There was a man in there who'd messed around with kids and the majority decided he could go home for the weekend. It was always group decisions but a small group of us turned round and said that, no, he shouldn't go home because we felt he would do the same thing again. Next thing you know on the Monday the CID were there, and he was being arrested because he was mucking around with kids still. But there was no group therapy for him, there was nothing. He wasn't getting any treatment there, none of us were.

'They were all terrified of the bloke in charge. And I had a go at him about it. He was one of those people who'd been everywhere, seen everything, done everything, you know, and he used to really piss me off. So I had a go – a verbal go – in one of the meetings. I told him he made me sick and when he asked why, I said because he'd been everywhere, done everything, seen everything. He hit the roof. Everybody else changed the subject. But he didn't like it that I'd confronted him: he was the boss. He was in charge and he didn't like being criticized.

'I'd already made my mind up I was going by then, anyway. I'd decided that as soon as my Giro came I was off. And it was due the next day. He knew what I was going to do. He knew, like, I was going to clear off. So it was a case of who could get to the post first. We got some of it and he came charging out and grabbed hold of me, the letters flew out of my hand. One of the other young girls had managed to shove some of the post in her jacket and run upstairs. Luckily she had my Giro. So he went charging up the stairs after her, but she managed to drop my Giro down to me and that was it, I was off. I wasn't supposed to leave because I was on borstal licence but they didn't do anything about it. I got the train and came to London. I was about nineteen. I came to London with another girl who knew some people in London. They were into drugs and I was into drugs, I got very much into drugs. All the time.

'I was never in trouble really with drugs until I started getting involved with barbiturates. Then I got involved with barbiturates and that was it. I hadn't been in prison for fourteen months yet I got sent to prison and I got a six-month sentence. And my reputation was still very much there. They put all the women in the holding room. And they said, "Right, Terri, are you going to get undressed" and I said, "Blimey, I've only walked in" – bam, on the deck. They brought more screws up to the reception area and yet I hadn't been inside for fourteen months, yet they were treating me as if the fourteen months had never happened.

'I also got done for beating up police, GBH. But you see the people I was staying with, they had a couple of kids, twins. And I couldn't cope, I didn't like the idea of being around babies at all. I didn't like the idea that I might hurt them when I was stoned so I cleared off. So I was homeless then, living round the West End, getting more and more into drugs.

'I went to that City Road place a few times, that's a crisis centre down by the Angel, to try and get myself sorted out. I had a girlfriend as well at the time. I went to Norwich for a couple of weeks and she went to Southampton, that was to give us a chance to decide what on earth we were doing with ourselves. Homeless Action had offered a place, a flat, for two women, and we were going to move in on the Tuesday after we came back.

'But we came back and we . . . what we call "Hit the doctor" – got a prescription out of the doctor by giving him a load of bullshit – and we got some barbiturates and we just took 'em. We fixed some of them and we were popping. With barbiturates you get to a point where you can't remember that you're taking them anymore but you're still taking them. And we had a bit of drink, couple of cans of lager and some whisky. We'd never drunk with barbiturates before . . . she died and I nearly died. We were crashed out on the street at the Angel and people were just walking over us. A member of the public who thought we were too young to be drinking called the police.

'And her heart had stopped. They got her going again. Then the ambulance came. She died in hospital, in casualty. I was bunged in the back of a police car. My heart had stopped but they got me going again and I was put in intensive care. I woke up on the observation ward with a member of staff of City Road (the crisis centre) sitting there. I was really too stoned so when they told me she'd died it didn't register and I just crashed out again. I remember them saying they'd be back at six o'clock to pick me up. St Bartholomew's Hospital, this was, and they were so nice there, they always have been.

'As I was walking out of the hospital with them at six o'clock suddenly my legs just went, just gave way, when it hit me that she'd died. We'd been going out together for two and a half years. That was the first time in my life that I'd cried. For about four days in City Road I just sat there and cried my eyes out. I believe those four days saved my life. I'd have gone out and just done myself in, but they knew that at City Road and they were concerned. Not long after that I was back in Holloway.

'There was a small group of us, five or six, just people I knew on the drug scene who got on really well and looked out for each other; I'm the only survivor. Within a period of eighteen months all these deaths happened, all due to drugs. The crazy thing is we were all trying to come off. That's always when you're at your most vulnerable, when you're trying to come off. You think one more fling won't hurt, it won't happen to me, so you kept going out having one more fling. It killed most of them apart from me. So there must be a reason, why me? Maybe so they can still be alive in some way. I like to see it like that. We were all so young. And it would have been just a total waste if I'd have died too, nobody would have known.

'One of the things you can't do is you can't make people change. The system can't do it, bunging you inside can't do it, courts can't do it – you have to want to do it yourself. And people can change, people do change but society won't let them change. Our culture here is to bung everybody in little boxes: you know, once a con always a con, once a junkie always a junkie. So for people like me it becomes very, very difficult when we do change. It's the easiest thing in the world, under the pressure you're given, to go back: it's much much harder to plod on and say, I have changed. You are constantly having to prove yourself, to prove that you can be trusted and that you're not the same as you used to be. And that's the pressure of society. That's why so many people end up going back inside, because it's easier. "They won't let me change, why should I?" – that's the kind of thing that happens.

'Then I was in and out of prison. I was in Homeless Action places. I always got on well with Homeless Action. I never used to abuse their places. If I knew I was going to screw up, if things weren't going well and I was on the rocky road again, I'd just leave.

'In 1984 I started a fire – attempted to start a fire. I did £2's worth of damage to an empty house, and £34's criminal damage to a police cell – I just took some wooden boxes from round the pipes – and got remanded in custody and got Section 37/41. Sent to Broadmoor. I was classed as having a psychopathic disorder.

'A 41 is a restriction order – it means you can be detained without limit of time. That was because of the £2 arson damage. But basically I got sent to Broadmoor because of my history. That's all I got sent for: they didn't know what to do so they wanted to lock me up and throw away the key.

'Suite 23 in Broadmoor is the lowest of the low, you can't get any lower than that. Suite 23, it's called, on Lancs 1. And they sent me there. Lancs House is classed as the intensive care unit in Broadmoor. But for people like me it's the punishment block. There's no treatment there, that's a load of crap. I got out of there despite, not because of, them. I had lots of people on the outside who were friends who came every weekend to see me. I never had any therapy there, nothing. But I started talking to my friends on my visits.

'I was made from an illegal junkie to a legal one. I was given injections every week, Clopixol. When I had it in tablet form I was on twenty-three tablets a day of all different kinds: Largactil, Tofranil — you know, anti-depressants, the lot, they just give them to you to control you. If you didn't take them you got 'em in the arse. I was given ECT. Everybody was shoved in the same boat. They had anorexics there. They didn't give a damn if you had eaten on the ward or whatever, if you missed a meal in the dining hall you were classed as depressed. And, of course, ECT was one of the main treatments for anorexics.

'I'd been there about five weeks when I had ECT. I was terrified because when you went for ECT they just bundled you in a room with a shutter across the window. Now to me, I'd been in prison, and to be locked up like that in prison was because you'd done something wrong.

'When I went to Broadmoor you were admitted to York 2. I wasn't even there twenty-four hours before I was on Lancs 1. Two nurses came to see me when I was admitted and all they told me was that if I mucked about on the sports field two great big strapping nursing officers would come and carry me off. And all I was being with them was honest. I told them that in a new situation, because I was frightened, I did one of two things. One, I shut up and say absolutely nothing, or two, I make my mark. And that was the response I got.

'Years later one of those two nurses told me that after coming to see me she told the other staff I wouldn't last a month on York 2, I'd be down on Lancs 1. So from the word go I didn't have a chance.

'To me Lancs 1 was a punishment block. You know, you had toilet rounds — everyone had to sit in the day room and when there was enough of you who wanted to go to the toilet two nurses would go down with you to the bottom of the corridor where the toilets were. And if you missed a toilet round you had to wait till the next one. That was what it was like. And of course in the rooms you had paper pots and plastic pots, you had no proper sanitary facilities. Shutters across all the windows. You slept in strong bedding — untearable canvas gowns and untearable canvas sheets. I remember once being locked in my room because I'd got in a bit of trouble with one of the nurses. I screamed for two and a half hours to go to the toilet because I had nothing to pee in, not even a paper pot, nothing. I ended up having to pee on the floor because I couldn't hold myself any longer. They just wouldn't let me out to go to the toilet.

'I'd got into self-mutilation too. Badly, by this time. I didn't like hurting people, no matter who they were – I didn't like being violent, I hated it, but that was the only way I could express myself. Eventually I stopped doing that and turned it in on myself, I started to hurt myself. It was like me being able to see how bad I hurt, and how upset I was, instead of lashing out in a physical way.

'I used to just scratch myself with pins when I was very young, when I was about twelve, but that was just like another form of crying for help. But it became quite serious. When I was about seventeen I started stubbing fags out on my face and on my arms and I set fire to my pyjamas – while I was still wearing 'em. But then it became a real sort of problem just before I went to Broadmoor. It escalated from there – I used to cut down to the bone. And what they used to do there, well anywhere, they stitch you up without an anaesthetic and they used to sew so tight that your hand used to swell up, your arm used to swell up. And because the stitches were too tight they'd rip and they used to go all full of pus because they were so tight.

'Their attitude when they stitched you up without an anaesthetic was you did it without an anaesthetic, you can be stitched up without an anaesthetic. I remember one time my body was shaking with shock but you wouldn't – it was one of them things again – you wouldn't show that it hurt. You would not show pain. Physically I can take a lot of pain but emotionally I can't.

'It was really just a form of torture. You see, people don't understand self-mutilation. Doctors an' that think it's just attention-seeking but it's not. It's not quite suicide but it's a really big cry for help. They come along and say you'll be able to play noughts and crosses on those arms soon.

'No one ever spent time – the whole time I was there no one ever asked me why I behaved the way I did, why I did the things I did. I think that's one of the major things that will always stick out, that all the way along the line, I've never ever been asked why, or what I wanted. Never. Never ever been asked. And that would make a helluva difference if they did. No one ever asks you ... the thing is in places like Broadmoor a nurse who likes someone who is diagnosed as a psychopath is what they call a 'patient lover'. They don't have any time for people who are classed as psychopaths, they see us as evil. To them we're just evil people.

'If I spoke to a member of staff for more than half an hour I was meant to be having a fling with her. I was seen as socially unacceptable because of the way I dressed and because I was a lesbian. They gave up on me in the end. I used to say I get heterosexuality shoved down my throat all the time. Before my time there was a doctor there who for ten years had made a woman, a lesbian, wear a skirt and make-up, otherwise he wouldn't let her out. And she did it. And they used to say they could see the pain in her eyes. And I used to say no way, I wouldn't do that. Because they couldn't keep me in there for not being heterosexual.

'They tried to stop my friends coming to see me but couldn't because my friends threatened to go to the papers. Same with Rastafarian women or Jewish women, women whose religion demands a special diet. Even in prison you're allowed special diets, to practise your own religion or culture but in these places you lose everything. You lose all identity completely.

'I wouldn't allow them to do it. On Lancs 1 you had to wear dresses. On all the other wards you could have your jeans. I asked why we had to wear skirts on Lancs 1 and they said because it was easier to strip you off if you played up. So I asked them if the men on the equivalent men's wards had to wear skirts too. I wouldn't conform, I wouldn't wear a dress or a skirt, because they wanted me to. I couldn't link arms with another woman going to the central hall even though other women were allowed to; but they were straight and they had boyfriends over the male side. I was classed as being offensive.

'I used to argue about going over the male side to socialize. I used to say I don't want to go over there and socialize with child murderers and rapists, would you? That was my argument all the time, I'd say I'll choose who I want to socialize with. I used to go over the male side but I'd sit with a group of women.

I went to a male work area and I got on with some of the blokes there; got on well with some of the male nursing staff, occupational therapists and so on. But their idea of getting on with blokes was to have a boyfriend and no way, no way. So I refused to conform in that respect and they didn't know what to do with me.

'I saw my Mum as well when I was in there. If you tell them you don't want your parents notified, you don't want to see them, they take no notice. They will not recognize anybody but your biological parents and they notify them. They notified my Mum I was there. So when I was twenty-five my Mum came to visit me. She offered me her friendship but I couldn't have that based on guilt, it was too late, you know what I mean, it was too late. You choose your friends but you can't choose your family. It was just too late really.

'I decided it was about time I got my life together myself. But I realized I hadn't helped myself by getting involved with drugs. There were certain things I could have not done but which I did, unfortunately. I wasn't at fault at the beginning. But I realized I'd enabled my family to destroy me for so long, by how they'd treated me . . . now it was up to me. And I just thought, well, there are some things you can never get answers to, some things are best left unanswered, some things you just work out for yourself. By the time you're twenty-five you think, "Well, I may never get an answer to that so I'm just going to have to start from here."

'And I then did a complete U-turn from one sort of behaviour to another. I just decided that was it, it was my time, I was an OK person – 'cos I always used to ask my mates, you know, why do you come and see me? Why do you like me? There was all this unsureness. I did all my talking and sorting out with my mates. And then I kind of got to realize that I wasn't such a bad person after all, there must be something about me.

'I had tribunals (to assess if a patient can be released). I nearly got my first one and my second one, which was about a year or so later, I did get. No matter what they threw at me in there I dealt with it. It was like water off a duck's back. They used to say to me is this for real or is it an act. I could never act, it would never last. But no matter what they did I just dealt with it. And of course I got out. The 2nd of March 1988. I was there nearly four years.

'I went to a probation hostel in North London and I got on really well there. Came out, got myself on a course at Camden training centre, building and maintenance part-time course. My probation officer rang me up and asked if he should have a word with them but I said no, if I can't get on the course on my own merit I don't want to do it. As a last resort I would have tried the educational places which cater for people who've been in trouble but I wanted to try the other way first. And I got on the course. Then I decided I wanted to do plastering so I went and did a full-time course. Then I applied for two jobs and got a job in Hackney.

'From the probation hostel I moved to a Homeless Action place and I was only there eleven months when I got nominated for the flat where I live now. Then Prue Stevenson and I set up WISH [Women in Special Hospitals, a very active support and pressure group] (see Useful Addresses).

'As part of my conditional discharge from Broadmoor I had to see a doctor and a probation officer, and after a year they could have written to the Home Office for my official release but they wouldn't, so I had to have a tribunal. That was after I'd been out two and a half years. And all they talked about at that tribunal was my badness, my past, nothing that I'd done over the two and half years I'd been out. Nothing of that was mentioned. I'd taken a work colleague along to the tribunal, for moral support. She was crying her eyes out when they said they'd be writing to me to tell me officially that I would be released. She was in tears and I just felt like I'd bloody earned it.

'We had a little celebration that weekend. So then I was totally free of them. Been out four years. All I want now is just to live my life.'

HEDDA NUSSBAUM

In January 1989, one year after Terri Simpson was released from Broadmoor, Joel Steinberg, a wealthy American lawyer, was convicted of beating to death his illegally adopted, six-year-old daughter Lisa. She had been battered before and sexually abused. Originally Steinberg's lover, Hedda Nussbaum, had also been charged but these charges were later dropped. She received psychiatric help, testified against Steinberg and, as they say in the States, 'walked free'.

No one knows whether Nussbaum also beat Lisa but one thing was clear: she herself had been appallingly beaten by Steinberg during the twelve years she'd lived with him. At the time of her arrest, she had deep gangrenous ulcers on her legs, a pulverized nose, a broken jaw, nine broken ribs, a cauliflower ear, a split lip and bruises on her back and buttocks. She was later revealed to have a ruptured spleen, a broken knee and minor brain damage.

Terri Simpson's and Hedda Nussbaum's stories exemplify the central themes of this book. Simpson was seen as a villain: rejected by her mother, she went from institutionalized care to prison, to 'Suite 23 in Broadmoor – the lowest of the low'. All through Terri Simpson's life people, especially those in authority, had found it all too easy to believe the worst of her.

The American public could not believe that Hedda Nussbaum, a woman – and a white, educated, middle-class woman at that – could have taken part in the abuse and killing of a child. The case brought female violence into the light of public scrutiny, but Nussbaum was seen as a victim – charges against her were dropped; she was given extensive psychiatric help and then released.

Could such a woman have done that? No, came the reply from many feminists; women don't do that, women are not violent. And the sub-text went: 'Hedda's not violent, we're not violent, we're the world's carers, the nurturers. You've told us we're not creative, not intelligent – leave us our caring.' Therefore, to be an acceptable woman, Nussbaum had to be seen as somehow not responsible for her actions, as a victim to be pitied, not a perpetrator to be blamed.

And it's true she was, as her supporters said, terribly badly beaten, and seemed very much under Steinberg's control. So much so that she was incapable of doing anything? Not even pick up the phone during the twelve hours Lisa lay dying at her feet? asked Joyce Johnson, in her book, *What Lisa Knew*. If that's what is being said then isn't women's moral autonomy being given away? Isn't that reinforcing the passive, infantilized role women have been struggling to escape from for years?

Only Hedda Nussbaum and Joel Steinberg know to what extent, if any, Nussbaum was responsible for the beatings Lisa suffered and her eventual death. However, the issues surrounding what happened both to Nussbaum and to Simpson, a self-acknowledged aggressive woman, have implications for all women, including those who commit violent crimes.

What the two stories show clearly is that a woman in the dock is going to be judged not only in the light of the crime she is charged with but also in the light of what sort of woman she is judged to be. Nussbaum was perceived as a victim, passive and helpless. She was also white, educated, middle class – in other words, the same sort of person as those sitting in judgment on her, the lawyers, the psychiatrists, the court personnel. She was one of their own, which would have helped.

She got sympathy, psychiatry and leniency to the point of dropped charges and freedom. Simpson's beginnings and the aggression she learned in order to survive the tough world of institutionalized care branded her as deviant from the outset. She wasn't passive, was determined not to be anybody's victim. In the end she too, like Nussbaum, was psychiatrized. But for her that meant Suite 23 in Broadmoor, not sympathy and freedom.

Simpson was deviant in two ways. First of all, she broke the law, which was seen as freakish for a woman anyway because not many do; and she was violent, thereby breaking the 'natural' law that women, far from being aggressive, are passive, nurturing and generally morally superior to the brute male of the species. 'What is the world coming to if women are starting to be violent!' For this double deviancy she was doubly punished.

First, she was more harshly treated than a man would have been for similar crimes – £2.00 worth of damage by fire to an empty house and £34.00 worth of damage to a police cell are what led her to Broadmoor – and second, she suffered a much greater stigma than a man convicted of a violent crime, simply because she was a woman.

Men who are violent are, of course, deeply disapproved of and punished by society but a violent woman is seen as being an unnatural woman. Since women are naturally passive, nurturing and better than men, for a woman to commit a violent act is evidence of her true degradation. *Women just don't do that.*

And, as Simpson discovered, it is much easier for a woman to find her way into a Special Hospital than a man: violent behaviour that is tolerated in a man causes panic, overreaction and sometimes a swift dispatch from prison to a maximum security hospital when displayed by a woman. Once there, a woman faces an indeterminate stay. Though women offenders' crimes are less, they remain longer in the Special Hospitals, on average, than male offenders.

However, as we saw with the Nussbaum case, the stereotype of helpless victim can work for a woman. The woman's gender is in the dock with her: how she is perceived to conform to notions of proper womanhood will affect how she is judged and treated.

A woman charged with a violent crime is already perceived as having behaved in a non-feminine way, because she's broken both the law of the land and the unwritten code for proper female behaviour. Let her then, in her own appearance, persona, circumstances and lifestyle, appear to be further deviant and the chances of her getting harsh treatment are very great indeed.

If she is accused of one violent act (or of a series of violent acts, as in Nussbaum's case) but otherwise fits the pattern of good wife and mother – leading a blameless and conforming life at home with her husband, the father of her children, in a conventional, nuclear family setting – and appears as a contrite victim in court, she may well receive leniency.

That Hedda Nussbaum lived with, rather than was married to, Steinberg, and that their lifestyle involved drugs, was counterbalanced for her by the fact that she had lived with him for twelve years and was very reluctant to testify against him – she talked about worshipping him, and not calling the police when Lisa lay unconscious because she didn't want to show disloyalty or distrust – and by the extent of the injuries which she had suffered. In spite of those injuries, it seemed, she loved him. She was a passive, loving woman devoted, above all else, to her man.

CHAPTER 2

Men, Women and Aggression

'I don't remember getting there. At the point of Ian opening the door I've forgotten I've got a knife. I ask him for my key. He tells Maria to get my key. And then he starts again, calling me names. But they all sound fuzzy. He raises his arm to me and says: "And don't come the fuck back down." And snap. I thump him. Because at this point I've forgotten about the knife.

'I realize he's stabbed. I see the blood. The only part I remember from when I see the blood till being in the police station, talking to a solicitor, is holding Maria by the hair.'

Jackie Child was found guilty of manslaughter and sentenced to three and a half years.

'We crept up behind the German sentries very, very quietly and cut their throats. When we blew up bridges while trainloads of German soldiers were crossing we thought: "That's a few less." '

An 83-year-old woman on Radio 4 describing the work of herself and other women during World War II.

Men are more aggressive than women. There's no argument about that. But that should not blind us to the fact that women too have the potential for violence, although they tend not to realize it as often as men. But why is this? Why are men more aggressive, more violent, than women? These questions to be considered in this chapter are only part of the larger question which has been asked for centuries: why do human beings do what they do?

Though it cannot be universally claimed that men have always, everywhere, been more aggressive than women, that has certainly been the pattern in Western society as far back as records go. For instance, women commit murder at a steady rate of '15 per cent of all murders for as long as anyone has kept records anywhere'.[1] And, as we shall see later, men in this country commit about ten times more violent crimes than do women. Broadly speaking, there have traditonally been two main sets of theories which seek to explain human nature: those which explain it in terms of nature and those which explain it in terms of nurture – thus, the 'nature v. nurture' debate.

Lately, a third view has emerged which I share. This can be most easily described as a dynamic combination of both the nature and the nurture schools of thought. It is an approach which accords importance both to hereditary and to cultural factors. It sees these factors as affecting each individual differently and interacting in a very complex way to produce behaviour which is itself so complex as to be unpredictable in all important ways.

I shall look first at what the innate aggressionist or 'pop ethology' school, and its modern successor, sociobiology, have to say about the causes of aggression. Both sets of theories can be described as being biologically determinist. To make clear what this phrase means: in answer to the question 'Why are individuals as they are?', a biological determinist would answer

> that human lives and actions are inevitable consequences of the biochemical properties of the cells that make up the individual; and these characteristics are in turn uniquely determined by the constituents of the genes possessed by each individual. Ultimately, all human behaviour – hence all human society – is governed by a chain of determinants that runs from the genes to the individual to the sum of behaviours of all individuals. The determinists would have it, then, that human nature is fixed by our genes.[2]

The sociobiologists, like the innate aggressionists before them, have a strong appeal to, and hold on, the public mind, legitimating, as they do, the status quo.

I shall then consider two other explanations for greater male aggression which also seek to explain 'the properties of complex wholes . . . in terms of the units of which [they] are composed',[3] namely, that males are more aggressive because of their possession of the male hormone, testosterone, or because they have a Y chromosome.

Finally, I'll review some of the cultural factors involved in greater male aggression. But all the evidence suggests that the behaviour of human beings in general, and the greater aggression of men in particular, is neither solely biologically nor solely culturally determined Men are no more 'naturally' aggressive than women are 'naturally' passive. The crucial point is that we can change our own behaviour. I reject the impression given 'by modern biological determinists that the simple objective facts of modern science force us to the conclusion that biology is destiny'.[4]

BIOLOGICAL THEORIES OF HUMAN BEHAVIOUR

The Innate Aggressionists

A group of ethologists which includes, for instance, Konrad Lorenz and Robert Ardrey came to be known in the 1960s as 'innate aggressionists'. From their research on animals and early human history they concluded that today men are, by their natures, inevitably aggressive, dominant and territorial because for millions of years they hunted and killed. The killer instinct is, as it were, bred into the genetic bone.

It's not always clear, when reading about innate aggressionist theories, just precisely what it is that is being claimed: that human beings are innately aggressive or that the writer is really thinking only about males as being aggressive. The innate aggressionists' focus is the male, the 'actor'. The female is secondary, complementary. It's another example of the androcentric fallacy mentioned in Chapter 1, and says a lot about the mind-set of the writers/researchers.

These ethologists used research on animals to 'show' that men's 'dominance', as a modern manifestation of aggression, is a natural characteristic. But how valid is it to draw inferences about complex human behaviour from the behaviour of animals? Doesn't the range and the complexity of the differences between us render any comparisons at least a little suspect? Surely the differences between us and animals – consciousness, language, our ability to understand, to conceptualize, to hypothesize, to learn how to innovate, to argue whether we *should* do so – are very much more significant than any similarities?

It must be acknowledged that there is evidence, based on research with rats and mice, that aggression between males is linked to testosterone levels. However, these were rats and mice in laboratory conditions designed to be stressful; in the wild, such aggression is rare. The setting obviously has something to do with the fighting: you can't separate the behaviour from the context.

There's an anthropomorphic circularity to the way animal research is used. When you talk, as some ethologists do, of baboons having harems and ants being slaves, you are anthropomorphizing the animals, treating them as if they had human traits under their animal skins. But the ants and baboons know nothing of these social institutions. They just live in a certain way. Then the researchers come along and 'understand' their way of living in terms of human behaviour and society, and say that the animal behaviour/social grouping proves the human behaviour/social grouping is 'natural'.

Sociobiology

The sociobiologists are the successors of the innate aggressionists. Sociobiology can be seen as the latest manifestation of the attempts to explain human behaviour, and male and female differences, in terms of its biological basis. It's an interdisciplinary science, combining work from genetics, anthropology, psychology and sociology.

Broadly speaking, sociobiologists believe that social behaviour, as it was and as it is, is not only the inevitable, but the best, result of genetic action since evolution selects the traits which lead to the highest levels of reproductive fitness to ensure the continuance of the species and its genes. These include aggression in men and nurturance/passivity in women.

For the sociobiologists, the pattern of successful hunter–gatherer societies – men go out and hunt and women stay home and look after children – provides a genetic blueprint for future generations. At the core of their thesis – and at that of their predecessors', the innate aggressionists – lies the belief that it is a natural given that men do and women wait, that men run things.

Various refutations can be made of the sociobiologist position. The hunter–gatherer description of early human groups upon which the theory is based has been challenged, as has the accuracy of the description of men's and women's roles within such a society. However, for the sake of discussion, let's concede that early human social groupings were characterized by such a pattern. The argument is that the male's strength and aggression (in killing animals) were rewarded by food and therefore survival. When the women were pregnant or breast-feeding they couldn't join in so had to stay home. Thus, today men still go out into the world to run things and women remain behind to look after the home and children. To try to change this would be not only difficult but also dangerous: it would upset the natural order and balance of things. In this way sociobiology simultaneously legitimates and lauds the status quo. If you accept its interpretation, it becomes a self-fulfilling prophecy.

Even if you accept that the picture of early human society underpinning this theory is accurate, you need not draw the same conclusions as the sociobiologists. There's more than one way to interpret versions of history. For instance, what can be seen in this picture of groups of hunter–gatherers is that they adapted their behaviour to fit the circumstances of their lives. The jobs the men and women did gave the whole group their best chance for survival *in those circumstances*. It's as easy to see them as models of community living and co-operation as societies which demonstrated the fundamental importance of the masculine aggressive drive. Furthermore, if the men hadn't been able to control their aggression, and had been violent to each other and the women, they might all have failed to survive.

One of the central weaknesses of the sociobiological view is that it talks in universals. If aggression is genetically determined, i.e. all men are aggressive, then what are we to make of anthropologist Peggy Sanday's cross-cultural study of ninety-five societies which 'revealed that 47 per cent of them were free of rape'? And of Robert R. Holt's report that 'there are at least thirty-three societies in which war as well as interpersonal violence are extremely rare'.[5] Can they all be temporary aberrations from the aggressive norm?

Various strands of argument have developed to explain how the original physical aggression of men is not always equally present in all men or societies. Some sociobiologists talk about a potential being already encoded with the trait in question, which is triggered only when 'the appropriate environmental cue is given'.

> Sometimes sociobiologists try to give both messages [i.e. genetic and environmental] simultaneously: 'Are human beings innately aggressive? . . . The answer . . . is yes. Throughout history, warfare . . . has been endemic to every form of society.' But as one reads on, it turns out that human aggressive behavior is 'a structured, predictable pattern of interaction between genes and environment'. But we are on dangerous ground for sociobiology here. If aggression is manifest only in *some* environments, then in what important sense is it innate and why do we not simply avoid the wrong environments? It is at this point that notions alien to genetics begin to appear.[6]

The determinism of sociobiology has a very worrying bearing for the problem of violent crime, be it male or female: determinism rules out any questions to do with justice. If we are driven by our selfish genes, if they make us necessarily what we are, and the world necessarily what it must be, then questions to do with individual and social justice are meaningless: 'The issue of justice arises only where there is choice.'[7] If we are not responsible for our actions we can be neither praised for good ones nor condemned for bad ones: 'right' and 'wrong' become meaningless terms. But they aren't, are they? Even though we argue about their precise meanings, does anyone seriously propose that they are meaningless?

Testosterone Makes Men More Aggressive Than Women

Both men and women have so-called male and female hormones

occurring naturally in their bodies. They do not possess mutually exclusive sex hormones; men tend to have more testosterone than women, women more oestrogen than men. It's a matter of proportional, not absolute, difference. And there's an important cause-and-effect, chicken-and-egg, question to be asked: when you find high levels of testosterone and aggression, how do you know which one caused the other? There is an assumption being made here that one *does* cause the other. Could it be that the presence of testosterone, where there is an aggressive reaction, is part of a physiological mechanistic process rather than the cause of that reaction?

In fact, we don't know much about testosterone levels and adult males. Such studies that have been done are inconclusive, because either they've not been properly designed, or 'aggression' wasn't clearly defined or it was not clear whether the aggression caused the testosterone levels to go up or vice versa.[8]

Dr Gwen Adshead, a lecturer in victimology, works on the Forensic Psychiatry Traumatic Stress Project at the Institute of Psychiatry in London. On the basis of her own work with violent men and of a recent search of the literature on the subject of violent offenders and testosterone levels she concludes that it is

> very hard definitively to show any connection between testosterone levels and aggression. It's even quite hard to show any connection between testosterone and sexual desire. It's by no means a linear relationship.
>
> There is no reason to suppose at the moment that testosterone has a simple relationship with aggression. For instance, there are case reports of men who've raped women after they've had their testicles cut off.
>
> Testosterone is only one factor in the expression and activity of aggression. And obviously, from the example I've just given, it is not an essential factor. We know today that there are people who've committed violent offences and people who are just generally violent who do not have raised levels of testosterone while there are men with raised levels of testosterone who are not violent. A link between testosterone and aggression is unproved.[9]

Over the last twenty-five years or so research on the testosterone/aggression link has tended to focus on the theory that it's the effect of testosterone prenatally which predisposes boys to be rougher than girls and to learn to be aggressive as they grow older.

A useful summary of the six most frequently cited studies on the role of prenatal hormones in the development of aggressive behaviour in humans is provided by Anne Fausto-Sterling.[10] None of the studies, she says, was unequivocal: 'The claim that clear-cut evidence exists to show that fetal hormones make boys more active, aggressive or athletic than girls is little more than fancy, although harmless it is not.'[11]

A big problem was observer bias, best illustrated by the Baby X revisited experiment. Researchers told one group that a baby was a boy and another group that it was a girl. The two groups were then asked to describe the baby's behaviour. 'All the observers ascribed sex-stereotyped behaviour to the infant.' For example, one observer, describing what he believed to be a girl (although it was really a boy), said: 'She is friendly and female infants smile more.'[12] This illustrates as neatly as anything can the difficulty, first, of separating the biological from the social influences and, second, the difficulty of measuring those two factors. Babies are being handled, reacted to, interacting with other people from the first second of birth: they are born into the world.

The case for testosterone causing aggression is, at the very least, not proven.

An Extra Y Chromosome Causes Male Aggression

Women have two X chromosomes, men have one X and one Y chromosome. Around the late sixties and early seventies there was interest in investigating men with an extra Y chromosome to see if they were more aggressive than normal men. The thinking behind this, I presume, was that because the Y chromosome is *the* male chromosome, then it must be the one that carried the aggression; so, if a man has an extra Y chromosome, he must be doubly aggressive. If that was the thinking, then the assumption had already been made that to be male was to be aggressive.

Efforts to prove this failed; it is now accepted that though men with an extra Y chromosome tend to be taller than other men, they are *not* more aggressive.

Muscles Maketh Man Aggressive

What, finally, of the everyday view which says men tend to be more aggressive because they tend to be physically bigger and stronger? There is something in this: if you are aware your body can be used to inflict pain then there it is, ready and able to demonstrate anger. I can see, therefore, that the temptation to lash out would be greater for men who are, overall, more aggressive than women. Maybe they always will be – if the way they are brought up and the society in which they learn what it is to be a man says that part of masculinity is being aggressive.

However, it is just too simple and overpredictive an explanation. Most men are bigger and stronger than women but most men are not physically aggressive. And some of the most muscular men, i.e. body builders, are no more aggressive than other men. Nor do we see a higher level of physical aggression amongst strong, well-muscled female athletes than amongst other women. It is as insulting to men to say they tend to be more aggressive because they are physically stronger as it is to say women are emotionally unstable because they have menstrual periods.

The greater aggression of men cannot be explained simply in terms of biology. Biology is part of the picture, as it must be, because we all have genes, hormones, and muscles, but the point is that we are not *just* these things, we are social beings with consciousness, with minds. We live in a world with which we interact from the moment of birth – some would say from the moment of conception. The biological and the social are constantly interacting. It's not a question of a lump of 'pure' genes preceding messy reality: the reality is the constant flux mediated by our consciousness, our ability to reflect and to choose.

SOCIO/CULTURAL/ENVIRONMENTAL PERSPECTIVES

What part do socio/cultural/environmental factors play in male aggression?

'Being able to give and take violence is part of what it is to be a man: it's a fundamental part of the construction of masculinity.'
Paul Wolf-Light, co-ordinator of the Everyman project in South London, which aims to help battering men understand and control their violence.

As we saw earlier with the Baby X revisited experiment, expectations and assumptions about gender shape our earliest interactions. The first question that is asked about a baby is whether it's a boy or a girl. (On one Greek island the question is still very often: 'Is it a child or a girl?', showing clearly the strength of androcentrism.) From the first moment of life the child is interacting with its environment; she/he is affecting it and it is affecting her/him. The human infant, with its highly complex brain, continues to develop biologically.

> During its long infancy, connections between nerve cells are formed on the basis not merely of specific epigenetic programming but in the light of experience.[13]

It's in this continuing interaction that the uniqueness of human nature lies.

> ... in organisms with less complex brains most of the neural pathways are laid down – genetically specified – to form rather rigid and preprogrammed connections. This invariance gives such organisms a comparatively fixed and limited behavioural repertoire,[14]

whereas the range of behaviour of human beings is enormously varied.

What happens in infancy and later in the child's life – the way it is handled, spoken to, cared for – will influence its development if, from the beginning, it is treated in a gendered way. This will form its notions of what is appropriate and inappropriate behaviour for it as a male or a female. It's a terrible thing for a little

29

boy to be called a sissy, but not so terrible for a girl to be described as a tomboy (she's merely aping her betters) as long as she grows out of it.

Boys are brought up to behave appropriately as men, and girls as women. Part of what it is to be a man has to do with being aggressive or, at the very least, with 'being able to handle himself'. The construction of the masculine gender in our society contains that.

All the way down from the macro level – men holding the vast majority of positions of power, media images of men as doers and deciders and women seen often only in reference to men – to the micro level – of being told not to cry, boys don't cry, only girls – the boy's world shows and reinforces what it is to be a man in that world.

GROWING UP TO BE FEMALE OR MALE

It is here I want to look now, at the upbringing of boys and girls and how they differ and how that results in men being more aggressive, more violent, than women.

I don't want to give the impression that, while I am *not* a biological reductionist, I am an 'upbringing' reductionist. I believe that the works of Heather Formaini, and Susie Orbach and Luise Eichenbaum, are crucial to understanding the effect this gendered upbringing has on us as adult women and men. It's an extremely important part of the picture. It's a necessary part of, but not a sufficient explanation of, what happens. It is not deterministic. It doesn't explain all men or all women. It's descriptive, not prescriptive. It shows how the influence of our interactions with our mothers tends to shape us as men and women.

For her book *Men: the Darker Continent*, Heather Formaini, a psychoanalyst, interviewed 120 men. Not one of them, she says, and none of the men she has seen in therapy 'feels himself to be masculine'.[15]

From what men tell me about their lives, and from all that I see of the way men behave towards themselves, and other men and women,

I conclude that masculinity forces upon men a split which cuts them off from dealing with their own personal experience. This convinces me that the split in men does an immense amount of psychological damage to individual men, to men as a collective group, and to men as they exist in history. This damage becomes apparent when men try to deal with their feelings. Their impulse towards love, the most human of all impulses, is somehow wounded. Having a split in their internal reality means that men have to use their energy to cover up the wound caused by the split.[16]

Eichenbaum and Orbach explain the upbringing of girls in *Outside In, Inside Out* as clearly as Formaini explains the upbringing of boys. They describe how mothers replicate their own upbringing by teaching their daughters to nurture others' needs while repressing and denying their own.

Boys grow up being taught, unconsciously, two things. First, they learn to devalue and reject the mother/feminine – necessary if they are to attain 'real manhood' – and to repress all feelings (because feelings are feminine) except for the one sanctioned emotional outlet open to men as men: anger, which may be aggressively expressed either verbally or physically. Second, they learn to automatically expect women to care about them and to look after them.

What you then have is a potentially explosive scenario. An important part of being a man is not being a woman, therefore, men need to be constantly on the alert for anyone who challenges their masculinity – and against any woman who threatens to weaken the grip they have on their emotions.

What I have described so far has been the effects on boys and girls of their interaction with their mothers. But children have two parents. Where is the father in all this? Fathers are traditionally authority figures, somewhat distant, and insofar as they are representing unemotional, rational, powerful masculinity, they are going to reinforce for boys their idea of what it is to be a man. To be specific, the tendency of fathers to play more roughly with sons and to encourage them to tolerate more roughness may prove to be a contributory factor to their greater aggression.

Moreover, when children have been naughty, it is twice as common for boys to receive physical punishment as it is for girls who are usually punished verbally, by the threat of missing a treat or of losing their parents' affection.[17]

Could boys thereby learn the lesson that hitting and being hit is 'masculine'?

Although Alice Miller doesn't lay any stress on gender in her book, *For Your Own Good: The Roots of Violence in Child-Rearing*, she does have something very important to say about the causes of violence. 'Poisonous pedagogy' is how she describes the method of bringing up children which is based on obedience, coercion, severity and lack of feeling. Children who experience such an upbringing learn, she says, to squash down – and to forget they have repressed – their feelings of rage at what they have suffered at the hands of their parents and teachers. However, those

who were permitted to react appropriately throughout their childhood – i.e. with anger – to the pain, wrongs, and denial inflicted upon them either consciously or unconsciously will retain this ability to react appropriately in later life too. When someone wounds them as adults, they will be able to recognize and express this verbally. *But they will not feel the need to lash out in response. This need arises only for people who must always be on their guard to keep the dam that restrains their feelings from breaking. For if this dam breaks everything becomes unpredictable* [my emphasis]. Thus, it is understandable that some of these people, fearing unpredictable consequences, will shrink from any spontaneous reaction; the others will experience occasional outbursts of inexplicable rage directed against substitute objects or will resort repeatedly to violent behaviour such as murder or acts of terrorism. A person who can understand and integrate his anger as part of himself will not become violent.[18]

Since boys are more likely to be hit than girls, is it any wonder that we find that more of them 'feel the need to lash out'? The societally approved model has an inbuilt imperative to be tough, which means splitting off from the feminine, from feelings; the father and other men encourage this. It's their job to show the boy how to be like them; part of the way of doing that is to toughen him up so he can 'take it like a man' and won't grow up to be a wimp, to be soft, like girls are.

All of Formaini's, Miller's, and Eichenbaum and Orbach's work helps enormously in understanding men's greater aggression and provides pointers as to how it might be lessened. Though early parenting, first influences, and how children are brought up, are very important, they are not sufficient to explain entirely the continuing dominance of both male aggression and 'masculinity'. There are all sorts of 'macro' reinforcers intermeshing with the influence of the parents.

Ann Oakley puts it succinctly when, quoting Harriet Holter, she points out that the early learning of gender roles is

> only one mechanism for maintaining sex differentiation in society. Others include sanctions applied to adults (as well as to children) when they deviate from their gender roles, and the sex-typed models provided by the mass media.[19]

The world, as far as western society at least is concerned, spins on an androcentric axis. The male is at the centre of the universe; woman is his helpmate, companion, defined in relation to him. Men run things. Men make the important decisions. Men are in the 'real' world of money, politics, products, performance. The ones at the top got there by being ambitious, aggressive – in the sense of ruthless, determined, single-minded, rather than in the physical sense – and by being completely in control of their emotions.

They have these emotions in check: feelings are not allowed to interfere with them getting what they want. Images of men from God down to Andy Capp proclaim male power. The young boy growing up sees the Pope make decisions for Roman Catholics; the president/prime minister make decisions for the country; his father make the decisions about where he goes to school, whether or not they are going to move house, whether or not he can have a new bike. The macro and micro forces which underpin the androcentric status quo are continuously, constantly interacting to reinforce each other. So, as the young boy grows, he learns that he is to have power, to be at the centre, in charge, running things, looked up to and cared for by women. However, the price for this is that he must cut himself off from his emotions, except for anger. Anger is permitted. So is aggression. They are even encouraged, which means they are more likely to be displayed when he's angry or afraid – they are his emotional outlet.

Of course, the picture thus painted overpredicts. Most men are not violent and don't lash out with their fists at either women or men. But the point is that men are much more likely than women to do so, since a willingness to be aggressive is seen as part of what it is to be a man. This tendency is strongly discouraged in girls, who are brought up to be gentle and nurturing so that they will be good wives and mothers.

CONCLUSION

Men are not more aggressive than women simply because of their genes, hormones or chromosomes, whatever the biological determinists tell us, but tend to be more aggressive because of complex and dynamically interacting factors which must include all the myriad socio/cultural/environmental elements of our world, one of which is the way our society has constructed masculinity.

To talk about human behaviour out of its social context doesn't make any sense: that's where it exists. Of course our bodies and how they work are going to be part of the explanation, but to say it is THE explanation is to leave out most of, if not all, the aspects of our lives which make us human. Such an explanation has nothing to say about consciousness, or language, or our ability to make significant choices, moral and otherwise.

Nevertheless, the biological reductionist/determinist explanation of human nature, including male aggression, has a powerful and enduring appeal. The pull of this type of theory lies in two things. First, it's so simple: one knockdown explanation for everything. Second, if it's true that men and women are fixed forever as, respectively, aggressive and passively nurturing, then the patriarchal status quo is unchangeable, and it's foolish to try to do anything about it. The 'sensible' women are those who know this and who know their place in the scheme of things: to look up to and to look after men.

For biological determinists we are unfree because our lives are strongly constrained by a relatively small number of internal causes, the genes for specific behaviors or for predisposition to these behaviors. But this misses the essence of the difference between human biology and that of other organisms. Our brains, hands and tongues have made us independent of many single major features of the external world. Our biology has made us into creatures who are constantly re-creating our own psychic and material environments, and whose individual lives are the outcomes of an extraordinary multiplicity of intersecting causal pathways. Thus, it is our biology that makes us free.[20]

CHAPTER 3

Stereotypes, Biology and Female Crime

The female is a female by virtue of a certain lack of qualities; we should regard the female nature as afflicted with natural defectiveness.
Aristotle (384–322 BC)[1]

Once a woman has descended from the pedestal of innocence . . . she is prepared to perpetrate every crime.[2]

The central argument of this book is that when women commit violent crimes they are seen to have breached two laws: the law of the land, which forbids violence, and the much more fundamental 'natural' law, which says women are passive carers, not active aggressors, and by nature morally better than the male of the species. Such a woman is doubly deviant. Not only is she being tried for her crime, but how she measures up to the idea of proper womanhood is also being judged. Whatever the outcome of her trial, more moral opprobrium will be heaped on her than on a man in a similar position. She will feel this societal disgust keenly, even though she may not be able to name it, and will suffer more because she is a woman.

This chapter focuses on how the women who commit violent crimes are 'understood' in terms of the ideas, prejudices, attitudes and stereotypes which govern the perception of all women. Very few women commit violent crimes. Their small numbers mean that they appear to be 'unnatural' and freakish.

I will also consider the impact on women who commit violent crimes of all women being seen as 'other'; as passive; as ruled by their reproductive biology; as being unstable, irrational, mad. And I shall look at how women are judged, albeit unconsciously, against the standards of proper womanhood, i.e. are they virgins/good wives/good mothers?

As well as considering the impact of the age-old stereotypes of mothers, virgins and evil temptresses, I will also discuss two newer stereotypes which have serious implications for women who commit violent crimes and indeed for all women. These are woman as victim and liberated woman as law-breaker.

Very few women commit crimes; even fewer commit violent crimes. Men convicted of indictable offences outnumber women by about eleven to one. One implication of the very small numbers of women charged with violent crimes is that when such a woman is in court she's seen as something of a freak just because she's such a rarity: 'The vast majority of women are law-abiding – so what's wrong with this one?'

Perhaps so little has been written about the subject because so few women commit violent crimes, or at least partly because, just as most criminals are men, so are most criminologists. More has been written over the last fifteen years or so as growing numbers of women researchers have turned their attention to the field. Whatever the reason for the past lack of interest, the public is still largely unaware of female violent crime which in turn has profound implications for the understanding of *male* crime. By leaving women out of the picture, the fact that crime is predominantly a male activity is masked. A couple of examples will illustrate this invisibility.

In 1993 the BBC announced an 'ambitious four-week season of programmes on BBC2', entitled *Crime and Punishment*. According to the press pack, the programmes would 'examine the workings of justice and the legal system on a scale unprecedented in British television. Programming from across the spectrum of BBC2's output will be supplemented by a complementary run of programmes on BBC Radio 4.'[3]

There was nothing in the 25-page hand-out sent to the press about women who commit crimes; women as victims were there, but women as perpetrators were invisible; the awareness of women's low crime rate was nil, its potential implications for the problem of *male* violence well over the horizon of the programme makers' consciousness.

A story in the *Guardian* reported the then Shadow Home Secretary Tony Blair citing a new book, *Crime and the Family*, based on European and US evidence, which Mr Blair said 'showed overwhelmingly that poor parenting and family disintegration led to crime'.[4] Well, whatever you think of that argument, it doesn't apply to girls and women – they are not the ones who commit the majority of crimes.

Women had remained invisible in both the television programmes and, presumably, the book to which Mr Blair was referring. Thus, the exploration of both women's and men's different levels of involvement in crime was rendered impossible, as was any investigation of what actually happens to women who commit crime.

IDEAS, ASSUMPTIONS AND STEREOTYPES

Before outlining some of the ideas, assumptions and stereotypes which shape the way women are perceived – whether violent or not – I must stress that most of us are unaware of the ways in which we dynamically interact and reinforce each other. For example, a group of magistrates will say – as they do later on in the book – with their hands on their hearts, that they treat men and women equally, that there is no discrimination. But the research shows that those same magistrates nearly always send the 'bad', not the 'good', mothers to prison.

While it's true that male criminologists haven't paid a lot of attention to women and crime, Cesare Lombroso and Guglielmo Ferrero published one of the earliest books on women who commit crime, *The Female Offender*, in 1895. It's worth mentioning here because it provides a useful introduction to the myths, prejudices and stereotypes that infect the study of women and crime.

Lombroso and Ferrero saw women as passive, men as active. The egg passively awaits the active sperm. Therefore, any woman who wasn't passive, i.e. true to her own nature, was acting in a masculine way and thus was a deviant woman.

Some of the other things Lombroso and Ferrero had to say about:

Women in general: 'Women are big children . . . their moral sense is deficient'; 'Their evil tendencies are more numerous and more varied than men's . . . and it is only right therefore that they should be kept in the paths of virtue by . . . maternity, piety, weakness.'
Mothers: 'In the ordinary run of mothers the sexual instinct is in abeyance.'
The female criminal: '[she shows] an inversion of all the qualities which specially distinguish the normal woman; namely, reserve, docility and *sexual apathy* [Heidensohn's emphasis].'[5]

What Lombroso, who became known as the father of scientific criminology, and Ferrero are demonstrating here is the strength of the unquestioned assumptions which have been made about the nature of women for centuries.

WOMEN AS 'OTHER'

The fundamental assumption that Lombroso and Ferrero made totally unconsciously was that women are 'other'. It's only if you accept without even being aware of your acceptance that male equals the norm, i.e. the male is the standard for what it is to be human, that you can think of women being defined by their reproductive biology – because this is what makes them 'other' than men.

Myriam Miedzian provides a good illustration of how this works and at the same time shows that the idea that women are passive by nature is still very much around.

> Psychiatrist Anthony Storr, in *Human Aggression*, argues that women are naturally passive. To understand the significance of this title one must reverse the situation. Is it imaginable that a book primarily about female passivity and very secondarily about male aggression would bear the title *Human Passivity*?[6]

HORMONES RULE: OK?

The idea that women are ruled by their biology – as distinct from men who are autonomous human beings, in control of themselves – is also still around, a hundred years after Lombroso and Ferrero published their book on female offenders. The use of Pre-Menstrual Syndrome (PMS) to explain and excuse female violence is the most obvious and high-profile manifestation of biological determinism applied to female behaviour in the late twentieth century. The seeming acceptance of PMS as an excuse for violent behaviour has appalling implications for women.

WHAT IS PMS?

Pre-Menstrual Syndrome (PMS) appeared on the scene in the 1950s. What exactly is it? Does it really exist? How many women does it affect and how badly? Can it really drive women to violence? – these are some of the questions that continue to be asked and argued over in the 1990s.

Dr Katharina Dalton is responsible for popularizing PMS. Classic PMS symptoms include mood changes, anxiety, tiredness, irritability and hostility. However, one hundred and fifty symptoms have been named as PMS-related, including food cravings, muscular pain and anxiety about relationships. You begin to wonder if almost anything you feel that you don't want to feel could be included.

As the name suggests, these symptoms appear in the days preceding a menstrual period, but there is argument about how many days prior. Also, how many women suffer how many symptoms and to what extent? Estimates vary between 5 per cent (severe) and 95 per cent. PMS has been described as being a cause of: women's poor performance at work, in sport and in childcare; suicide; psychiatric admissions; accidents; violence and murder.

Dr Dalton on PMS: ' "If we don't have enough progesterone premenstrually we end up with PMS . . . The disease of PMS is a disease of the progesterone receptors." '[7]

Dr Jane Ussher, lecturer in psychology at University College, London, and author of *Women's Madness: Misogyny or Mental Illness?*:

With both PMS and PND (post-natal depression) there is no clear evidence for a simple hormonal aetiology – the raging hormones just cannot be pinned down . . .[8]

[they] certainly seem dangerous: the picture painted of the premenstrual woman is certainly of one who is 'mad'. Yet there is no consistent empirical evidence for any of these supposed deleterious effects.[9]

Ussher goes on to quote studies which show that performance is not significantly affected by menstruation, that there is no consistent evidence of mood variability, increased psychiatric admissions, accident, suicide or cyclical violence.[10]

Whatever the causes, nature and symptoms of PMS are, what is most worrying is the way it seems to be becoming almost routinely accepted by the courts as excusing, at least partially, women's crimes. Such leniency is alarming because of the implications for women in general: if aspects of the normal functioning of women's bodies are almost routinely accepted as excuses for irrational and/or criminal behaviour, what does that say about women? That we are all pretty unstable much of the time, because from our teens to our fifties we are at the mercy of our hormones?

This acceptance of PMS as excusatory is evidence of an all-too-easy slippage: from some women having some problems just before their period to hormones explaining women's behaviour and excusing wrongdoing. Some women do have PMS, but how does that explain their behaviour? Why does it excuse wrongdoing? And why have the courts accepted with apparent ease that it does both? Could it be because the notion that women are inherently unstable – especially at certain times of the month – is as old as the hills and that PMS is just a modern name for an old myth? Why do we never hear of men being excused on the grounds that their hormones made them do it? Men have hormones too. But hormonal explanations are only for women.

Helena Kennedy, a practising barrister for over twenty years:

I have used the condition [PMS] in relation to my client's mental state only once. In murder cases it can be raised only where evidence is strong that the hormonal imbalance is so extreme that the tests for diminished responsibility are fulfilled. There are probably just as many cases where exceedingly high testosterone levels in the male might account for outbursts of violence. It is just that, as usual, we are more predisposed to explore psychiatric explanations for women.[11]

Why we are so predisposed needs to be part of the broad framework of any future research on PMS.

Using PMS to excuse wrongdoing leads to excluding women from moral agency. If hormones *rule* us, then we are not full human beings responsible for our moral choices and for our actions. That's what's potentially at stake when PMS is used to excuse female wrongdoing.

If we are not responsible for our actions at certain times of the month, maybe we should not be allowed to drive or be allowed to make important decisions at these times, which rules out any job that needs a reliable and responsible person – i.e. nearly all jobs. Maybe it would be '. . . better after all to let the men do the driving and make the decisions, just to be on the safe side, because you never know with periods, they can come early or late so you're never quite sure when you're going to go a bit loopy.'

Maybe it would be better if we just stayed at home and cleaned and cooked and brought up the children. But running a home and bringing up children are highly demanding and responsible jobs. How come we never hear our hormones make us unfit for them? Could it be because our female natures, which render us natural homemakers and mothers, natural carers, override the hormones so that it's all right for us to be trusted in our own sphere, where our natures protect us from our natures?

It doesn't make any sense but it does serve to keep us in our place.

All Women are a Little Bit Mad But Some . . .

The myth that women's biology renders them unstable is enhanced by the perception of women as more emotional and less rational than men. Interestingly, the word 'emotional' is pejorative, implying weakness, a surrender to emotions: whereas 'rational' is objectively descriptive.

Freud gave this theory a boost when he wrote:

> I cannot evade the notion (though I hesitate to give it expression) that for women the level of what is ethically normal is different from what it is in men. Their super-ego is never so inexorable, so impersonal, so independent of its emotional origins as we require it to be in men . . .
>
> They show less sense of justice than men . . . they are less ready to submit to the great exigencies of life . . . They are more often influenced in their judgements by feelings of affection or hostility.[12]

What is Freud doing here other than revealing how completely and utterly his thinking is permeated by the unconscious acceptance that male equals good equals the norm? Man is the norm, man is rational, therefore what is not the norm is deviant, inferior, i.e. women and their emotions.

A study described by Allison Morris, lecturer in criminology at the Institute of Criminology, Cambridge University, illustrates where this view of woman as other/emotional can lead.

> A group of clinicians were given a questionnaire in which they had to rate certain traits as representing healthy male, healthy female or healthy adult behaviour. The results were that, for all the clinicians, the concept of a healthy man approximated to that of a healthy adult. However, the concept of a healthy woman differed: she was described as excitable, submissive, emotional, dependent: the opposite of the healthy adult. What this means is that if clinicians adhere to this standard of mental health, women are likely to be viewed as unhealthy adults, *simply because they are women* [emphasis in original].[13]

The view that women are 'other' and inferior and unstable, because of their hormones and emotions, makes it all too easy to see them as being, by their very nature, unstable, irrational, neurotic or mad. What can happen to a woman who is perceived as violent and then labelled as mad is shown by Kim Andrews's experiences. She was sentenced to prison on drug-related charges in 1970. While there, she was aggressive although, she says, she never hit anybody in her life before going to prison. Within the year she was transferred to Broadmoor Special Hospital. She spent fifteen years in Broadmoor and Rampton.

'It took them two minutes to label me as an aggressive psychopath,' says Andrews, 'and it's taking me the rest of my life to get rid of that label. I will never agree to that label of aggressive psychopath or that I was mad. Yes, I was a bad little bugger but I was not mad.' Kim Andrews's case is a severe example of what can happen to women because of the tendency to psychiatrically treat women who commit crimes.

The following case, where a man and a woman are involved in the same crime, illustrates both a wider tendency to 'psychiatrize' women who commit crime and a deep reluctance to similarly treat men who commit crimes.

A young girl is robbed in a London street. Her assailants, a man and a woman, are jointly apprehended, jointly charged, and jointly brought to trial. Both are middle-aged, unemployed and black; both have extensive criminal records; both claim amnesia for the events in question, and are remanded for psychiatric and social reports.

On psychiatric examination, the woman is found to have a disturbed background, a history of drug and alcohol abuse, and various physical ailments, but is not regarded as ever having been psychiatrically ill. To quote from the psychiatric report:

There is no history of psychiatric illness . . . When I saw her she was very cooperative, answered questions as well as she could, and expressed regret at the events which led to her being charged . . . There was no evidence of any gross abnormalities in her mental state, in particular she did not appear to be experiencing hallucinations or suffering from delusions, and in spite of her assertion that her memory is impaired, I could find no evidence of definite intellectual deterioration . . . There is in my view no evidence of formal psychiatric illness.[14]

The man, by contrast, is found to have a considerable psychiatric history, and to be suffering from a major mental illness at the time of the report:

> His psychiatric history dates back to 1968 [fifteen years prior to report] when he was treated at Hospital 1 with ECT. At that time he was depressed and had persecutory ideas. Two years later he was seen at Hospital 2; by this time he had developed auditory hallucinations with many neurotic symptoms ... He was considered to show evidence of a personality disorder and to be an hysterical psychopath. In 1976 he was referred to Hospital 3 with symptoms of depression with paranoid ideas again; he was similarly referred to Hospital 3 in 1978; at that time he was considered to show unequivocal evidence of a schizophrenic illness. He was treated as an in-patient for two months and given injections to control his illness ... He was treated at Hospital 4 as an in-patient between August 1982 and February 1983 ... he was considered to be suffering from mental illness, expressed bizarre delusional ideas that he was Prince Charles and that Princess Margaret was his mother, he claimed to hear the voice of Jesus. He responded to the appropriate treatment ... [and following his discharge] I was asked to take over his outpatient care ...
>
> This defendant has shown evidence of mental disorder for at least fifteen years with unequivocal evidence of schizophrenic illness ... It is quite impossible here to categorically state whether or not he is/was responsible for his actions. In my mind there is a reasonable doubt.[15]

Hilary Allen's book, from which this case is taken, goes on:

> Each of the two defendants attempts to blame the offence on the other, but the jury decides that both defendants were participants in the crime, and both are convicted of it. The man is sentenced to two years' imprisonment. The woman is placed on probation, with a condition that she receive psychiatric treatment.
>
> Viewed in relation to the particular medical findings of this case, the discrepancy in the sentencing may seem remarkable, even bizarre: a mentally ill offender is imprisoned for his crime, whilst his mentally fit accomplice is released to psychiatric care. Viewed against the overall pattern of criminal sentencing, however, the case is no more

than an individual example of a much more general trend, whereby female defendants are consistently more likely than males to be referred for psychiatric examination, to be assessed as suitable subjects for psychiatric treatment, and ultimately to be dealt with by psychiatric means.[16]

Not that this happens in many cases. Allen found that psychiatric disposals are rare – somewhere between one case per thousand and four and a half cases per thousand. Nevertheless, the trend from 1950–85 was consistent: women were twice as likely as men to be dealt with by psychiatric means. And this is not because, she says, the courts see the women as mad.

> . . . the courts tend to go on perceiving their female offenders as 'relatively normal women', and it is often their apparent conformity and competence that make them so acceptable as psychiatric patients.[17]

THE STEREOTYPES

We've seen that women are perceived essentially as: 'other', passive by nature, defined by their gender, less rational than men, given to emotional outbursts, and unstable by virtue of their emotionality and their hormones, almost by their very nature.

We've seen how breaking one taboo by acting aggressively led one woman to be labelled as mad, with appalling consequences for her. And we've seen how the tendency to regard all women as somewhat unstable leads to a higher proportion of women than of men receiving psychiatric disposals when they appear in court.

The stereotypes of women which have emerged over the centuries have their roots in a view of women which is determined by their sexuality. These stereotypes are crystallized conventional notions of what is a 'proper' woman and a 'fallen' woman. It is by how closely they approximate to the former, and by how far they are removed from the latter, that women are judged.

Except for two stereotypes – woman as victim and newly

liberated woman as lawbreaker, which have emerged only recently – the others are so instantly recognizable, so widely known, that they require little in the way of description.

The good mother She is, of course, always married and it goes without saying she is a good wife to her husband, as defined by him. This is perhaps the most powerful of all the stereotypes. A mother who is seen as a bad mother can expect vilification. It's natural for women to be good at caring; they are designed for motherhood – it comes naturally to them. So when a woman is a bad mother she is being perverse, unnatural, defying her own instincts: truly wicked.

It's my personal belief that it's the strength of the hold this stereotype has on the minds of many young mothers – and how far it falls short of reality – that accounts for much of the distress which gets labelled post-natal depression, and the numbers of disillusioned women having to cope, usually alone, with several young children.

In *A Doll's House*, Nora's decision to leave her children still leaves many people deeply uneasy. Barrister Helena Kennedy acknowledged the force of the stereotype when working on the television drama *Blind Justice*. She and playwright Peter Flannery needed to create a scandal in the past of the character, Katherine Hughes. Flannery suggested they invent a child left behind with a previous husband. But Kennedy felt that 'to have her abandon a child, however good her reasons, would completely lose her . . . audience sympathy . . . In court no reason is good enough to justify a woman leaving her children'.[18]

The virgin What a girl should be on her wedding night – is it an old-fashioned idea? Within the last few years I have heard a man in his late thirties bemoaning the fact that, when he did eventually marry, it would be too much to hope these days that he would find a virgin. I was amazed to hear him say that. He was amazed that I was amazed. Didn't I realize that deep down all men would prefer to marry a virgin?

Stray far from the path of virginity – i.e. lose it and be openly sexually active – and you'll run the risk of being called any or all of the bad names reserved for women of 'easy virtue': slut, slag, slapper, scrubber, etc. Get a 'reputation' and you lower your value on the marriage market – and risk being left on the shelf, a shop-soiled, unwanted commodity.

The madonna Standing on top of the pedestal, this combination, canonized in the form of the Virgin Mary, poses an impossible ideal. The madonna is a serenely beautiful, totally good woman who is simultaneously a mother and a virgin.

The sexual temptress Eve, at the opposite end of the spectrum from the madonna, is the quintessentially evil sexual woman. Manipulative and deceitful, she uses her sexual wiles to entrap and ensnare men who are powerless to resist her. A she-devil who both fascinates and repels.

Woman the deceiver Being manipulative and deceitful forms part of one stereotype of female criminals. Since women, unlike men, can control their sexual urges, use their bodies to tempt men, and to fool them, i.e. fake orgasms, and since a man never really knows if he's the father of the child, they are not to be trusted. And when a woman turns to the bad, i.e. to crime, then watch out because she has all that innate capacity for manipulation and deceit at her disposal.

'The famous fifteenth-century manual for witch-hunting, *Malleus Maleficarum*, claimed that the Devil sought out women because they were impressionable, and innately prone to malice, sensuality and deception',[19] which will certainly ring bells in this century with anyone who's seen the film *Fatal Attraction*.

The evil monster This epithet is reserved for those who commit horrific, inexplicable crimes, such as those committed by 'The Moors Murderers', Ian Brady and Myra Hindley. While it can be applied to men as well as women, there is a deeper opprobrium and disgust when it is used to describe a woman, especially one who is the object of both fascination and revulsion. It's Myra Hindley's name and photograph, not Ian Brady's, that are still appearing fairly regularly in newspapers and magazines, thirty years after her arrest in 1965. It is partly because she seeks release whereas he does not, but also because she's seen as so much worse than he because she's a woman. Since women are 'naturally' kinder and more caring than men, especially towards children, it follows that, to participate in the torture and murder of children, Hindley must be unnatural and truly evil to have chosen to go against her own womanly nature. Such a woman is beyond understanding, beyond redemption, hardly human at all. We must place her as far as possible away from all other women, from all of us.

Woman as victim This is one of the newer stereotypes. Over the last twenty years or so a lot of work has been done by women to raise the profile of women as the victims of domestic violence. Hedda Nussbaum, whose case was described in Chapter 1, had at first been charged with her partner, Joel Steinberg, in connection with the death of their daughter, Lisa, but was finally seen as a victim and given psychiatric treatment.

However, by overemphasizing women as victims, you run the risk of depriving women of their moral agency. Part of what it is to be a victim is passivity and blamelessness: it's the pedestal-plus-passivity stereotype in a new guise. I am not saying women are not victims of male domestic violence; obviously hundreds of thousands throughout the western world are. But we mustn't let our sympathy and support for them blind us to the knowledge that women do have a potential for both wrongdoing and aggression.

As awareness of this 'victim trap' is growing, women who work with victims of male violence are beginning to talk of such women as survivors, seeking to emphasize, encourage and support a woman's own strength to resist and to shape her own life.

Liberated woman as law-breaker This is the latest stereotype. Twenty years ago (in 1975) a book by Freda Adler, *Sisters in Crime*, was published in New York. In it, Adler said that as women had become more emancipated in western society they were entering masculine areas of operation such as crime; the rising level of recorded female crime proved it.

Adler did not simply say the feminist movement would lead to a new breed of emancipated, i.e. feminist, criminals but in this context she did conflate the women's liberation movement with lots of profound social changes occurring concurrently. And she did expect to see that, *as women became more like men* [my emphasis], because of these liberating forces they would commit more crimes, both violent and otherwise.

The book kicked off a moral panic about the new female

criminal who would be created if the women's libbers got their way. The notion that lodged firmly in the public mind was that feminism was turning good women into bad women and that we should expect a female crime wave as increasing numbers of liberated women turned to crime.

So, twenty years on, where are all these new liberated female criminals? They're not in evidence in the courts and the prisons. Female prisoners tend to be traditional-type, non-liberated women, which is what you'd expect since 'the women's movement has its greatest impact on white, middle-class women; crime and the criminal justice system has its greatest impact on black and working-class women'.[20]

Allison Morris, who is Director of the Institute of Criminology at Victoria University, Wellington, New Zealand, also describes a study which shows that 'girls with a high potential for delinquency . . . were less likely to commit delinquent acts if they held feminist attitudes'.[21]

To be fair, Adler herself describes Marge, a female offender she saw as typical of the members of the new '"liberation movement" spreading through the ranks of the nation's female offenders', as being unlikely to 'accredit her actions to any sort of a "liberation".' Like the majority of women in prison, says Adler, Marge is from a lower socio-economic group and is very pro the traditional view of women. She will not tolerate any mention of women's lib which she equates with lesbianism.

> Ironically, her feelings are similar to those expressed by countless prison administrators, police officials, and other law-enforcement authorities who believe that the women's liberation movement is in no way connected to the sharply rising crime rate in America.[22]

There are three basic flaws in Adler's thesis: she conflated the ideas of being a 'full human being', being 'male' and having a capacity for, and a willingness to use, violence, and she misunderstood both the nature of the women's liberation movement and the significance of the rising figures for female crime.

Adler had assumed that male equals the norm from which females deviate. Being a full human being does not equal being male to the exclusion of the female, even though society operates as if that were true. We all have a capacity, a potential, for violence. That potential is encouraged in boys, frequently with disastrous consequences for all of us; it is rigorously discouraged in girls, with the consequence that most girls grow up repressing their anger and suffer later on in their lives. If you bring up children, encouraging them to be tough and aggressive and violent, they're more likely to end up like that. But is that how we want any child to be brought up, female or male?

Adler misunderstood the nature of the women's liberation movement, or the women's movement, as it's now more often described. Feminism is not about freeing women to become men. Women are not being liberated (and I don't think there are as many around as Adler seems to think in any case) to be pretend-men, to swap feminine stereotypes for masculine stereotypes. The women's movement is about creating a world where women and men have as much choice as possible about what to do with their lives and talents. It's not a question of taking off a woman's apron and discovering a real human being, i.e. a man, underneath. It's about liberating all of us from such false notions so that all of us can have the freedom to shape our own lives and to live them as fully as possible.

And the female crime figures: were they rocketing up?

While some prisons planned new facilities for the expected influx of violent women, feminists in criminology and the criminal justice system were quick to respond to Adler with convincing arguments. They maintained, and rightly, that Adler's figures were misleading precisely because women commit so few crimes. When the number of crimes is small, only a few more may account for a large percentage increase; but Adler cited those alarming percentage increases without recording the low absolute numbers. She pointed to a shocking rise of 277 per cent in arrests of women for robbery between 1960 and 1972; but the 1973 *Uniform Crime Reports* of the FBI reported only 5,700 women arrested for robbery that year, compared with almost 95,000 men. Across the board women were arrested in 1973 for about 15.3 per cent of all crimes committed – not a high rate, and certainly not an alarming one, for a group that makes up more than half the population. Adler's critics also noted that there has been *no* demonstrable increase in crimes of violence committed by women.[23]

Jones goes on to say that the

> greatest increases in women's crimes have been in the areas of larceny and fraud, particularly welfare fraud; and these are not violent crimes but economic ones easily attributable to the growing financial needs of poor women, most of whom have children to support . . . In any case, the so-called new woman criminal was likely to be – like the old woman criminal – young, poor, and black or Hispanic.[24]

However false this stereotype is, it has gained a hold on people's imagination. This became obvious over the four years I was researching and writing this book. People who couldn't have cared less about feminism and/or the causes of female crime would trot out this notion that now women were liberated they were just as bad as men – maybe even deadlier than the male – 'see, so that's where feminism's got you', being the sub-text.

This new myth is proving durable precisely because it provides yet another stick with which to attack women who are working to improve the position of women in our society. It's a new – again unconscious – way of blocking that improvement, a new way of keeping women in line.

CONCLUSION

All of the so-called explanations of women's crime which rely on and are informed by the perception of women as other/ biologically determined/passive/unstable/mad, etc., fail because these perceptions of women are false. Even asking for THE explanation of women's crime, violent or otherwise, is misleading. Why expect there to be one explanation of women's crime when we don't expect there to be one explanation of men's? My impression is that most property crime by both men and women results from need or greed, but when it comes to violent crime men and women's motivations differ.

To come up with helpful answers about the causes of women's crime, both violent and non-violent, we need research and analysis which combines work on individual women's lives and the circumstances of women's lives in our society, from a combination of 'micro' and 'macro' elements, to use a concept described by Loraine Gelsthorpe,[25] university lecturer in Criminology at the Institute of Criminology, Cambridge University, and Fellow of Pembroke College.

One very useful source of such research would be female offenders themselves. Research based on interviews with women who have committed crimes, violent or otherwise, must be part of the way forward. Such research could well yield patterns which would be helpful in understanding why women commit crimes.

All of the above applies equally well to male crime and male offenders. We need to look at male and female crime both separately and together if we are to understand why some people, and not others, commit crime. The problem which needs to be addressed most urgently is that posed by male violent crime. Studying female violent crime throws light on this.

CHAPTER 4

What Kind of Crimes Do Women Commit and Do They Get Off Lightly?

I came out of there [Styal prison] once again. I came out in winter, my second time in a year. I was in a pub and this man wanted me to have a drink with him and I said no, I didn't want to have a drink with him. He kept pestering me all evening and so I said leave me alone . . . and I'd got a glass in my hand and I'd forgotten . . . . and I went to punch him and I split his face open with the glass. I ran away and then I saw him being brought out by the ambulance man. I waited until all his mates had stopped looking for me and then I gave myself in to the police and told them I was the one that did it.

June Clarke, Ashworth Special Hospital, January 1993

The central themes of this chapter are: what kind of crimes do women commit? How many women commit crimes, violent or otherwise? And how are these women treated by the courts? Much of the discussion of their treatment will centre on the so-called leniency or chivalry argument, which maintains that women are treated more leniently than men simply because they are women.

Though there are elements of 'chivalry' in the courts, just as there are in society at large, such chivalry is unlikely to be extended to women who don't conform to stereotypical notions of proper womanhood. This is particularly unlikely for women who commit violent crimes because, by the very nature of their crime, they have offended against the passive/nurturing stereotype of good womanhood.

However, the rebuttal of the leniency argument cannot consist of a straightforward accusation of upfront sexism on the part of the courts; it's more complex than that. And there are ways in which the law can operate leniently towards women. The way the courts sometimes psychiatrize women *can* lead to leniency, as can the way the law deals with women who kill their children, but how well the woman conforms to proper, conventional stereotypes will influence the extent to which the court approves or disapproves of her and will be reflected in how she is dealt with.

HOW MANY WOMEN COMMIT WHAT KINDS OF CRIME?

It has already been said: very few women commit crimes; even fewer commit violent crimes. In 1991 more than five times as many men committed offences as women: 1,269,100 men compared with 236,000 women. The largest number of offenders for both men and women falls into the category of theft and handling stolen goods, followed by burglary for men and fraud and forgery for women. Violence against the person is the third largest category for both sexes: 43,300 men were found guilty of such crimes in 1991, compared with 3,900 women, the men outnumbering the women by more than eleven to one.

The Home Office confirms this overall picture:

> ... women commit fewer crimes of all types, and proportionately fewer serious and violent crimes than men. Seven per cent of the female population will have had a conviction for a serious offence by the age of 31 compared with 33 per cent of males.[1]

There is little research available comparing men and women's crimes within the category of violence against the person, other than statistics relating to killing, and these don't go back beyond the 1980s: another instance of women's invisibility in the study of crime. However, one researcher who studied a sample of 326 women in prison during the mid-eighties found that fewer than 39 women (12 per cent) were there for robbery (which *Chambers Dictionary* defines as theft from the person, aggravated by violence or intimidation). However, the women's role was usually auxiliary.

Just over 29 women of her sample (9 per cent) had assaulted

someone. Two-thirds of the assaults happened when the woman was trying to escape arrest for another offence, had been drinking heavily, or was involved in a family quarrel. The final third were premeditated and had been organized either with men (predominantly) or with other women.[2]

Women Who Kill

In 11 per cent of currently recorded homicides for 1983–90 the principal suspect was female.[3] So male killers outnumber their female counterparts over this period in the ratio of nearly ten to one.

During the eleven years from 1982 to 1992, 527 women were convicted of homicide. That figure breaks down thus: 174 women were convicted of domestic homicide – 33 per cent; 184 of child homicide – 35 per cent; 137 of homicide of a suspect other than the first two categories who was known to the victim – 26 per cent; and 32 of homicide where the suspect was not known to the victim – 6 per cent.[4]

Because so much controversy centres around domestic homicide and battered wives who kill, I shall deal with the subject in detail in the following two chapters. Suffice it to say, a woman is much more at risk of being killed by her spouse/partner than vice versa.

To sum up: as far as numbers are concerned women commit fewer crimes than men and far fewer violent crimes. Their offences are petty and trivial; it's unusual for them to be convicted of causing physical harm.

TREATMENT OF WOMEN BY THE COURTS

The leniency or 'chivalry' argument is that women are treated more leniently by the courts simply because they are women. My argument is that, while chivalry may well be extended to some women – those who conform to approved stereotypes – leniency will not be shown to 'deviant' women.

'If a woman conforms to a judge's idea of what is appropriate for a woman he will have trouble convicting her,' Helena

Kennedy told a conference at St George's Medical School in 1991. '"Chivalry" exists but it is very much limited to those women who are seen to conform.' She added that a woman who showed anger would be viewed as threatening by the court, which puts women who've been violent at particular risk of being treated more harshly than women who are perceived as conforming to notions of what constitutes proper womanhood.

Aggression and violence are seen as much more essentially masculine than mere law-breaking, so violent women must be 'unnatural' and are more likely than men fitting the same description to be psychiatrized, labelled psychopathic and to end up in a Special Hospital like Broadmoor. These women are treated more harshly than comparable men since an *indefinite* term in a Special is a much more frightening option than a fixed term of imprisonment. And women tend to stay longer in the Specials than men.

Dr Gillian Mezey, Consultant Psychiatrist at St George's Hospital and Medical School:

> For example, if somebody has committed a stabbing in the pub . . . and a man has done it, then you look at it and think, 'Oh God there's an argument involved, it's a drunken brawl' – most of the time these people don't get psychiatric disposals made. If a woman has done it . . . people immediately sit up and take notice . . . the solicitor thinks it's unusual . . . she gets referred to a psychiatrist . . . The impact of what she's done may well be translated from a sort of statistical abnormality, because so few women do it, into a psychological abnormality. She is unrepresentative of the majority of women and therefore something must be wrong with her.[5]

However, it seems that my case is contradicted by, and the leniency argument supported by, current statistics:

> In 1990 the average sentence length of prison sentences awarded for indictable offences at the Crown Court was 17.7 months for women aged 21 or over, and 20.5 months for men. *The average length was lower for females convicted of violence against the person* [my emphasis],

burglary or robbery and theft and handling, but higher for criminal damage and drugs offences.

In 1990 the average sentence length for women aged 21 or over sentenced at magistrates' courts was 2.3 months compared with 2.6 months for men. *The average sentence length for women was lower for offences of violence against the person* [my emphasis] and burglary, but higher for criminal damage and fraud and forgery and drug offences. For theft and handling both sentence lengths were similar.[6]

But what force have these statistics? How 'true' are they in the sense that they give us the whole picture? The Home Office itself seems a little hesitant about its findings:

On the face of it, these statistics suggest that the courts are inconsistent in their treatment of the sexes. However, consistency in sentencing does not mean that all offenders convicted of crimes within a particular offence category should automatically receive the same sentence.

Sentencing courts may legitimately take into account a large number of other factors in addition to the offence category, such as the seriousness of the particular offence when compared with other offences of the same general type (measured, for example, by the value of goods stolen), the circumstances of the offence and any other aggravating or mitigating factors. This is clearly an issue for which more detailed research is needed and further thought is currently being given to how this might be done.[7]

Criminologist Frances Heidensohn, speaking at the St George's Conference on Perspectives on Female Violence in 1991, had issued a 'criminological health warning' along the same lines, on the reservations one must have about criminal statistics and criminal data. In *Women and Crime* she states the position clearly:

Scepticism about both the validity and the reliability of criminal statistics is now more or less universal. The police themselves point to changes in recording procedures and public attitudes which can affect reporting of crime and the annual British *Criminal Statistics* publication makes a point of stressing the limitations of the data it presents.[8]

Having established that it's wise to put less than complete confidence in the statistics, I want to criticize what they appear prima facie to show under two main headings: the seriousness of the offence factor, and the extent to which stereotypical prejudices, assumptions and attitudes may quite unconsciously influence convictions and sentencing.

THE SERIOUSNESS OF THE OFFENCE FACTOR

The Home Office booklet (quoted in note 7) talks about other factors in addition to the offence category which the courts might take into account 'such as the seriousness of the particular offence when compared with other offences of the same general type . . .'

In a paper on whether or not men and women in England and Wales are sentenced differently, David P. Farrington and Allison Morris describe a review of the American literature which found that in general women were sentenced more leniently than men.[9] It should be noted that the American researchers were not focusing on violent women, nor were Farrington and Morris in their research based on the records of Cambridge City Magistrates' Courts. Their research concluded that, when it came to magistrates' decisions, the sex of the defendant did not have any direct influence on the severity of the sentence or the probability of reconviction. It seemed that women got more lenient sentences only because they had committed less serious offences and were less likely to have previous convictions than the men. So, once you take into account the seriousness of the offence and the number of previous convictions of the defendant, any apparent leniency towards women may well disappear.

Farrington and Morris say they couldn't detect any leniency towards women in Cambridge City Magistrates' Courts. They acknowledge that more research is needed to test how far their results can be generalized to other kinds of courts and to other offences.

less serious

STEREOTYPICAL PREJUDICES, ASSUMPTIONS AND ATTITUDES

Another point to bear in mind when analysing statistics of conviction and sentencing rates is the influence of conventional stereotypical ideas and assumptions about women.

The conviction and sentencing figures represent the end of a long process which begins with somebody deciding what is a crime and what isn't. And, throughout that process, there are opportunities for the operation of assumptions, value judgements, stereotypes and prejudices – not only to do with gender, but also to do with, for instance, class and race. How do you measure the influence of such, perhaps largely unconscious, assumptions and value judgements, etc.? They are inevitably going to be part of the process leading to conviction and sentencing but what can conviction and sentencing figures tell us about how much they were influenced by the process, resulting in a certain outcome in a particular case?

Farrington and Morris noted that

> some factors (notably previous convictions) had an independent influence on sentence severity and reconviction for both men and women . . . others only had an influence for one sex. In particular, marital status, family background and children were more important for women than for men.[10]

Morris also found that divorced and separated women received relatively severe sentences, as did women coming from a deviant family background.

> These may be the kind of women whom magistrates, especially female magistrates, disapprove of: they are women who do not conform to notions of 'respectable' women.[11]

She then refers to the work of Kruttschnitt who analysed more than a thousand cases involving female offenders and found that 'the more "respectable" a woman was, the more lenient her sentence. "Respectability" referred to a good employment record, no alcohol or drug use and no psychiatric history'[12] but, no matter what the offence, the less 'respectable' a woman was the more likely she was to get a severe sentence. She also found that 'the more economically dependent a woman was, the less severe her disposition'.[13]

Working lawyers I've spoken to agree with these findings, and tell me that chivalry is very much limited to those women who are seen to conform. The criminal lawyer, the probation officer and the psychiatrist all know how the system works: judges and magistrates make decisions based on a division of 'good' and 'bad' women, so the defence team tailor what they do and say to try to ensure their clients approximate to that stereotype as closely as possible.

Lawyers may well be aware that these strategies are locking women into traditional stereotypes and may even question what they are doing to women in general. But their job is to do their best for the client. Helena Kennedy discusses these methods with women clients, trying to give them choices about what they want to do, telling them that if they turn up in a broderie anglaise blouse or a nice Marks & Spencer's dress they will be dealt with in a rather different way than if they turn up in bovver boots, sporting a spiky hair-do.

She agrees that the appearance of male defendants also has an influence on how courts view them but not nearly to the extent it influences the way a woman is treated. 'How a woman looks is seen as somehow much more crucial to who she is: she is being seen first and foremost as a woman and women are judged to a large extent by their appearance.'[14] And to illustrate how notions of good and bad mothering influence the way a woman is treated, she cites a case with which she was involved in 1990.

It concerned a series of armed robberies in which there was a 'Bonnie and Clyde' relationship. The couple had been holding up banks and places throughout the country. The judge asked about the woman, who, twelve years earlier, when she was in her teens, had had an illegitimate child. The child had been fostered and there had been little mention of it in the inquiry report. But the judge was at great pains to ascertain whether this woman had ever visited her child, whether she had shown any care for this child, whether she had maintained any contact with this child; he wanted to know what kind of mother she was.

None of this bore any relation to the offences she was in the dock for. And even if you say, 'Well, it's not irrelevant to ask those questions, it might tell you things about who she is as a person', those sorts of questions are never, but never, asked about men.

The nature and quality of parenting by men is not a subject judges ever ask about but it is always on the agenda in relation to women. It's the way in which women either pass or fail the test of good motherhood or pass or fail the test of good wife – i.e. not divorced – that determines whether or not they will be perceived as being appropriate women. And it is on that basis, whether or not they are seen as being appropriate women, as well as on the basis of the nature of their offence, that they will be judged.[15]

Pat Carlen, Director of the Centre for Criminology at Keele University, found, in her study of women's imprisonment in Scotland, that the women most likely to be sent to prison were those who were seen as 'women, mothers and wives' who had 'somehow stepped out of place'.[16]

The fifteen sheriffs and two stipendiary magistrates she interviewed about how they decided whether or not to send a woman to prison said they particularly hated sending women there.[17] However, what her interviews revealed was:

> when the sheriffs I interviewed are faced with a sentencing dilemma in a case where the offender is female, they mainly decide their sentence on the basis of their assessment of the woman as mother [emphasis in the original].[18]

'If she's a good mother, we don't want to take her away. If she's not a good mother, it doesn't really matter.' – Sheriff No. 13. The sheriffs also saw husbands as useful means of control: 'If she has a husband he may just tell her to stop it.'[19]

So, if you appear to be a good wife and mother, have a husband and children and live in a semi-detached in Surbiton, and your offence constitutes a momentary lapse about which you are duly contrite, you should get lenient treatment. You're rather less likely to receive it if you're divorced, unmarried, have no children or children in care, are black, lesbian, live in a commune, and display neither fear, tears nor remorse in court.

The leniency which the statistics would indicate the courts are practising towards women may well fade away when the seriousness of the women offenders' offences are brought into the picture because women's crimes tend to be less serious, and their previous convictions fewer, than men's.

However, I want now to look at two ways in which stereotypical assumptions and 'understandings' of women can lead to them being more leniently treated than men. I'm referring to the greater likelihood of women being given psychiatric disposals than men, and women who kill their children being likely to get more lenient treatment than men who kill their children – as long as they don't step outside of what it is to be a good mother.

The work of Hilary Allen, whose PhD is in sociology and law and who was also Chair of the campaign group Women in Special Hospitals (WISH), shows that women offenders are twice as likely as men offenders to be given a psychiatric disposition by the criminal justice system. And since a psychiatric probation order would be preferred by most of us to, for instance, a three-month prison sentence, a psychiatric disposal often means more lenient treatment.

Allen's work is invaluable; it shows that this tendency to give women psychiatric disposals didn't arise because the courts saw women as crazy in a conscious and sexist way, but because the male-made system which had evolved, higgledy-piggledy, from the interactions of medicine, psychiatry, the law and common sense, has developed a certain way of dealing with women. But, while it may be lenient to certain women offenders, it is based on a premise grossly insulting to all women. And, as Allen points out, this way of dealing with women leaves many male offenders who are obviously in need of help denied it and sent to prison.

However, women are more likely to be treated as 'mad' not because they are offenders but because they are women. 'Some of the ways in which female behaviour is discussed, for example, seem to present the female subject in fundamentally pathological terms, as naturally irrational, unstable and out of control', writes

Allen. Yet when a male offender is – rarely – diagnosed as mad he is seen to be 'really mad'. I would postulate that that's because such men are seen to have deviated from the true normative behaviour of the rational human being, i.e. the male, whereas women are perceived as being a bit unstable to begin with.

Two points need to be made clear here. As Allen herself points out, less than one per cent of female offenders are dealt with by psychiatric measures, so we are talking here about fewer than one in a hundred such women. Also we've seen that for some violent women at least psychiatrization can lead to a Special Hospital and a 'sentence'. (The women themselves see it as an indefinite sentence even though strictly speaking they are there as patients to be treated, not punished.)

What part did conformity to stereotypes play in Allen's research? She does have something to say about the treatment of lesbians and the force of the 'good wife and mother' stereotype. She found that in many ways the treatment of lesbian women differed from that of heterosexual women but with only 4 of the 129 cases she studied involving lesbians it meant she couldn't generalize. Nevertheless, the way these few women were treated is illuminating and could provide a starting point for much-needed research.

The lesbians, it seems, got the worst of both worlds, male and female. Like the other women they were treated as if they were sick in some way, but unlike them they did not escape legal and moral blame; although they were diagnosed as being disordered they didn't get any medical help, and although their crimes were 'treated as evidence of their disturbance [they were] still dealt with (unlike the vast majority of female offences) by means of severe custodial sentences'.[20]

Allen describes the force of the 'good wife and mother' stereotype as 'blinding'. She discusses the case of a woman convicted of causing grievous bodily harm to her 18-month-old daughter. Since the birth of her daughter the woman had been diagnosed as depressed and had been in hospital three times.

For more than a year, Allen comments, the woman had been

officially regarded as likely to commit homicide. The officials involved in the case have decided that she should none the less remain in the most intimate proximity to her anticipated victim, and they have knowingly arranged for her to spend many hours each day alone with this completely helpless child. She then fulfils the expectation, by attempting to stab the child to death . . . None the less, the officials concerned still insist that the desirable course of action is to reinstate the existing pattern of management, and as soon as possible to restore the offender to her original position of responsibility for her victim's safety and wellbeing. This is regarded as the ideal situation for all concerned.[21]

The woman is never seen as violent and continuingly dangerous, nor is she perceived as someone for whom brief hospitalizations and community treatment have

manifestly and devastatingly failed. What grounds the report [on the woman] is the apparently blinding construction of its subject *as a woman, as a mother, and as a wife* [emphasis in original]. Home and family are her proper place. Caring for her husband and children are her rightful activities. Tenderness towards her child is her natural emotion. The technical possibility of disrupting this domestic idyll by the preventive detention of the woman is dismissed in half a sentence. The report neither anticipates nor encounters any judicial opposition: the woman is ordered to her local hospital, with no restriction on her discharge.[22]

The motherhood myth, it seems, is powerful indeed. Another researcher who also found that myth to be particularly potent is Ania Wilczynski who, for part of her PhD at Cambridge University in 1993, examined twenty-two English cases where women had killed their children. She found that these women were treated more leniently than fathers who killed their children. Similarly, a study conducted by Dr Maureen Marks and Professor Channi Kumar of the Institute of Psychiatry, London, on infanticide in England and Wales, found that mothers convicted of infanticide were treated much more leniently by the courts than fathers who killed their children under one year old.[23]

The Infanticide Act 1922 (amended 1938)

created the offence of infanticide in the case of a woman who caused the death of a child under 12 months while 'the balance of her mind was disturbed by reason of her not having fully recovered from the effects of giving birth to the child or by reason of the effect of lactation consequent upon the birth of a child'. For a conviction to be one for infanticide, therefore, a court must be satisfied that the above conditions apply.[24]

It is pretty well accepted now, says Wilczynski, that there's 'no association between lactation and the development of mental disorder' but there is some evidence of a *temporal* association between child-birth and the development of mental illness . . . A first-time mother has a 35 times greater chance of developing psychosis in the first month of delivery than at any other time of her life' [emphasis in original].[25]

Puerperal psychosis – serious mental illness occurring usually within a few days or weeks of childbirth – affects about one in a thousand new mothers. However, it is rarely the cause of a mother killing her child – perhaps in only five cases a year.[26]

Wilczynski concludes that about half of the women found guilty of infanticide in her study would not have satisfied the definition of mental disorder recognized elsewhere in the criminal law, i.e. diminished responsibility.

The definition of the offence would appear to be an almost infinitely elastic one, which can (if the lawyers and psychiatrists involved so choose) cover almost any case where a woman kills her child under 12 months. Virtually any type of mental or social stress or distress can be invoked if required, including that which has very little or no connection with the birth of the child.[27]

NUMBERS

Given the amount of time that women spend with their children and the fact that normally they have primary, if not sole, responsibility for their children, the number of women convicted of killing their children is small.

Over the eleven years from 1982–92 inclusive, 184 women were convicted of killing their children; roughly an average of seventeen per year. And the Home Office has pointed out to me that the number of convictions for infanticide had not been more than ten in any year since 1981.[28]

MOTHERS WHO KILL THEIR CHILDREN: TWO MYTHS COMBINE

The belief that women are inherently unstable because of their reproductive cycle combines with the pull of the 'women are naturally good mothers, that's their primary function in life' belief to produce lenient attitudes towards mothers who kill their children. The two myths combine – the same way that they did in the case described by Hilary Allen – and render it virtually impossible to see a mother as being both rational/responsible and capable of harming her child.

> The basis for this leniency lies in the court's inability to believe that any normal woman could commit such a deviant act as filicide. She must have been *mad* to kill her own child. [Emphasis in original][29]

In the twenty-two cases Ania Wilczynski studied, it was clear that distinctions were drawn 'between "good" and "bad" women and, more particularly, between "good" and "bad" mothers'.[30]

Fourteen of the women were seen as 'good' mothers for whom something had gone tragically wrong. (That's another thing you notice when reading about women offenders who are sympathetically treated: like Victorian heroines, things are always happening to them, they are the passive, recipient, hapless victims of events who never seem actually to do anything.) These fourteen were given probation or hospital orders; the ones who got hospital orders spent some time in an ordinary psychiatric unit. The vast majority of women who kill their children get such an unrestricted hospital order: most of them receive treatment in an ordinary – as opposed to a secure – psychiatric hospital and are often there less than a year.

Sara, for example, allegedly suffocated her eleven-month-old child while she was acutely depressed, then tried to commit suicide. She denied manslaughter, arguing that the death was a cot death, but was convicted of manslaughter on the grounds of diminished responsibility. At Sara's trial, it was stated that her child had been healthy and happy and that all who knew her regarded her as a loving and caring mother. The judge seemed to agree and gave Sara a three-year probation order, saying: 'You are in need of help and not of punishment'.[31]

However, the eight other women in Wilczynski's sample went to prison.

These women tended to be viewed as having acted in ways inconsistent with traditional concepts of women's behaviour. That is to say, they were viewed as 'bad' women and 'bad' mothers – selfish, cold, neglectful, uncaring and sexually active.[32]

Morris and Wilczynski then quote the case of Susan Poole and her common-law spouse (as described by journalist Yvonne Roberts) who, in 1988, were convicted of the manslaughter by starvation of their ten-month-old son and the wilful neglect of their two-year-old son.

They were given seven years' and ten years' imprisonment respectively. Susan Poole was described by the popular press as 'evil', 'callous' and 'vile', and was said to have referred to her child as 'it'. The jury were told that she sometimes left the children alone while she accompanied Frederick Scott to the pub which was a hundred yards down the road, that she had severely neglected the housework, and that although she was grossly overweight, her son had starved to death. Mr Justice Owen, at the trial in the Central Criminal Court in London, commented that she must have seen the pleading look in her son's eyes: 'When one thinks of the extraordinary maternal sacrifice and care shown by lower animals, one has to wonder at her apparent selfishness.'

Yvonne Roberts, a journalist who interviewed Susan Poole after her conviction, presents her in a very different light from the popular perceptions of her. She describes her as a young, immature woman from a chaotic, abused and neglected background who in the two months before her son's death became increasingly despondent and depressed because of her deteriorating relationship with her violent and unsupportive partner, her social isolation and her feelings of being unable to cope with the care of the children.[33]

The seven year sentence given to Poole appears to have been more a reflection of the negative image created of Susan Poole as a mother than of the medical evidence presented. On appeal, the period of imprisonment was only reduced to five years, as was her common-law husband's.[34]

Wilczynski believes that one reason for the leniency extended to mothers who kill their children is the huge stake society has in upholding the mythical status of motherhood. 'It's less potentially disruptive to the system to attribute causes of deviant behaviour in mothers, in time-honoured fashion, to women's inherent instability, rather than to look at the circumstances of real women's lives.'

She remains concerned about the mothers who kill who

cannot present themselves as 'disturbed' or 'good', or are not perceived in such ways. Women and mothers who 'step out of line' or 'let the side down' are penalized accordingly. They run the risk of punitive sanctions. This cannot be right or fair, since objectively the situations, background and mental state of at least some of these women appear to be not dissimilar from those of the women who are dealt with 'sympathetically'.[35]

CONCLUSION

Women commit fewer crimes than men and many fewer violent crimes. This means they can look 'freakish' in court and being exceptional women in that they have broken the law run the risk of appearing to be very, very bad.

The small numbers of women offenders is probably one of the reasons why criminologists weren't much interested in them until recently. It could also be because, until recently, most criminologists were men. Whatever the reason, the result is that not much is known about women offenders, yet their offences tend to mask the *masculine* nature of the vast majority of crime, especially violent crime. It has been virtually impossible to conceptualize masculine crime, which is the big problem that needs studying if we are ever to find a way of tackling it effectively.

The idea that criminal justice is simply chivalrous to women on the grounds they are the gentler and morally superior sex and therefore to be treated in a privileged way is far less real than the figures make it apppear. If you take into account that men's crimes tend to be more serious and more frequent, such leniency may well disappear. However, where women can be shown to be mentally and emotionally unstable, they are likely to be treated more sympathetically than men. This viewing of women as unstable, though it may be advantageous to individual women, is a high price for all women to pay insofar as it is premised on a belief in women's inherent instability *per se*. It also raises questions about the unfairness of treating men as if they had no inner lives and therefore of denying psychiatric help to men who could benefit from it.

Even when mothers commit infanticide – a category of crime tailor-made for leniency on the grounds of instability – they are very likely, if they do not conform to traditional ideas of good motherhood, to be more severely treated than other women. Along with other violent women offenders they are judged not only on the crimes they have committed but on the extent to which they are perceived by those involved in the criminal justice system as proper women.

Two final points: men and women being treated the same may not be just when you consider that the lives of men and women are hardly equal in reality.

'Paper justice' involves giving like penalties to women and men for like offences, but real justice involves taking into account the impact of a penalty: for example, the fact that, at least in this culture and at this time, child-rearing *is* primarily the responsibility of women and that women earn less than men, or the possibility that imprisonment *is* a greater punishment for women than for men.[36]

Prejudice other than that against gender, such as that against class and race, complicates perceptions of offenders, whether male or female. It's not only black women who are overrepresented in prison – so are black men. However, it seems to me that there is much greater awareness of prejudice based on race, class and religion than of prejudice to do with gender, especially where it affects women. A major reason for writing this book was to draw attention to how much women's success or failure to conform to traditional roles influences their treatment within the criminal justice system.

CHAPTER 5

Battered Women Who Kill

In 1987 Thomas Corlett received a three-year sentence for killing his wife. She had provoked him by moving the mustard-pot to the wrong side of the table.

In 1988 the Reverend Shirley Freeman killed his wife after she had refused to tune in to his favourite radio programme, *Desert Island Discs*. His plea of provocation was accepted by the judge who gave him a suspended sentence.[1]

Joseph McGrail killed his drunken, abusive common-law wife by repeatedly kicking her in the stomach as she lay in an alcoholic stupor. He had finally snapped after 10 years of torment during which Marion Kennedy went on massive drinking binges and became addicted to sleeping pills 'to enhance the mental effects of the alcohol'. She had repeatedly sworn at him and forced him to feed her vodka habit during the years they lived together in Kingstanding, Birmingham.

Last week McGrail was found guilty of manslaughter and walked free from Birmingham Crown Court with a two-year suspended prison sentence. The judge, Mr Justice Popplewell, said the woman he had killed 'would have tried the patience of a saint'.

Two days earlier, Sara Thornton's appeal to have her murder conviction for killing her husband Malcolm changed to manslaughter was heard. She had stabbed him in the stomach as he lay, like Marion Kennedy, in an alcoholic stupor at their home in Atherstone, Warwickshire. Mrs Thornton had been repeatedly battered by her husband during their 10-month marriage. He had once knocked her unconscious and threatened to kill both her and her 12-year-old daughter. On other occasions, he had punched her in the eye and on the back of the head, broken a glass over her hand, threatened to throw her through a plate-glass window and smashed furniture when he was drunk. The court also heard that only two days before she stabbed him Mrs Thornton told a friend: 'I'm going to kill him.'

Her appeal was rejected and she returned to Bullwood Hall prison in Essex to continue her life sentence for murder.[2]

The focus of this chapter is battered women who kill; it is around their treatment that controversy rages most fiercely. The two reasons for this are: first, that these women have not only killed, they have killed the men who were their husbands or lovers in their own home. They've flown in the face of the natural order of things, so they'd better have a very good reason for doing so; second, that a battered woman who kills her batterer can be convicted of murder and go to jail for life. This, say campaigners, is in effect punishing her twice. First, she endured possibly years of battering from a man and now the male-made law says she must be branded a murderer and serve a life sentence. Whether or not she is convicted of murder will have something to do with how, apart from her crime, she measures up in all other respects to the standards of proper womanhood.

A LITTLE LEGAL/MARITAL HISTORY

The first known 'law of marriage' was formalized by Romulus (who was credited with the founding of Rome in 753 BC) and required married women 'as having no other refuge, to conform themselves entirely to the temper of their husbands and the husbands to rule their wives as necessary and inseparable possessions'.[3]

The marital template of male authority and female submission can be seen underpinning ancient English law that laid down that a man who killed his wife was to be charged with murder, but a woman who killed her husband was to be charged with petty treason – as was 'a serf who killed the master'.[4]

And under the common law of England, up until the late nineteenth century, husband and wife were treated as one person. Once married, the woman simply ceased to exist as a legal entity. So how could she own property or bring a legal action, when legally she didn't exist? It was only in 1946, 274 years after the introduction of provocation as a partial defence to murder, that 'an English court finally stated that wives who killed their husbands or their husbands' lovers could also avail themselves of the defence'.[5]

Up until 1991, the law in this country acknowledged that rape in marriage could take place only where a decree of judicial separation or a decree nisi was in existence, or in certain circumstances where there was a separation agreement or an injunction restraining the husband. Previously an 'I do' meant you had to whenever he wanted to, so there could be no such thing as rape within marriage since rape means sexual intercourse without consent and married women were deemed to have given their consent at the time they married, to cover all future occasions.

In one of the south-western states of the USA things were worse until quite recently. In Texas, until 1974 it was the law that

> homicide is justified – not a criminal act, and therefore subject to no penalty whatever – 'when committed by the husband upon the person of anyone taken in the act of adultery with the wife, provided the killing takes place before the parties to the act of adultery have separated'.[6]

And not only in Texas:

> Elsewhere, this is the 'unwritten law', and cases both in Texas and other states with analogous practices based on precedent have considered the justification to extend to lethal assaults upon the errant wife, the rival, or both.[7]

THE POSITION TODAY

All of this reveals the androcentric nature of the law which is itself defined by being conservative, relying in part on tradition and precedent. So-called 'objective' justice is, in truth, fundamentally male-centred, male-defined and male-made, which means that when a woman comes into the dock, subconsciously she is perceived as 'other', but the conscious claim is that she is being dealt with objectively. The hidden gender factor was revealed by the actions of the Scottish sherriffs mentioned in Chapter 3 who could honestly say they did not discriminate against women, and then send 'bad' mothers to jail and let 'good' mothers, with husbands, go home.

It is also why you don't hear judges agonizing over whether *men* acquitted of killing wives are being given a licence to kill, whereas they do express such doubts in the far fewer cases involving women who kill men. For example, Lord Wheatley said, passing a life sentence on Mabel Patterson, who was convicted of murdering her brutal husband in 1983, that so many wives were subjected to rough treatment it would be dangerous to establish a precedent for them to take the law into their own hands.[8] Contrast that with Mr Justice Popplewell's remarks to Mr McGrail quoted at the beginning of the chapter.

PATTERNS OF DOMESTIC VIOLENCE

It was only in the 1970s and 1980s that feminist research and campaigning began to reveal the extent of domestic violence suffered by women. Before that it was a hidden crime, one that existed in the family so that it wasn't strictly a crime at all.

In 1980, a survey found that almost a third of women who had suffered domestic violence replied, when asked if there were circumstances in which a man had the right to hit his wife, 'Women may deserve to be hit if they neglect the children, are sleeping around, or fail in various ways to take care of their husbands.'[9] That such a high proportion of women who had been abused thought it right for a man to hit his wife, even if only in certain circumstances, indicates the strength of the unconscious acceptance of the husband as master and rightful chastiser.

It's difficult to predict who's going to be involved in violence within a marriage. Although wife-beating takees place at all levels of society it is, however, more likely to be found amongst

75

the poor. Men are more likely to become abusive husbands if they have seen their own father being violent in the home when they were growing up.[10]. They also tend to have low self-esteem, poor verbal skills and to be prone to depression. They frequently lack, for instance, such things as social standing, friends, money and education, all of which can confer status.[11]

Alcohol is often involved. For instance, the abusive husband may be the sort of man who spends most of his leisure time drinking with his mates in the pub and who has traditional ideas about being master in his home, with his wife there – in the home – to look after it, the kids and him, without nagging.

Domestic Violence That Ends in Death

In this country about a hundred men a year and about twenty-five women are convicted of killing a spouse or lover,[12] but we don't know in how many of those killings domestic violence played a part.[13] However, Angela Browne, an American social and forensic psychologist, quotes various researchers to show that around 70 per cent of women who killed their husbands had been physically abused by them.[14] And Jeremy Horder, a lawyer who wants to see the law changed in this area, believes there is no reason to think the proportion would be significantly different in the UK.[15]

Research in Australia backs up Browne's contention. Bacon and Lansdowne investigated cases of women who had been convicted of killing their husbands and boyfriends. They found that in fourteen out of sixteen cases the woman had been physically assaulted and subjected to repeated violence.[16]

WHY DO MEN KILL?

The killing comes typically at the end of a pattern of repeated batterings: but this time it's lethal. As to the question of what triggers the violence in the first place, one survey of women in UK refuges found that while 33 per cent of women blamed drink, the next biggest category (19 per cent) said anything could provoke an attack. The author of the study said she got such a wide range of rationalizations as 'to make any single explanation an erroneous reduction. The message is, as the women themselves expressed it, that "men are violent".'[17]

The Dobashes, who like Edwards have done a great deal of work in this field, have concluded that where women are abused by violent husbands the 'only pattern discernible ... is that the behaviour, whatever it might be, represents some form of failure or refusal on the part of the woman to comply with or support her husband's wishes or authority'.[18] It's an explanation, along with the notion that a man owns his wife and his fear of having his dependency on his wife and his emotional vulnerability exposed, which recurs.

According to Wilson and Daly, intensive studies of the conflicts that culminate in spousal homicide 'are unanimous in confirming that male sexual proprietariness constitutes *the* [emphasis in original] dangerous issue in marriage regardless of whether it is the husband or the wife who is finally slain.'

They describe research on seventeen cases of killing or seriously wounding a legal or common-law spouse, six of which were attributed to psychiatric disorders. However, the authors were so impressed with the essential similarity of the remaining eleven that they entitled their report 'The Spousal-Homicide Syndrome'. All eleven of these attackers were men, and they all said they were deeply in love with their victims.

Ten of the 11 attacks were precipitated by 'an immediate threat of withdrawal', and 8 of the 11 victimized wives had left the offender at least once previously, only to return. In all 11 cases the victim was having an affair or had led the offender to believe that she was being unfaithful to him.[19]

Barnard, Vera, Vera and Newman, who described the most frequent type of male homicide [i.e. that committed by men] as 'sex-role threat homicide', also see such men's 'unspoken dependency' on their wives

as the key to this type of homicide; as well as the sex-role stereotypes that encourage men to believe they have the right to control their wives' whereabouts and activities . . . [which] lead them to express the pain of separation or rejection in aggressive, rather than more sensitive, ways.[20]

The three most dangerous things that a woman in an abusive relationship can do are: to threaten her husband's authority, e.g. by talking back and/or not being a good wife and mother, or to strike back; to give her husband any reason to believe she is being unfaithful, e.g. by chatting to a male friend at a party; to threaten to make him face how much he needs her, e.g. by announcing her intention to leave him.

WHY DO BATTERED WOMEN KILL?

In 1984, two-thirds of the homicides between partners were of husbands killing wives, while one-third was of wives killing husbands. Given the finding that women are more likely than men to kill in self-defense, and that physical abuse by the man precedes many spousal homicides regardless of the perpetrator, it seems probable that a high proportion of these cases represented the culmination of a battering relationship. As Susan Jacoby points out, in many homicides between partners, the woman kills as a 'desperate, final response' to physical threat and attack whereas the man kills as a 'logical extension of the . . . abuse he has been dispensing for years'.[21]

Although in 95 per cent of the cases involving injurious assault between a couple it is the women who are hurt, studies of severely battered women suggest they aren't usually violent towards their spouses, and one who kills is extremely rare.

In order to study the differences between battered women who killed and those who didn't, Angela Browne compared 42 women who had been charged with either killing or seriously injuring their partners with 205 women who, while they had been in abusive relationships, did not take lethal action against their spouses or lovers.[22] She found no dramatic differences. The women who killed were slightly older than the women in the comparison group and came from a slightly higher-class background. Employment and education patterns didn't differ significantly.

Comparing the men who were killed with those who weren't, Browne found that the former group used drugs and got drunk more often, threatened and assaulted more often, threatened to kill someone other than themselves, abused children as well as wives, and their abuse of their spouses was more 'more frequent, more injurious and more likely to include sexual assault'. In other words their spouses or lovers had had even more to endure than the women who hadn't killed their respective partners.

The women who killed, 'like victims of other types of trauma', says Browne, 'responded to these assaults with reactions of depression, denial, shock and a sense of helplessness and fear'. They tried to deal with the assaults by withdrawing, by trying to understand, and by adapting their behaviour to avoid future outbreaks of violence. They showed care and concern, and felt it was important to maintain the relationship with the abuser. However, none of the strategies worked. For most of the women in the 'homicide group', the violence got worse and happened more often.[23]

The typical killing was not planned and occurred while threats were being made either before an assault, during a violent episode, or during an attempt to escape which failed. But, responding in the way Sara Thornton and Kiranjit Ahluwalia did, by killing when the man was asleep, is not uncommon, given women's fears of provoking greater violence if they respond during an attack.

As we shall see in the following chapter, such a delayed response is going to lead the woman into serious legal battles: that's not the way to behave when you are provoked. That's not how men behave when they are provoked. Suffice it to say, whether that is how she responds, or whether she responds during threats which she knows typically precede an assault, or during violence, or while trying to escape, it is likely this is her single violent response to a prolonged period of abuse.

Interestingly, there's research which shows that, whereas men's aggression rises fairly steadily in response to stress, women's aggression remains low until the stress levels get very high and then the aggression level leaps up dramatically. 'The researchers' graph is a visual testament to women's snapping point, which occurs suddenly at high levels of tension.'[24]

Typically, the few battered women who kill their abuser do so out of sheer desperation when they can see no other way out. They have probably tried to get help and/or tried to find somewhere else safe to go but have failed. They kill when suddenly they can take no more.

Predictors of Risk

Browne has identified several factors which suggest it's possible to predict which couples are

> at particularly high risk for a lethal incident (at least one perpetrated by the female victim) . . . frequency of assaultive incidents by the man, severity of injury, frequency of alcohol intoxication or other substance abuse by the man, forced or threatened sexual assaults of the woman partner, the man's threats to kill, and suicide ideation by the woman.

She goes on to suggest that many of these variables 'could be useful in identifying high-risk relationships in general, not just those in which the woman kills in self-defense'.[25]

The Role of the Police

Browne's findings are enormously important. Accepting that American society is to some extent different from English society, they could still be very useful to police responding to pleas for help by battered women, in helping them to assess the likelihood of a lethal attack in the future. They would, of course, have to take seriously what the woman told them about the assaults and would have to take the attitude that *any* domestic assault is unacceptable. Sadly, this is often far from being the case. 'Typically there have been numerous calls for assistance to the police before the fatal event.'[26]

However, there are signs that things are changing. A Home

Office circular on domestic violence was issued to the police in 1990, urging chief officers

> to review their force procedures for dealing with such cases and to issue revised policy statements based on a positive, interventionist and informed approach. The circular also made a number of practical recommendations of ways in which procedures might be enhanced, primarily drawn from examples of good practice which had already evolved in some forces. A detailed evaluation by Home Office researchers is now in progress.[27]

The police also launched a major campaign in autumn 1994, stressing the seriousness of domestic violence.

Pragna Patel of Southall Black Sisters[28] (see Useful Addresses) acknowledges that while there is a growing awareness on the part of the police that domestic violence is an issue they should address

> that growing awareness isn't really matched by an enhanced and better practice. The police still betray an attitude which is very much that domestic violence is not really a criminal offence. So what you tend to see is that while women are being treated more sympathetically, which is good, they are still being encouraged to take civil action, instead of the police taking action themselves. In other words the incident is still not being criminalized. Whilst this continues what we are getting is a re-legitimization of domestic violence as a private problem.[29]

The Perennial Question: Why Didn't She Leave?

Before considering the question, 'Why didn't she leave?', which is so often asked of battered women who kill, let's look first at the case of one woman who did leave: Balwant Kaur Panesar.

Balwant was in hiding at the Brent Asian Women's Refuge, having left her violent husband after ten years during which she was repeatedly abused. Balwant had taken out injunctions against her husband on at least two previous occasions, the second one with a power of arrest attached. This followed an incident in which Bhagwant Singh Panesar had attacked her with a screw-driver and kicked her in the stomach during a pregnancy. Her solicitor, Amrik Singh Gill, described how he had made eighteen telephone calls to agencies and charities, looking for somewhere for her to go. Despite the stipulations of the Housing (Homeless) Persons Act, Redbridge Council, like so many councils on too many occasions, refused to accommodate Balwant and her children, instructing her instead to return home since she had the 'protection' of a non-molestation order. When Mr Gill finally found that Brent Asian Women's Refuge could offer her a place to stay, he gave her twenty-five pounds and put her into a taxi with her daughters and the carrier bags of clothing they had escaped with.

> On the 22nd of October 1985, she was stabbed to death [in the refuge] in front of her three daughters, all of whom were under the age of six. Another Asian woman who worked at the refuge was also injured as she tried to fight off the killers. Balwant's husband was thought to have been assisted by an accomplice, but only he was apprehended and convicted for the killing . . .[30]

Broadly speaking, a battered woman doesn't leave until it's too late – either for her husband, or more likely for her – for three reasons: she stays because she wants to go on trying to make the relationship work and believes that, if she tries harder, she can make it work, can make it like it perhaps once was. She believes deeply in her own ability to love the man better. And, since it is this relationship, along with her relationship with her children – and there usually are children – which is at the centre of her life, it is inordinately difficult to give up on it and walk away.

Sara Thornton's account from prison of her experience answers the question why she did not leave as follows:

> I loved him. Sober, he was a warm, funny, caring man who never hit me. I did not realize how much his drinking made him hate me. Constant fear of an unprovoked attack distorted my perceptions of reality and logic.[31]

In the experience of most people it is still true that a man is defined by what he does, a woman by how successful she is in her primary roles of wife and mother. If she leaves her home, her marriage, what does that say about her? What will her life be like alone? A single, perhaps homeless, mother does not enjoy high status in our society. Will she be able to manage? Will she be able to keep the children? Will she lose everything? A battered woman may well have contacted the police, the social services, the family doctor, the church and a solicitor. She may have been told she has no remedy in law. All such attempts to get help are pretty common.

She stays because she — and her children — have nowhere else to go and no money to go with. Relatives and neighbours don't want to take on a possibly permanent burden: they may simply not have the room or the resources to cope. They may not want to get involved in a 'family' dispute; they may fear the man's violence; they may feel the woman's duty is to stay with her husband.

She is also afraid, afraid that if her husband catches her trying to escape he will beat her and may even kill her, since the attempt to leave often provokes the final, lethal assault. And even if her attempt is successful she will still be afraid that, wherever she goes, he will find her and beat her, perhaps even kill her. That fear is not irrational. Threats by husbands to hunt down wives if they ever leave are far from idle.

> ... separated women report higher levels of violence committed against them than do married women still living with their mates.[32]

Nor are court orders much use:

> Court orders of restraint are not merely difficult to enforce; they are downright provocative, because they signal yet another challenge to these men's control of their wives.[33]

The possible presence of all three factors interacting on a woman who is being physically beaten and is probably emotionally exhausted and at her wit's end is likely to lead to her feeling she has the strength to do nothing other than survive from day to day – if she can.

To sum up, men are more likely to kill than be killed where there is domestic violence. In about 70 per cent of spouse killings by wives, there is a history of battering. Men who batter and kill their wives tend to be insecure in themselves as men and may see themselves as lacking in status. They may also be hypersensitive to any suggestion of a threat to their authority as men or to their sexual ownership of their wives. They may need them so much, a need which as men they must hide from themselves, that an attempt by a wife to leave triggers a bout of violence which may prove fatal.

If this deeply repressed emotional vulnerability threatens to break through, it must not be allowed to. She is the cause of all the trouble: the only permitted emotional outlet is anger. And in an established battering situation, anger means violence. Women, on the other hand, who can no longer tolerate the abuse, snap, strike back in desperation, and kill. This is typically a one-off act of violence.

The response of the police and other agencies can often be inadequate, betraying a reluctance to upset the status quo which traditionally makes the man head of the household and puts what happens in the family beyond the reach of those outside. All of this contributes towards making it extremely difficult for women to leave, which might also prove more dangerous than staying.

THE QUESTION OF LENIENCY

A concise way of covering the leniency controversy is through a consideration of some of the points in a powerful feature by Russell Miller which sums up the campaigners' position, and the official response to it from the Home Office in the form of a letter from the Head of Research and Statistics, Christopher Nuttall.

Miller's piece appeared in the *Sunday Times* in May 1993. It was about the way the law discriminates against battered women who kill. He discussed how the law on provocation effectively safeguards only the interests of men. Courts frequently decide that men were provoked by women, but rarely decide that women were provoked by men ... The defence most likely to succeed for women who kill is that of diminished responsibility.[34]

Miller goes on to say that

the Home Office claims that women are more likely than men to be charged with the lesser offence of manslaughter and that men usually receive longer sentences. Crown Prosecution Service statistics present a very different picture: no less than 40% of men who kill their partners have their conviction reduced to manslaughter, usually on the grounds of provocation, while only 24% of women have their convictions reduced.[35]

Before going on to talk about the Home Office response, I must clear up the confusion surrounding those Crown Prosecution Service figures quoted by Miller. First of all, the 'Crown Prosecution Service' statistics are *not* from the Crown Prosecution Service, although they have been widely quoted in various newspapers and magazines as having come from there.

Trying to track down the source of these statistics, since they appear to be central to the argument, I recalled that, in 1991, Dr Susan Edwards of Buckingham University had used somewhat similar figures at a conference that I had covered for the *Guardian*, on the subject of female violence.[36] She had said that figures for 1987 showed that women who killed their husbands were more likely to be convicted of murder (37.5 per cent) than men who killed their wives (26.6 per cent).

I wrote to Dr Edwards, saying her figures seemed similar to the 'Crown Prosecution Service' figures, and asking where hers came from. Dr Edwards responded that the 37.5 per cent and 26.6 per cent figures given in my *Guardian* article referred to a special computer run done for her by the Home Office for the year 1987.[37] She added that she suspected the 40/24 per cent divide was a rounding up and down of 'those same figures quoted randomly by people from my original figures published in the *New Law Journal*'.[38]

'The 40/24 per cent divide is the figure for 1987 – this is the *same*. My figures refer to spousal homicides only. They are Home Office figures and must be *correct*.' Dr Edwards further commented that the Home Office had 'masked this 1987 reality by combining figures in such a way and interpreting them in such a way as to make it appear as if women are treated leniently'.[39] (When Dr Edwards's original article was published, in 1990, 1987 was the latest year for which figures were available.)

I shall not refer to these figures any further. They were for 1987 and, because the actual numbers involved are so low, I don't feel confident relying on them.

The figures in the Home Office letter responding to Miller's piece are based on an analysis of 1,071 domestic homicide killings by women (defined as killing husbands, partners, lovers)[40] which took place between 1983 and 1991.[41]

This analysis shows, says the letter, that the belief that women accused of domestic homicide are treated more harshly than men accused of the same crime is not true.

The nub of the problem is contained in that statement and needs to be made clear. Miller's piece was about the unfairness of the law in its treatment of battered women who kill. The Home Office letter responding to it refers to domestic homicides. But Miller and the Home Office are at cross purposes. Domestic homicides are not synonymous with killings involving battering scenarios. All killings involving battering are domestic homicides, but not all domestic homicides involve battering.

The Home Office figures do not distinguish which domestic homicides involve battering;[42] this means that when we are talking about convictions for murder or manslaughter and about sentencing we don't know whether the crimes under discussion involved battering or not.

A further, very important point must be made before turning to the letter itself. It talks about the belief that women accused of domestic homicide are treated more harshly than men accused of the same crime. There is another area of confusion here. Domestic homicide is killing of spouse by spouse. Same title, same crime. Maybe. Sometimes. For instance, a wife and her lover kill the husband for her freedom and the insurance money, or a husband and his lover kill the wife for his freedom and the insurance money – on the face of it, the same crime.

However, in a substantial number of cases of domestic homicide, according to what campaigners, lawyers and researchers have told me, the husband kills the wife as the culmination of a battering relationship. Statistical estimates already referred to indicate that in around 70 per cent of domestic homicides where women killed spouses, these spouses had been beating them. It seems highly likely, therefore, that the majority of domestic homicides involve battering. The pattern of this majority of cases is that where the husband kills it is a graduation from a series of inflicted beatings; where the wife kills it is a single desperate response to the husband's prolonged battering.

The crimes being compared are not similar but about as dissimilar as you can get, given that both involve husbands and wives killing each other. It would hardly be just for the perpetrators of what are, when seen in context, such different crimes to be treated equally. Thus, what might appear to be leniency to women disappears when you take into account the seriousness of the crime and the context in which it occurred.

Another statistical warning: we need to be aware of the impression which can be conveyed by the use of percentages when we are comparing similar numbers of men and women. There's a danger, if you talk of 25 per cent of A compared to 25 per cent of B, of giving an impression that these percentages represent equal numbers, whereas we know from HO figures that on average about a hundred men and twenty-five women a year are convicted of killing their spouse or lover. Four times as many men as women kill spouses; of the women who kill spouses, it seems that almost three-quarters are responding to male violence.

A discussion of six of the points raised in the Home Office letter to the *Sunday Times* follows:

1 *At the trial, 22 per cent of the women but only 5 per cent of the men were acquitted of all charges. We do not have complete data on the reason for acquittal, but for those women who did not deny the killing*

and for whom we have information it appears that the most successful defence was one of self-defence.

The 22 per cent and the 5 per cent figures presumably reflect the context of the killing about which we know nothing. But how representative are these figures for battered wives who kill, when we don't even know if battering was involved?

If the figures represent some women who had been battered and who successfully pleaded self-defence, they must have responded 'immediately' to the husband's violence. For research conducted by Professor Katherine O'Donovan, of Rutherford College, University of Kent, on the law reports concerning women who were battered and who killed their abusive partners, shows that where there is a delay between the latest battering and the killing there has never been a successful plea of self-defence: 'Which is not surprising given that English law cannot contemplate the use of self-defence where there is a delay,' says Professor O'Donovan.[43]

Quite possibly the women who pleaded self-defence successfully responded to the latest of a series of batterings immediately, thus falling within the law on self-defence. Or, quite conceivably, if there was no history of battering, they simply struck out to defend themselves during the course of a single attack. We don't know because we don't know the context of these particular cases.

2 *At the trial, of those found guilty of unlawful domestic killing, 81% of the women were found guilty of the lesser charge of manslaughter, whereas only 62% of the men were.*

Wouldn't you expect these figures if, when men kill, most of the killings follow a series of batterings? They don't show that women are being treated more leniently for a similar crime: they are far more likely to show that when men kill women as a final act of battering they are less likely to have the charge reduced to manslaughter than is a woman who, typically responding after suffering prolonged battering, strikes back and kills her attacker.

Since the male crime is nearer to murder and the female crime nearer to self-defence, wouldn't you expect more women to be found guilty on a lesser charge?

3 *Of the men found guilty of manslaughter and for whom we have* *information about their defence, 47% used the defence of diminished responsibility, 32% provocation and 21% no intent to kill.*

Here I profess myself nonplussed. I haven't been researching men's defences to domestic homicide but I was surprised to see that almost half had been found guilty on the grounds of diminished responsibility because, during the three years I'd been researching the subject, people working in this area – academics, campaigners, lawyers – had all talked matter-of-factly about provocation as the man's defence and diminished responsibility as the woman's.

Again, it's difficult to know how to respond without knowing in what circumstance these killings were committed. Were these cases which involved battering? At least some of them must have been. However, Sue Lees, Co-ordinator of the Women's Studies Unit at the University of North London, who has researched and written about violence against women, points out that the concept of diminished responsibility can be

used in such a way as to condone male violence. For example, I have seen a diagnosis of depression accepted as evidence for diminished responsibility when there was no evidence that the defendant was undergoing any kind of treatment or suffering any significant symptoms . . .[44]

In the case of Fares, in March 1988 at the Old Bailey, a man was charged with the murder of his common-law wife and two young children, whom he set fire to by throwing petrol over the house, soon after he had separated from them. He was in regular employment and was not under a doctor. He had writen in his diary that he planned to kill his wife and children by setting fire to them. He was sentenced to six years for manslaughter on the grounds of diminished responsibility.[45]

A complicating factor, says Lees, is that defence lawyers often plead more than one defence; if the jury decide the person is guilty of manslaughter, it's up to them to say on what grounds. 'They are often confused by the differences between the defences and make some strange decisions.'

4 *Of similar women found guilty of manslaughter, 33% used the defence of diminished responsibility, 34% provocation and 33% no intent to kill.*

I would like to point out again that the women, in most cases, present the opposite profile to most men convicted of killing a spouse, but we don't know the context. Maybe none of the 34 per cent who pleaded provocation were battered wives. I'm working on the basis that around 70 per cent of domestic homicides where women killed involved battering; it's possible that 34 per cent of women involved in domestic homicides weren't involved in battering scenarios.

Maybe all the women convicted on the grounds of diminished responsibility were involved in battering scenarios, and were responding finally to years of abuse – we just don't know.

As Lorraine Radford, a senior lecturer in Social Administration and Women's Studies at the Roehampton Institute, London, says:

> There is no way of learning from the *figures* the circumstances underlying men's and women's claims of diminished responsibility and provocation. We would need to know the circumstances leading up to the pleas of provocation and diminished responsibility to make conclusive empirical claims about discriminatory practice. Reported cases of provocation and diminished responsibility currently show that when the circumstances leading up to homicidal acts are examined, justice for battered women who kill is at the very best inconsistent.[46]

5 *As for differences in sentencing those guilty of domestic homicide: between 1989 and 1991, 73% of men convicted of manslaughter received a prison sentence compared with only 29% of women. The average sentence length for men found guilty of manslaughter was 56 months; for women it was 47 months. And 59% of women were sentenced to either probation or a suspended sentence compared with 12% of men.*

As for the differences in sentencing, once again, given the differing backgrounds to most of the killings, you'd expect such a pattern.

6 *The issues presented to courts in cases of domestic homicide are frequently complex and distressing. No statistical analysis can bring out in full those complexities, and how they affect individuals' lives.*

I agree.

To sum up: I have argued that the figures can't be relied on because they conflate domestic homicide and killings involving battering, but tell us nothing of the circumstances of the particular cases.

One final point: it would not surprise me to learn that a woman who came across as a devoted wife and mother, but had snapped after many years of brutality, received a lenient sentence. For instance:

> There was mercy yesterday for a slave wife who turned on her master. She raised an axe to the brutal husband who had battered her into submission for fourteen years but was placed on probation. Her counsel described her as a wonderful mother to her five children. Her teenage son told the court. 'I would say she is the best mum in the world.' Yet despite all the cruelty she still loved her husband deeply.[47]

The slave wife who killed her brutal husband still loved him deeply and measured up particularly well to the good mother stereotype.

But what of Pamela Megginson, the 65-year-old mistress of 79-year-old Alec Hubbers? He told Megginson he had found a new mistress, half his age, and that he intended to live with her. She said she felt 'churned up and humiliated'. They had a 'ghastly quarrel' over dinner and then went back to the flat.

> 'I got into bed with him and had oral sex which he always wanted. I was doing it partly because of routine and partly because I wanted my position back.' As soon as she began making love to him, he pushed her away and told her she was not as good as his new love, nor as beautiful. 'He was shouting. "I don't want you. I only want her." I lost my head and went completely crazy. I reached out of bed for the champagne bottle we had for lunch and hit him a number of times.'[48]

Compare her case with that of Doris Croft, 'a very gentle, well-loved soul who killed the publican with whom she lived when she discovered he was having an affair with someone else.

Doris was not sent to prison at all.'[49] How closely a woman conforms to the approved stereotype is relevant, since she is being tried as a woman as well as a defendant. It's impossible to believe this had no bearing on the case of the 'articulate, fiery and poised' Sara Thornton.[50]

THE LAW AND BATTERED WOMEN

Bisla Rajinder Singh, aged 44, a clothes-shop owner from Erith, Kent, was given an 18-month sentence suspended for a year, after being cleared of murder by a jury at the Old Bailey. He said he had killed his wife, Abnash, 'to shut her up'. Judge Neil Dennison said, 'You have suffered, through no fault of your own, a terrible existence for a very long time. I do not see that sending you to prison is going to do you any good and, more importantly, is going to do your children any good.'[51]

Carol Peters killed her husband with a knife during a fight that left her in hospital for seven days. He had constantly threatened to kill her and their three children while they were sleeping. She was so terrorized that at one point he made her carry cans of petrol out to their car, telling her that he was going to set her on fire and make it look like an accident. She was charged with murder, found guilty and sentenced to life imprisonment.[52]

In the case of *Wright* (1975), who killed his wife with a hammer as she lay in bed one morning, what counted as provocation was that he'd had to put up with his wife's '"Saturday night and Sunday morning" activities with boyfriends'.[53]

It is not my contention that the law *routinely* treats harshly battered wives who kill their abusers. I accept that, as Helena Kennedy puts it, 'in the majority of cases, women who break under the pressure of domestic violence are treated with mercy'.[54] However, I do contend that there's a problem with the inflexibility of the law on provocation and how it operates in the context of battered women who kill; that the law itself, being founded on male experience and interpreted predominantly by men, operates unaware of its own gendered assumptions and often fails to take account of women's experiences; that the women's conduct and behaviour *as women* can influence the verdict and sentence they receive.

> Justice is likely to remain a lottery while so much depends on the woman's fulfilment of society's expectations. One of the factors which undoubtedly affects the outcome of murder trials is, as always, the persona of the woman in the dock. It is my view that this is what really determines the outcome. Women who conform to the conventional image of the cowed victim fare better than those who come to trial angry that they are being blamed for what ultimately took place.[55]

DEFENCES TO MURDER

There are three possible defences to a charge of murder for battered women who kill:[56] self-defence – a complete defence in that if it succeeds the defendant walks free from the court – and the two partial defences of provocation and diminished responsibility, which reduce the charge from murder to manslaughter on those grounds.

Self-defence

The history of the law of self-defence goes back to the thirteenth century. It's posited on a man's right to defend himself from attack. I use *him*self here because the law was framed in the context of one man attacking another and the attacked man having the right to defend himself. The picture was of one-to-one combat between men, and women were not part of that picture. Women were not out in the world, doing, deciding and sometimes fighting, but at, or working close to, home and looking after the children.

There was no need for any law of self-defence to consider women: men were the norm and women didn't fight; anyway, women were in the charge of their fathers and then of their husbands, the father having 'given away' the woman to the man in marriage.

Yet women weren't completely out of the picture. Katherine O'Donovan notes some relevant background to the way wives who kill husbands are seen by the law:

> . . . in the past the killing of a wife by a husband was regarded as a less serious offence than the killing of a husband by a wife. The wife was charged with petty treason [as when a serf killed the master] whereas the husband was charged with murder.[57]

If you put the historically enshrined idea of woman/subordinate : man/master together with a law of self-defence rooted in the idea of two males fighting each other, you can begin to glimpse where the problems for some battered women who kill their husbands might arise.

As the law of self-defence evolved, it stressed that the attack must make one fear for one's life, and that the force used to repel the attack must be proportionate, i.e. comparable, not excessive, which fits with a scenario of two grown men fighting each other. A woman who kills a man in the midst of a fight, when he is attacking her, is unlikely to be found guilty of murder because she will be able to enter a successful plea of self-defence or provocation.

However, this is rarely how women respond when they have been beaten over a period of time, as we saw earlier. Although some do, in general women do not meet force with force. We're brought up to please and placate, to avoid confrontation, anger and certainly fighting, not to react with a similar show of instant aggression. Responding to an attack just doesn't feel right to most women who are also, as a rule, smaller and less strong than men. And in the context we're interested in, domestic violence, the attack is not a single, one-off attack by a stranger outside the pub, or a fight with a fellow schoolboy in the school yard. The attack is typically one of a series, probably increasing in severity over time, by a man whom the woman may well love, in her own home.

There are further crucial differences. What if, after each beating – which you hope will be the last, if only you can figure out how not to provoke him – he cries and tells you he's sorry, he loves you so much and swears it will never happen again? What if he's big enough – and mad enough when he's drunk – to break down any doors you might slam behind you? What if the kids are asleep (you hope) upstairs? What if you've tried to leave before and that ended up in an even worse beating than you've ever had? What if you've nowhere to go if you do escape?

And what if, the next time he attacks you, it's the worst beating yet and he threatens to kill you but doesn't and instead falls asleep? It is not as strange as it may sound since drinking plays a large part in many battering scenarios. You know or believe you know that next time he might well do it and that you won't be able to defend yourself so, in fear for your life, you pick up a knife and stab him before he gets the chance to start again, not intending to kill but to stop him from killing you.

In such circumstances, the law of self-defence will not be available to you. It will not apply to what you did because you didn't respond to the fear of immediate harm to yourself. You didn't use proportional force in the midst of an attack which had led you to fear for your own safety. Although the law doesn't insist, as it used to, that you ought to retreat, if you can, from immediate danger, the fact that you didn't leave may well influence the judge in his summing up and/or the jury's verdict. As I've said, the question that's always being asked is: 'Why didn't she leave?'

A Word about the Reasonable Man

The concept which underpins the law, in the context of self-defence, is that the amount of force judged to be properly proportional and acceptable when responding to attack is assessed in terms of how the reasonable man would respond. 'Man' as in 'reasonable man' is used to cover men and women; 'the courts have attempted to say that the term "reasonable man" is inclusive of women'.[58]

When people in a male-dominated culture use 'man' to mean men and women they are unconsciously subsuming women into that male culture; the normative, the standard, is the rational male, as opposed to the emotional female. The interpretation of a 'reasonable man' is still being made in terms of what seems reasonable to *men*, in the light of the experience of their own lives.

'Graff suggests that many "decades of 'reasonable' men shooting and clubbing each other to death produced common law of self-defence which adequately speaks to men's needs." '[59] But what about women's needs? The law of self-defence is blind to the experiences of battered women, and knows nothing of women's life experiences. These were not thought of as the law of self-defence was shaping over the centuries. Women were part of 'mankind' and, in the context of the law of self-defence, invisible. Women did not have to defend themselves in armed combat: men were there to protect women. Women were under the charge of fathers and husbands: it was up to them to keep their own houses and womenfolk in order. However, if a woman did kill her husband, she would be charged with a more serious offence than if he killed her. She was seen to be attacking her master, i.e. her husband. In 1866 [in USA] the actions a husband could legally take against his wife were amended, giving a man the right to beat his wife 'with a stick as large as his finger but not larger than his thumb'. In this instance we see the law traditionally condoning some beating of a wife by a husband. It wasn't until 1891 that it became illegal in this country for a husband to beat or imprison his wife.[60]

Put all of those factors together with women's upbringing, which heavily discourages physical aggression, thus rendering most women unlikely to respond immediately to an attack, and it becomes clear why self-defence is an extremely problematic defence for battered women who kill. Self-defence is a complete defence. If it is successfully argued the person is acquitted. And, as Katherine O'Donovan said earlier, as far as she knows, it is not a defence that has ever succeeded in England for a battered wife who killed, where there was a delay.[61]

Yet, say the campaigners, this is what the woman herself is doing, finally defending herself. It is not how the law sees it.

Provocation

If successful, the partial defence of provocation, unlike self-defence which is a complete defence, can reduce the charge from murder to manslaughter. Whereas the judge has discretion about sentencing for manslaughter, a conviction for murder carries a mandatory life sentence in England, so the successful partial defences of provocation (or diminished responsibility) to murder can mean the difference between a life sentence and probation – or even a conditional discharge.

This definition of what constitutes provocation comes from the judgement on *R* v. *Duffy* in 1949:

Some act, or series of acts, done by the dead man to the accused which would cause in any reasonable person and actually causes in the accused, a sudden and temporary loss of self-control, rendering the accused so subject to passion as to make him or her for the moment not master of his mind.[62]

Mrs Duffy had been convicted of the murder of her husband. There was a history of violence by Mr Duffy; Mrs Duffy killed him after a violent quarrel while he was in bed. At the appeal Judge Devlin said:

A long course of cruel conduct may be more blameworthy than a sudden act provoking retaliation, but you are not concerned with blame attaching to the dead man . . . It does not matter how cruel he was, how much or how little he was to blame, except in so far as it resulted in the final act of the appellant.[63]

Mrs Duffy had not acted immediately: her plea of provocation failed. And her case set the pattern for what was to come.

There are three requirements which must be satisfied if a defence of provocation is to succeed.

The things said or done must first of all constitute provocation; the action causing the death of another must be committed in the heat of the moment; and the retaliation to the provocation must be appropri-

97

ate. All these conditions must be satisfied, and each involves a subjective element in the first instance.[64]

First of all, what is seen as likely to provoke the 'reasonable man' is the basis of the judgement as to what constitutes provocation. You can say 'man' includes women but the viewpoint is male. As Edwards points out:

> Precedent in the UK, USA and Australia has mapped out precisely what situation and circumstances the courts consider to constitute justifiable provocation. At the top of the list in all these jurisdictions is the situation in which a husband kills his wife who has had another sexual relationship, or taunted him over his sexual prowess.[65]

Second, the heat-of-the-moment response by the battered woman:

> The very nature of prolonged violence, the apparent initial tolerance by the victim [in a battering scenario] and her failure to respond violently immediately is contrary to the 'heat of the moment' quality which is required by the current definition of provocation.[66]

There is also a risk involved of immediately fighting back against a probably much larger, stronger man who is frequently violent, whereas for the women responding it may be a single, first, tentative attempt. And aren't women warned, when raped, not to respond aggressively lest they suffer more injury?

Three, the force used in response must be proportionate. This goes back to the idea of 'trial by combat and duelling'. And how do women fit into that scenario? '. . . what is the equivalent of male force in female conduct?'[67]

To return to point one: it is up to the judge in a particular case to decide what constitutes provocation. If he decides that battering over a long period does not constitute provocation in the legal sense then he can deny that option of manslaughter on the grounds of provocation to the jury. When that happens they are left with a choice between murder and acquittal.

However, says Katherine O'Donovan,

in the case of *R* v. *Rossiter* Mr Justice Russell in the Court of Appeal criticized the trial judge for failure to leave for the jury's consideration the issue of provocation. And he said: 'We take the law to be that wherever there is material which is capable of amounting to provocation, however tenuous it may be, the jury must be given the privilege of ruling upon it.'

So I claim that there's been a slight change from Duffy in the sense that they're more cautious now, they're afraid of being criticized for withholding the question of provocation. So they're going to leave the question of provocation – however tenuous the evidence is – to the jury.[68]

She also points out that there's been reluctance on the part of juries, since the Sara Thornton case, to convict for homicide in cases of cumulative provocation. She sees this as evidence of public opinion differing from the law's definition of provocation.[69]

Jeremy Horder, of Worcester College, Oxford, believes 'the common law on provocation is at present unclear and that it 'may be operating harshly against some of those who have received very grave provocation but whose angry reaction was not instantaneous'.[70]

He sees the extra legal requirement, introduced in *R* v. *Duffy*, that the killing should immediately follow a 'sudden and temporary loss of self-control', as having narrowed the basis for a successful defence based on provocation. Previously a killer had only to plead that he/she had acted in hot blood. Thus, he maintains, the ruling in *Duffy* excluded from the scope of mitigation offered by the partial defence of provocation 'the many defendants who only boiled up after a few minutes' reflection on the provocation. Yet previously [i.e. before the Duffy case in 1949] such defendants were permitted to plead provocation because they acted in hot blood'.

He considers that the narrowing of the 'simple and workable distinction between acting in hot and cold blood was narrowed without due consideration and deference to several hundred years of legal authority',[71] and further points out that the Appeal Court ruling which set Kiranjit Ahluwalia free contradicts the earlier *Duffy* ruling and leaves future judges with two opposing rulings to 'guide' them on the interpretation of the law on provocation, '. . . thus the law is now uncertain and confused'.[72]

He would like matters to revert to the pre-*Duffy* situation and has suggested that this can be done simply by amending the relevant section of the Homicide Act 1957 which would not so much change the law as 'reassert unambiguously the older, pre-*Duffy*, legal view'. The rider (to section 3) which he suggests is: 'There is no longer any rule of law that a provoked loss of self-control must be sudden as well as temporary.'[73]

However, in a book published in 1992, Mr Horder goes much further and calls for the doctrine of provocation to be abolished and for the effect of provocation in murder cases to be left as a matter 'for mitigation in sentence, should the mandatory life sentence for murder ever be abolished'.[74] That would be the option preferred by many commentators and campaigners who are less happy about merely 'tinkering' with the defence of provocation, which is how they regard the dropping of the word 'sudden' from the requirement that response to provocation be as a result of 'sudden and temporary loss of control'.

For instance, the loss of self-control would still remain

central to provocation. This is because the law remains based on adult men's experiences, or stereotypes built on male models which assume that men traditionally act spontaneously and in rage using methods like choking and strangling. It takes no account of the differences in women's socialization and circumstances, nor specifically of the fact that women's choice of methods and use of weapons can rarely be spontaneous because of the fear of being overwhelmed by a physically stronger man.[75]

In the view of the Rights of Women (see Useful Addresses) 'relaxing the rules around provocation is far more likely to enable even more men to use this defence than currently, without fully addressing the circumstances of women who kill'.[76]

Katherine O'Donovan also has reservations about changing the law on provocation and cites a change to the law in Australia.

New South Wales has amended its law relating to provocation in order to reflect an increased awareness of domestic violence. The

Crimes (Homicide) Amendment Act 1982 allows any past conduct of the deceased towards the defendant to be the basis of provocation. However, encouraging pleas of provocation in such cases may have certain drawbacks. Arguments which blame the victim may also be encouraged. Attention, which should focus on cumulative violence and the appropriate response thereto by the law, the police, the community, may shift onto the victim.[77]

It is fear, she says, which leads to delay in responding immediately to violence, and this is simply not acknowledged or reflected by the law as it stands at the moment. She wonders whether one possible way forward would be the acknowledgement by the law of the idea of the slow burn, of cumulative rage, as a response to cumulative violence. 'It has some purchase in California, though it has not been accepted in English law.'[78]

The feeling overall is that the way the law on provocation operates in the context of battered women who kill is too complex and too deeply rooted in the male-equals-the-norm ideology for any mere modification of it to be sufficient to rid it of its discriminatory bias against such women.

Both provocation and diminished responsibility evolved as partial defences to murder in light of the mandatory life sentence for murder. Before going on to consider how ending the mandatory nature of the life sentence might help I want first to look briefly at that second partial defence, of diminished responsibility, and then at what we can learn from events and research in the USA.

Diminished Responsibility

Diminished responsibility is widely regarded as the battered woman's best bet, just as provocation is regarded as being tailor-made for men who use violence to keep women in line, especially as far as sex and staying in the relationship are concerned.

Kiranjit Ahluwalia killed her abusive husband by setting fire to him in May 1989. She had suffered ten years of abuse on an almost daily basis. As well as beating her and pushing her downstairs, her husband had sexually abused and raped her, tried to strangle her, and had threatened her with a knife on more than one occasion. Threats from his family had stopped her from enforcing court injunctions she had obtained against him. Since he was constantly threatening to kill her she was terrified of him.

On the night she killed him he had hit her and threatened to burn her face with an iron and he'd tried to break her legs. She was found guilty of murder but, in 1992, her conviction was quashed on appeal; not, however, on the grounds of provocation but because a medical report saying she was suffering from depression had been overlooked at her trial.

At the re-trial, the prosecution said they accepted that she had been suffering from mental illness when she killed her husband and that this had impaired her responsibility. Her action was not seen as a reasonable response to ten years of torture and terror; neither her husband's abuse of her over ten years nor his actions on the night counted as provocation. The defence which succeeded finally was the partial defence of diminished responsibility.

In order to plead diminished responsibility successfully, a defendant must show she or he is suffering from an abnormality of mind resulting either from sickness, injury or a developmental problem and that this abnormality meant that her or his responsibility at the time of killing was impaired. Since pleas of diminished responsibility have been successful for battered women who kill, what's wrong with women using them? Why all the fuss about provocation? First of all, there's a risk for the woman herself and also a serious implication for other women: if too much is made of the 'abnormality' of mind then it is a psychiatric explanation that is sought for women's deviant behaviour.

But is it unreasonable for a woman, subjected to years of brutality and terrified for her life, to snap, finally, and react by attacking or even by killing her abuser? Given that she's tried everything else she could think of to stop him and is now in despair, and again in fear for her life, can her behaviour be described as irrational? To be content with women pleading diminished responsibility is to be content with women continuing to be defined in terms of their inherent instability and not in terms of rational adults responsible for their actions. The defence of diminished responsibility fits neatly within the old biological determinist explanation of strange female behaviour.

I am not saying that diminished responsibility is always an inappropriate defence in these circumstances but, because it fits so well with stereotyped 'understandings' of women's behaviour, and says nothing about the justice of the woman's action, the question of justification is side-stepped.

THE LAW IN AMERICA

In the USA there have been moves already to widen the law on defensive killings and new partial defences of imperfect self-defence and extreme emotional disturbance have been recognized in some states, while the acceptance of Battered Woman Syndrome has proved helpful to some women.

Widening the Law on Defensive Killing

As far back as 1977 American courts acknowledged 'the problems which battered women face in retreating and escaping from a situation of "imminent danger"'. Over the last eighteen years cases have been

> won in America, based on an acknowledgement of the importance of the differences between a man involved in a street fight and a woman in fear of an attack from her abuser ... Beginning with appeals where women had defended themselves against rapists, a series of cases relaxed the imminent danger and proportional force principles, thereby allowing women room to argue self-defence when they had performed a 'pre-emptive' strike to ward off an anticipated attack.[79]

In 1974, Yvonne Wanrow was sentenced to two twenty-year terms and a five-year term for wounding one attacker and killing another whom she believed was a rapist and child molester. At a new trial in 1977, the original conviction was overturned 'partly on the grounds that the jury had not been properly instructed on self-defense'. The Washington Supreme Court's landmark decision in the Wanrow case made it possible to argue that 'a woman who killed to save herself or her children from imminent danger of death or great bodily injury might be acting in a *reasonable* and *justifiable* manner' [emphasis in original].[80]

It also seriously dented the 'reasonable man' standard with its implications for women who used weapons. As it was a landmark decision it's worth quoting:

> [The instruction as given by the trial court] leaves the jury with the impression the objective standard to be applied is that applicable to an altercation between two men. The impression created – that a 5' 4" woman with a cast on her leg and using a crutch must, under the law, somehow repel an assault by a 6' 2" intoxicated man without employing weapons in her defense, unless the jury finds her determination of the degree of danger to be objectively reasonable – constitutes a separate and distinct misstatement of the law and, in the context of this case, violates the respondent's right to equal protection under the law. The respondent was entitled to have the jury consider her actions in the light of her own perception of the situation, including those perceptions which were a product of our nation's 'long and unfortunate history of sex discrimination' . . . Until such time as the effects of that history are eradicated, care must be taken to assure that our self-defense instructions afford women the right to have their conduct judged in light of the individual physical handicaps which are the product of sex discrimination. To fail to do so is to deny the right of the individual woman involved to trial by the same rules that are applicable to male defendants.[81]

Cases since Wanrow have extended the principles established in that case to cover defensive killings by battered women. While a history of victimization is not enough 'by itself . . . to establish a case of self-defence' what tends to happen is that the courts 'assess a woman's perception of imminent danger not in relation to the standards of a "reasonable man", but as a "reasonable battered woman".'[82] Rights of Women, in this country, has called for an end to reasonableness being defined in terms of the 'reasonable man', and suggests instead that '"honest belief" replace the concept of reasonableness'.[83]

Two New Partial Defences

Another possible way forward for the law might be offered by the concept of '"imperfect self-defence" where an honest but unreasonable belief that the attack must be responded to with deadly force mitigates a murder charge to manslaughter'. Certain states in America recognize this concept and it is, believes Katherine O'Donovan, 'worthy of further investigation'.[84]

Helena Kennedy points out that in parts of the United States a defence which

> encapsulates both provocation and diminished responsibility is that of Extreme Emotional Disturbance, which reduces murder to manslaughter. A re-evaluation of the law of homicide could consider a similar defence which would embrace the desperation that can drive men and women to kill.[85]

Battered Woman Syndrome and Expert Testimony

Battered Woman Syndrome arises from the work of American psychologist Dr Lenore Walker, whose theory is that a woman who is repeatedly abused 'learns helplessness' and is effectively paralysed by fear. This is why, says Walker, women who suffer cumulative violence don't leave. The 'cycle of violence' described by her has three phases: 'tension building', where the woman is aware of the man's feelings of aggression and attempts to calm things down; 'acute battering', and a final phase which is characterized by remorse on the part of the abusing mate who promises it won't happen again.

Battered Woman Syndrome gives expert witnesses a chance to explain to the jury how a woman can come to believe she is in imminent danger of being killed even if it might not seem so to the jury, 'even if the circumstances of the killing do not involve the kind of immediate threat traditionally seen within the scope of self-defence'.[86]

In 1984, Walker's evidence of Battered Woman Syndrome was accepted for the first time by an American court. In the *State* v. *Kelly*, the New Jersey Supreme Court said some women became so demoralized and degraded by the fact that they could not predict or control the violence that they sank into a state of psychological paralysis and became unable to take any action at all to improve or alter the situation.

However, there are problems with the Battered Woman Syndrome and with the use of expert testimony. If the syndrome explains women's paralysis – that they are unable to take any action – how do they manage to strike back? It also makes me uneasy that it fits so neatly into the historical and traditional pattern of pathologizing women, of somehow locating the reason for what happened within the woman, not with the perpetrator of the abuse which precipitated the act. And its gender-specificity bothers me: there aren't many, if any, syndromes to explain men's behaviour.

Helena Kennedy too is wary of the gender-specific name, Battered Woman Syndrome; it also concerns her

> that an acceptance of a rigidly defined syndrome can exclude those who do not completely conform to its criteria. Women find such varied ways of surviving that behavioural checklists do not always work. What is clear from the now extensive research is that all sorts of women are subjected to abuse, deal with it in a multiplicity of ways and put up with it because complicated dynamics are set in motion. However, putting the name to one side, it is crucial that the *principles* of 'battered woman syndrome' should be acknowledged by the courts in Britain, as part of an educational process to dispel myths about domestic violence [my emphasis].[87]

Although I do accept that Battered Woman Syndrome gives experts a chance to explain how a woman might come to believe she's in imminent danger of being killed even if it doesn't appear so to the jury, expert testimony can prove to be a double-edged sword. If we wholeheartedly welcome the experts who would explain and testify to the effects and implications of Battered Woman Syndrome do we risk opening the door to what can happen with psychiatric expert testimony: the defence 'expert' confirms the woman is suffering from BWS and the prosecution 'expert' denies it.

In fact, research in the States has led some feminists to be nervous of syndrome defences: first of all it's up to an 'expert' to decide whether a woman comes within the category or not; then there's a question of 'which "expert testimony" the juries are prepared to accept and which they reject'.[88] All of these developments in the United States offer the possibilities for fruitful exploration. We can learn from their advances as well as from what may well prove to be their mistakes.

Self-Preservation

Perhaps the most comprehensive attempt to capture women's experiences within the law is contained in the proposal by the Rights of Women (ROW): that a new partial defence to murder, that of self-preservation, be created. It would be of comparable standing to the partial defences of provocation and diminished responsibility.

Avoiding reforms aimed at changed existing defences, the Rights of Women bases the new defence on women's experiences. Having listened to 'personal testimony from women who have killed abusive/violent men' and having drawn on research in the United States, they say the common theme which emerges is that

> women who have been subjected to continuing abuse/violence reach a point where they come to believe that it is a question of 'it's my life or his'. Both the history of violence, and the many attempts women make to avoid or escape it, play a part in their reaching this desperate and despairing conclusion.[89]

They stress they are not arguing that such killings should be either condoned or made lawful but they are arguing that they shouldn't constitute murder or carry a mandatory life sentence. Their proposal is intended to offer 'a way into the legal system for women and would allow the jury to be in possession of all the relevant facts and circumstances to reach their decisions regarding the applicability of this defence without being constrained by legal definitions and concepts which were devised to deal with different situations'. The judge could then pass sentence according to his discretion, as happens with other manslaughter verdicts. ROW says

> what is important about this proposal is that it would allow women's different experiences and circumstances to be recognized in law. The new defence would reflect the particularity of women and children's experience of sexual/domestic violence and abuse, in the same way that provocation is currently structured around men's situations.[90]

The new defence is not, however, defined in sex-specific terms and could also be used by men.

ROW summarizes its proposed change to the Homicide Act 1957 thus: Self-preservation is a partial defence open to persons who
1 kill a partner or someone in a familial or familiar intimate relationship who
2 has subjected them to 'continuing'[91] sexual and/or physical abuse and intimidation to the extent that they
3 honestly believe that they have reached a point at which there is no future, and no protection or safety from the abuse, and are convinced that they will not continue to live while the aggressor is alive.

ROW would include sub-sections to allow for the following situations:
i a person acting in the protection of a child being subjected to abuse;
ii a child or young person acting in the protection of a mother or sibling being abused, as in the case of a child or young person victimized by sexual abuse acting to prevent the abuse being carried on to a sibling;
iii a household, or family members, acting together against a household/family member who is abusing all of them.

To use this defence defendants would have to provide evidence of a history of violence or abuse. This would take the form of testimony from the person herself with or without corroboration.

> Testimony from other members of the household, including children, friends and neighbours, would count as corroboration, as would documentors' or police reports, legal statements, court orders, or evidence from other agencies.[92]

While in sympathy with the aims of ROW, working barrister Jacqueline Gilliatt feels that their proposal of self-preservation is just 'too radical to be acceptable. It contains some interesting ideas and it helps broaden the debate but on a scale of one to ten the chances of getting it into law in ten years would be zilch. And in twenty years not much better.'

The third of the sub-sections she finds totally unacceptable. 'You could end up with the kids plotting to kill Dad; it's too far away from the idea of defence.' She also finds a problem with point 3 which allows the defence of self-preservation to be used by persons who 'honestly believe that they have reached a point at which there is no future, and no protection or safety from the abuse, and are convinced that they will not continue to live while the aggressor is alive'.

> Either that amounts to self-defence or it means nothing. And it doesn't get over the immediacy problem of the defences of self-defence and provocation.
>
> You have got to think about the jury. If the guy was unconscious they are going to wonder why she didn't leave while he was, as they see it, safe. You have to convince the jury that because of the state she was in at the time, killing him was the only option she could see. There's not much distinction between this and diminished responsibility. As I see the problem it is that the woman doesn't fit diminished responsibility because she is not temporarily mad. But she is in a real state. However, she doesn't fit the provocation defence because she doesn't react immediately. She falls between the two partial defences. Yet to convict such a woman of murder, to label her as a murderer and place her in the same category as someone

who kills cold-bloodedly out of greed, and to give her the same sentence, life, is obviously not just.[93]

Speaking generally about the law and battered women who kill, she says

the least preferable option would be to try and redefine provocation. The most preferable would be to drop the mandatory life sentence and at the same time to introduce degrees of murder. You would then no longer require the partial defences of provocation and diminished responsibility as they are presently defined and applied.

The ROW proposal would be a useful starting point for sentencing guidelines to make sure that the abolition of the life sentence was not merely a cosmetic change so far as the treatment of battered women who kill is concerned.[94]

Dropping the Mandatory Life Sentence

The suggestion that the mandatory life sentence for murder be dropped is favoured by lawyers, and at least some of the campaigners, and is my own preferred solution. While it doesn't take into account women's experiences *per se*, it would, I believe, lead to the greater flexibility needed to accommodate their different circumstances. And, of course, without the mandatory life sentence there'd be no need, as Gilliatt pointed out, for the problematic defences of provocation and diminished responsibility which evolved as an alternative to it.

Support for the scrapping of the mandatory life sentence for murder came from a report produced by a committee chaired by the Former Lord Chief Justice, Lord Lane, and published in December 1993.

As of today, all those convicted of murder – from the 'mercy killer' and the battered wife to the terrorist and armed robber – are sentenced in the same words. I cannot believe there is public support for this. It is quite wrong to require judges to sentence all types of murder in the same way regardless of the circumstances.[95]

At present anyone convicted of murder, irrespective of the circumstances, must be given life imprisonment; it is the mandatory sentence under the Murder (Abolition of Death Penalty) Act 1965.

'Life imprisonment' need not mean for the rest of the person's natural life. In exceptional circumstances, life imprisonment can mean that a person *does* spend the rest of his or her life in prison. However, 'the median period served before release on licence is between 11 and 12 years'.[96] After the trial, the judge sets the tariff – the number of years – to be served. This can be added to by the Home Secretary, taking into account the person's dangerousness and the public acceptability, in the Home Secretary's view, of the release of that person. No mandatory lifer can be released without the permission of the Home Secretary. He has the veto on their release. However, judicial review of his decision is possible and, indeed, is likely should he refuse release to open conditions. The Lane Committee's report was especially critical of the 'public acceptability' criterion announced by the Home Secretary, Michael Howard, in July 1993, when he said he would have to consider it before any lifer was released on licence.

The committee commented that:

> the introduction of a third phase, after punishment is complete and dangerousness is no longer an issue, bids fair to alter the whole framework of the system . . . Experience teaches that when politicians resort to 'public opinion' as a basis for a change of policy or a fresh course of action, it is advisable to scrutinize the proposals with particular care.[97]

The force of 'on licence' is that the person can be recalled to prison at any time, once they have been released. They need not even commit a minor offence: they are on licence. Anyone can call them to the attention of the police and they risk being put back in prison. In that sense 'life' means life.

The Lane Report clarified a common misapprehension about murder. Most people believe that someone can only be convicted of murder if that person intended to kill.

In fact, only a minority of people convicted of the offence have that intent: it is sufficient for the prosecution to prove an intent to cause serious injury. If death ensues, however unexpected, however unintended, the offence is made out and the mandatory life sentence must follow.[98]

The committee also had something to say about the law of provocation.

... cases of provocation, particularly those involving long-term domestic violence and abuse, where the strict legal requirements of provocation are not present and a conviction for murder therefore results, undoubtedly highlight the inappropriate nature of the mandatory life sentence. It is fundamentally wrong in principle that a judge should be required to pass upon the wife who has been maltreated for years by a brutal husband and eventually kills him, precisely the same sentence as that judge passes upon the ruthless shotgun robber who kills in cold blood.[99]

The only reservation I have about the dropping of the mandatory life sentence is that it still leaves the sentencing to the discretion of the judges, some of whom seem to have little understanding of the realities of women's lives. The only remedy I can see for this would be the sort of gender-awareness training Dr Gillian Mezey wants to see introduced for psychiatrists. And if psychiatrists, why not also judges, magistrates, police? As Helena Kennedy has said, bringing judges and members of other professional bodies together to help broaden their understanding of women's experiences in our society would help, although she cautions that persuading judges to be self-critical will have to be done in a 'goodwill' way if they are not to become defensive.[100]

CONCLUSION

The law, male-made, male-centred and rooted in that androcentric tradition, is particularly ill-equipped to accommodate battered women who kill, hence the controversy and the campaigns.

Those few women who kill their abusers do so typically as a single act of violence when they finally snap after perhaps years of abuse, whereas the killing by a man of his spouse is usually the final act after a long series of attacks. They are the same crime in that a spouse has killed a spouse; but much more unlike than like in that the woman has suffered much and her act is closer to, if not actually in, self-defence. The man, on the other hand, has caused much suffering, and has finally killed his spouse; his act must be seen as closer to, if not actually, murder.

This incomparability of what superficially and statistically appear to be the same crimes is at the root of my counterarguments to the official position. However, what figures can never show are: the circumstances of individual cases, what actually happened, and the extent to which a woman's conformity to approved stereotypes influences how the court perceives her and how she is judged.

CHAPTER 6

Women in Prison

JACKIE CHILD: ONE WOMAN'S VIEW FROM THE INSIDE

HMP Holloway: winter 1993/4

'Some women are in four-bed dorms, some are in single cells. I am in a single cell. You're woken at 7.00 a.m. and the doors open at seven-thirty. If you're not up and dressed by then for a third time, you're down the punishment block, which usually means you end up being fined – which is a hardship if you smoke.

'If you've got a job you go off at 8.15 a.m. Jobs in the prison are gardens, gym orderlies (which is what I do), wing cleaning, laundry, stores, sewing room, library, cleaning all over the prison. If you don't work you can go to education. There are so many courses to do you're spoiled for choice. I am doing a Community Sports Leaders' Award (CSLA) course, which is a qualification I can use outside. And I'm studying psychology.

'Holloway has a few petty rules but basically you can make it work for you; in fact it's like a boarding school. If you are issued a red band, which makes you a trustee, you can walk to where you are going unescorted.

'We come back to the landing at 11.20 a.m. which is dinner-time. The food here is not very healthy, as there's too much starch. Then you're locked up from 11.40 a.m to 1.10 p.m. when you go off back to work. Back on the landing at 3.20 p.m. for tea, locked up from 3.40 p.m. to 5.00 p.m. then you can go off to education, gym or association. Full association is from five until eight or it could be either only five o'clock to half-past six or half-past six until eight o'clock. Weekends are the boring times as there's a lot of bang-up in the evenings with no association.

'Surprising for a woman's prison, but it's rather dirty here. Basically it's what you make of it. The worst thing for me, is being separated from my children, that's all.

'But when I first came in I was in C1, the psychiatric unit – that's a different story altogether. I was on C1 for five months. That was because of the nature of my charge; people who are charged with murder are assessed [psychiatrically], also people who are charged with arson. But they're not usually kept for five months. Why I was I don't know.

'From what I saw it's the saddest place to be. It's run by nurses and screws. There aren't enough nurses and there certainly aren't enough good ones; they simply can't cope. And they're not qualified to look after disturbed patients. If they can't cope with a particular inmate they simply leave her locked up. There is far too much bang-up. Then they wonder why so many women cut up. While I was there, Donna, a girl I'd come to know and like, hung herself. All she needed was the right help but she would never have got it in Holloway. Since I've been on normal location another woman has hanged herself.

'The screws are there to keep order if someone flips. I must say, when I was there, there were some good screws who did try to help inmates, but it's an impossible job. These women need stimulation and so much love but unfortunately these are definitely the forgotten ones. Even the girls on ordinary location [that is not in the hospital but in the main body of the prison] call them names like 'fraggles' and 'muppets'. Through their own ignorance they label these women who then won't go to education because they know when they say their unit, C1, to the officer at the door, the stupid remarks will start.

'They shouldn't have psychiatric units in prison; they don't work. In fact, in my opinion they do more harm than good. The nurses don't care, all they do is give out massive doses of medication to keep the women quiet. It's like someone giving me a drink, so I can forget for a while. But the problems never go away, that way; they only become more desperate.

'It would be nice if someone from the Home Office could

spend some time on C1 — but only someone who would truly care; unless someone does something it'll never get any better.'

The first time I met Jackie Child was a week or so before her trial; she'd been on remand in Holloway for many months. She was warm, funny, open; afraid of the forthcoming trial, anxious to get it over with, but holding herself together well. She impressed me with her unselfconscious candour and honesty. She looked fine and seemed to be doing OK, so I wasn't surprised when, having asked her to write and tell me in her own words about life in Holloway, it was a pretty upbeat description.

At her trial she was calm and composed.

The next time I saw her was six weeks before she was due to be released. I expected her to be bursting with energy and impatience to get out. The trial was behind her and soon prison would be too.

Her appearance shocked me. She looked ill. Her face was blotchy and pink, puffy round the eyes. She was still warm and cheerful but she explained straightaway why she looked so bad. She couldn't stop crying. She'd been on a second home visit. It had been a disaster. Of course, seeing her little daughter had been wonderful but her nearly grown-up sons had managed without her while she'd been in prison. She was glad they had, of course, but they'd told her that when she moved to go to college, miles away from Luton, they wouldn't be going with her. 'It's time to let go, I know that, I know', but you could see it was going to be a wrench.

She'd also found that not only had she nothing to say to any of the people at home in Luton anymore, they weren't interested in what she had planned for her life; their talk of their lives meant nothing to her. That was her old life, a life of prostitution and heavy drinking. That life was dead. She wasn't going back to it. 'I just don't fit in there anymore. I've changed.' But would she fit into her new life, alone with her tiny daughter? What would it be like? Would she be able to manage? What if she couldn't and slipped back?

She had faced prison, had coped with that, but what about the rest of her 'new' life – could she manage on her own? She had an enormous transition to make from her old way of life to something that was unknown. Prison had given her the space to distance herself from her previous existence. She had realized she didn't want to go back. But did she have the confidence to go forward? She'd fitted into the prison routine, she'd coped with prison, but could she cope with leaving prison?

Jackie's description of life in prison touches on most of the themes of this chapter: women's anxieties about their children; the question of the over-prescribing of drugs in women's prisons, and women's nervousness and apprehension about whether they are adequately prepared for leaving prison; but it does not mention the fact that there is more 'aggro' in women's prisons than in men's.

PRISONS

There are twelve establishments for women prisoners in England and Wales that, as of November 1991, provide 1,774 places.

● Six closed prisons: Holloway in London, Styal in Cheshire, Cookham Wood in Kent, New Hall in Yorkshire, Bullwood Hall in Essex, and Durham men's prison where the maximum-security H Wing houses only a handful of women.

● Three open prisons: Drake Hall in Staffordshire, Askham Grange in Yorkshire and East Sutton Park in Kent.

● Three remand centres: Low Newton in Durham, Puckle-church in Bristol and Risley in Cheshire.

Five of the prisons include young offender institutions – Styal, Bullwood Hall and New Hall provide closed conditions; East Sutton Park and Drake Hall provide open conditions; and three of the prisons between them – Holloway, Styal and Askham Grange – provide thirty-seven places in mother-and-baby units.

NUMBERS

On 30 June 1991 there were only 1,038 women in prison in contrast to a figure of 28,283 male prisoners.

How Many Women Commit What Kinds of Crime

Very few women commit crimes; even fewer commit violent crimes. They are, typically, petty offenders. The single largest category of offenders, for both men and women, is theft and handling stolen goods; next is burglary for men and fraud and forgery for women. Violence against the person is the third largest category for both sexes, but men outnumber women in this category by more than eleven to one.

According to the National Association for the Care and Resettlement of Offenders (Nacro), almost half of women first-offenders are imprisoned for offences to do with drugs, while the largest single group of men imprisoned as first-offenders have been convicted of violent offences. Research in Scotland found that around half the women in Cornton Vale, Scotland's only female prison, were there for failing to pay a fine. For women over twenty-one sentenced directly to prison, a third had been convicted of breach of the peace and a third for crimes against property without violence.[1]

Women in prison are less likely than men to have had previous convictions: 13,044 (about 46 per cent of) men had no previous convictions, or these were not recorded, compared to 683 (about 66 per cent of) women. Nacro figures show that of the sentenced women in prison on 30 June 1990 for whom information about previous convictions was recorded, 222 (33 per cent) had no previous convictions compared to 2,409 (11 per cent) of sentenced men.[2]

However, according to Carol Hedderman and Mike Hough, *Does the Criminal Justice System Treat Men and Women Differently?*,[3] you cannot use prison statistics on their own to draw a valid comparison between the numbers of male and female first-time offenders in prison. The comparison must be based on the proportion of male and female first-time offenders being *sent* by the courts to prison. When you make such a comparison, it becomes clear that women first-time offenders at court are less likely to go to prison.[4]

I would say here that these figures show us nothing of the context of these first offences or their seriousness. Commenting on Hedderman and Hough's booklet showing that the courts imprison a smaller proportion of sentenced women than sentenced men in most offence categories, Paul Cavadino of Nacro says that this

> in itself proves little: broad categories such as theft, actual bodily harm, etc., cover offences of a wide range of seriousness and the statistics could simply reflect the lesser gravity of women's crimes.[5]

I want to look briefly at one final point in the Hedderman and Hough booklet which is particularly relevant to women in prison before going on to look at women violent offenders *per se*.

Remand

It's to do with the numbers of male and female prisoners on remand. Hedderman and Hough state that fewer women offenders, proportionately, are remanded in custody than males, and that fewer women remanded in custody (30 per cent) than men (40 per cent) are subsequently sent to prison, which raises one very important question for men and women: why are they in prison on remand in the first place?

Both the Howard League for Penal Reform and Nacro believe the remand system is being overused for both women and men. There is powerful evidence, according to Adam Sampson, formerly of the Prison Reform Trust, and now Assistant Ombudsman for Prisons, that

> women are more harshly treated than men at the remand stage of the court process.
>
> A survey of over 1,000 unconvicted women in London recently revealed that women were twice as likely as men to be denied bail when charged with offences involving drugs. When the case involved dishonesty, women were more than three times as likely as men to be remanded into custody.[6]

In their conclusion, Hedderman and Hough outline three caveats. The first acknowledges that when individual offence categories are examined this could show that the statistics mask differences between men and women in the seriousness of their offending. And they point out that the question remains whether 'there is equally suitable provision for women as for men throughout the criminal justice system'. They also say they have not considered disparities in treatment *within* [emphasis in original] gender, a major theme of this book.[7]

Something which greatly concerns reformers is that, because there are fewer alternatives to custody for women than men, they tend to have a shorter system of tariffs to move through and therefore get into prison quicker. For example, whereas the more intensive form of supervision provided by probation day-centres might be used as an alternative to custody for a man, such options are much less available to women. Generally speaking they are not seen as places for women and courts, even if they consider such an option, are probably reluctant to send one woman to an establishment that caters mainly for a male population. Hence the tendency for women to move faster through the tariff system from, for instance, conditional discharge, via probation to custodial sentences.

Women Violent Offenders

As has been said repeatedly, the overwhelming majority of women in prison are not there for violent offences. For instance, one researcher, Dr Alexandra Mandaraka-Sheppard, found that 11.6 per cent of the women she interviewed in prison were there for robbery but usually their role had been auxiliary. Just over 9 per cent had assaulted someone.

Eighteen of the 326 women in her sample (5.5 per cent) had committed murder. Three had killed their children. Of the fifteen murders involving adults, almost half – seven – were of spouses or lovers, as the women finally responded to 'unbearable treatment'. Three were committed during a robbery, two under the influence of excessive alcohol or drugs, and three, together with men, deliberately, for money.

The experience of violent women in prison can best be described by putting them into three categories: those who kill spouses, or lovers; those who kill or do violence for financial gain; and those who harm or kill children.

Women in the first group are indistinguishable from other women prisoners and are not treated any differently in prison. Jackie Child, imprisoned for the manslaughter of a friend's boyfriend who had beaten her up, told me there was no discrimination against a woman convicted of the murder or manslaughter of a man who had been violent towards her:

> I have always spoken very openly about what happened in my case and every woman who has heard my story says he got what he deserved. Personally I don't believe that because I have to live with the fact that I've taken someone's life . . .[8]

However, talking about the disapproving and censorious attitudes on the part of women prisoners towards two women convicted of murder for financial gain, Jackie Child says: 'The women felt that [financial gain] was simply not a good enough reason to kill. So those women are kept at a distance and regarded as cold, unfeeling and greedy. They knew what they were doing.'

As for the child killers and child abusers, says Child,

> these women are put on Rule 43, the same as men who do that. They are segregated from all the other women and called 'nonces'. I myself have spoken to a few of these women and my own opinion is that they are either very uneducated, very sick in the mind or they have continued a pattern in their own lives: having been abused they have become abusers.
>
> I haven't met one who I would consider evil. I am sure there must be evil ones, but not very many. Mainly I think they are just very sad. They carry a very heavy burden all of their own that no one else can understand. To take a life is wrong, to take an innocent life is unforgivable but . . . I don't want to judge them.
>
> If some of the women got hold of them though, god alone knows what would happen.[9]

Jill Matthews of Nacro adds that not all women sex offenders or child murderers are shunned by other prisoners or put on

Rule 43.[10] And Chris Tchaikovsky of Women in Prison (WIP) (see Useful Addresses) points out that the response of the tabloid press has had an effect on the victimization of vulnerable prisoners 'particularly when there are references to "monsters", etc.'

She recalls a particular case when the tabloids referred to the woman as a monster.

> She had neglected her baby and her baby died. But what didn't come to light, what wasn't said in the tabloids, was that she had attempted suicide when her baby died. And though she was overweight she was herself, in fact, suffering from malnutrition. She was in what I heard described as a hypermanic paradoxical state. And she was suffering very severe depression. She was absolutely ill and totally broken down and she grieved terribly over the loss of her baby, whom she had loved. No doubt about that.
>
> Because of the tabloid vilification of her she was put on the Vulnerable Prisoners' Unit and was subject to the most appalling verbal abuse. The VPU was near the remand wing, which was a very foolish place to have put it. So you had these young rough, tough cream puffs coming in, very mouthy, shouting off, wanting to seem tough. They were shouting stupid things like 'If we get hold of you we'll rip your womb out'. Which is pretty horrendous.[11]

Tchaikovsky thought that women who were in prison for having finally turned on partners who'd been battering them for years might well come in for a little bit of extra respect. 'It's not hero worship at all, more a feeling of "I wish I'd have the nerve to strike back too".' An attitude which, she says, is hardly surprising when it seems nearly half of women in prison (48 per cent) 'had suffered severe and continuing violence for years and the largest single group of perpetrators were boyfriends and husbands.[12] Posen thought it significant that women discounted what they considered mere "knocking about" and that "injuries such as cracked ribs, broken and dislocated shoulders, and stabbings featured frequently".'

She thinks the figure of 48 per cent is very conservative, 'because you only get parole if you say you have a stable home background. So you're not going to admit to being beaten up by your partner, are you?' and believes a more recent Canadian figure of 83 per cent of women in prison having been battered would be a truer figure.

And the behaviour of the very few violent women in prison? Each woman has a choice, she says, whether or not she feeds into that small group of macho, angry prisoners. But she'd be taking a big risk.

> She'd find herself on a hiding to nothing though, in a women's prison, because the end of that particular road is the special hospitals. If a male is violent and has strategies of resistance – like Jimmy Boyle or John McVicar – they become folk heroes. Women don't become folk heroes – they become sectioned. Exhibit a violent response, violent actions, in a women's prison and you just get nutted off (sectioned under the Mental Health Act).[13]

Put bluntly, the kind of women who go to prison are – not aristocratic. When a member of the aristocracy was arrested for having drugs in 1993 the *Daily Telegraph* ran a story with two colour pictures plus a background feature on the 'flawed dynasty'. The Marquess of Bristol getting ten months for possessing heroin and cocaine at his stately home is news. Rarely does a member of the aristocracy go to jail.[14]

There are no surprises as to where the women and men who fill the jails come from. As any fan of Tolstoy's novel, *Resurrection*, would expect, the prisons are not full of wealthy, well-educated people with stable and fulfilling lives. These are the people who sit in judgement. Women in prison are likely to be young, i.e. under thirty; to have children and to be single, divorced or separated. The biggest single group in terms of work are likely to be unemployed, with most of the rest being housewives or skilled manual or semi-skilled workers.[15]

Elaine Genders and Elaine Player interviewed 254 women prisoners and Youth Custody trainees about their backgrounds. They found that nearly two-thirds of the adult women and a quarter of the trainees had dependent children, 'yet two out of every three of these women did not live within a traditional nuclear family setting . . . The family lives of the women tended to be characterized by divorce and separation . . .' They also drew up a category of non-conventionality based upon criteria which included:

> frequent and brief marriages or relationships with men; children by different fathers; being separated from children; serious family violence; alcoholism; in-patient psychiatric treatment, and attempted suicide.
>
> In order to be rated 'non-conventional' women had to qualify on at least three criteria. In the event, over half of our sample, including six in every ten who had dependent children, fell within this category, and most women qualified on four or more of the criteria.[16]

Alexandra Mandaraka-Sheppard found a similar picture for a large proportion of the women inmates whose lives she studied. These women's lives were characterized by neglect; rejection by their families; being brought up by only one parent or in a maritally discordant home, and overcrowding and poverty which had led some women

> into involvement in a sequence of unhappy, unsatisfactory relationships and subsequently to confusion about their own lives. Usually these women had been in residential care from an early age, were immature, had grown bitter, perhaps involved in bad associations and had turned to drink or crime.[17]

However, a quarter of the women prisoners she investigated had come from happy family backgrounds; others had rebelled against too strict an upbringing. She identified at least one common element 'among women prisoners before they were involved in criminal activities: this seemed to be their financial difficulties and their inability to find other ways of livelihood.'[18]
The race factor As far as race goes the woman prisoner is more likely to be white although black women are overrepresented among the prison population. Sixteen per cent of Mandaraka-Sheppard's sample were black, but black people make up only five per cent of the population.

Home Office statistics for 1992 show that they [black people] make up 22 per cent of the prison population. Indeed, 29 per cent of the female prison population is now black.[19]

And black women serve sentences that are, on average, twice as long as those of white women. Acknowledging that a reasonable proportion of the black women in prison are jailed for the importation of drugs from abroad, Helena Kennedy says this doesn't provide the full explanation. Their overrepresentation in prison lies partly, she believes, in their failure to conform to appropriate ideas of womanhood.

> To some judges and policemen the lifestyles of many black women in Britain today, particularly Afro-Caribbeans, seems unorthodox. The set-up is often matriarchal, lacking the 'restraining male influence', for which judges tend to look.[20]

Nor are judges favourably impressed by, in particular, young black women who arrive in court angry, and who 'see no reason for colluding in a system which discriminates against them'. Their anger is often misunderstood and is taken for aggression and lack of deference.[21]

When you put those factors together with the fact that discrimination means more black people in general have lower-paid jobs, higher unemployment and worse housing than white people, then you begin to see why black women are over-represented in the prison population.

Asked about the differences in the backgrounds of those women in prison who have, and those who have not, committed violent crimes, Chris Tchaikovsky, Director of Women in Prison and herself an ex-prisoner, says she doesn't think there's any evidence of any qualitative differences. However, she wouldn't be at all surprised if it turned out that a link could be shown between violent women and unstable backgrounds and violence and abuse when they were children.

> There's some research which shows a very strong link – it may even have been a hundred per cent – between women who commit arson,

which is an angry and violent act, and the experience of sexual abuse as a child.

Look at the women in prison. Look at their lives, their backgrounds. Anybody who's had a warm, read-to-in-bed, happy home in a happy family – no violence, no abuse – they're not going to end up risking their liberty by turning up at King's Cross, turning tricks, raising fires, doing drugs, cutting their arms. They've got too much to lose.

I'm not making excuses for crimes by women, violent or otherwise: I'm not justifying them, I'm trying to understand, to explain them.[22]

The pattern of the lives of many of the women who end up in prison is succinctly described by Pat Carlen. Writing about the path from rejection at home to a residential 'home' to prison, she puts it like this:

The prematurely institutionalized women who once hoped that Care might provide an alternative Home from home subsequently recognize each other in penal institutions all over the country. Another generation of state-raised working-class women has passed from Care to custody.[23]

Women's Experience of Prison

In the summer of 1994, 23-year-old Michelle Pearson hanged herself from the curtain of her cell in New Hall Prison, near Wakefield in Yorkshire, which has been described as one of the leading women's prisons in the country. Pearson, the mother of two children, aged two and four, had been serving her sentence at another prison, Askham Grange. However, after returning from weekend leave at home, she had been very distressed and had 'cut up': deliberately cut herself. Consequently she was transferred to New Hall and put into a single cell. That night she hanged herself with a curtain cord.

'The real agony of imprisonment for women,' says Chris Tchaikovsky, 'is the agony of separation from children, family, loved ones. Every time you have to leave them it's a fresh hurt.'[24]

Alison Liebling, a senior research associate at the Institute of Criminology at Cambridge University, has been studying suicide amongst women prisoners and has discovered that the rate of suicide for them is as high as for men prisoners and on the increase. She has speculated that a

> factor which may increase the specific vulnerability of women prisoners to suicide is the particular impact of a prison sentence upon women. The devastating and gender-specific effects of custody upon a woman with dependent children or other equivalent family ties are undeniably part of the dynamics of female prisoner suicide. It is clear that family and children are often an essential part of the explanation for each death or attempt.[25]

The photograph accompanying the story about Michelle Pearson's death in the *Yorkshire Post* shows a woman prisoner in her cell at New Hall. The room has soft furnishings, a bird cage, and lots of flowers, cards and photographs. Sunlight streams through the net curtains on to what looks like a dainty floral bedspread. The impression is of a homely and chintzy bedsitter. But we shouldn't be fooled by such photos, argues Tchaikovsky.

> Certainly things have improved over the last twenty years, it would be wrong to say they hadn't. But beyond that pleasant-looking cell is the reality of prison life: the walkways, the corridors, the fear, the strangers you live with, the coldness of some officers, the shouting of others. Some officers are kind but there is little they can do to ease the agony of not being able to hug your kids, of worrying what's happening to them.[26]

Superficially women do seem to have an easier time of it in prison than men, for instance, there's less 'slopping out'; most can bathe or shower every day and they are allowed to wear their own clothes.

Jill Matthews of Nacro says,

> ... in all the most important ways – emotionally, psychologically – women don't have a better time in prison. Many are single parents,

separated from their children with all the heartache that causes. They are subject to petty, trivial rules and regulations which men wouldn't stand for. And on top of that they are more likely to be a long way from home.[27]

The fact that women's prisons are fewer and far between means greater difficulties for families and friends who want to visit. Women also have fewer leisure, work and educational opportunities – the emphasis is still on domestic work.

This is what the Chief Inspector of Prisons had to say in his 1989 report:

> It is often said that imprisonment is a punishment for both the offender and the family, that if a man goes to prison things will be hard for his family but the wife will hold things together – she will cope. The reverse is not necessarily the case if a woman is sent to prison, and many women in prison do not have stable family backgrounds. Their children tend to be lodged with in-laws or relatives, and in some cases they are taken into care. Such situations can place tremendous strains on what remains of a family. Women prisoners naturally worry about their children while those responsible for the children have to cope with the sudden and additional problems involved with endeavouring to visit at every opportunity.[28]

The women's prison system has been described as the poor relation of the men's system. There are so few women prisoners that they tend to get tagged on to the end of whatever is provided for the much larger numbers of men.

Jill Matthews of Nacro: 'There is no director-general of women's prisons; they're treated like substitute men and it just doesn't work. There's no proper strategy. The whole thing needs re-thinking.'[29]

She, like other reformers, is concerned about high levels of tension in women's prisons. In 1986 the House of Commons Social Services Committee noted that:

> the tension in women's prisons is marked. 'Acting out' is common, even to the extent of self-mutilation. Women seem to suffer more

than men from the emotional strain of imprisonment and separation from their families. Women prisoners have no access to the few specialist psychotherapeutic units in the prison service. The level of prescription of psychotropic (mood-altering) drugs to women prisoners is very high.[30]

WHY ARE WOMEN MORE AGGRESSIVE THAN MEN IN PRISONS?

Alice's Story

A group of us kicked our doors because they wouldn't let us out to go to the toilet, using the potty all the time – it just seemed pointless. Why were they so wicked? They'd be walking around, laughing and joking – their keys rattling. And you'd say, 'Oh can I go to the toilet?' And their policy is – you let one out you have to let everyone out. So what? I had an adjudication and the governor gave me a terrible punishment, she gave me 14 days' loss of remission, 14 days down the block and 14 days' loss of pay and this was just for kicking my door. I wasn't the only one. That was the punishment she gave all of us. On the adjudication I was very upset. I stood up and I was banging the table. You know you don't realize what you're doing. It must have looked like I was climbing over to grab her. They all just jumped on top of me and I was defending myself and in defending myself I bit an officer and I lost 28 days for that. And the rumour just went round that Alice tried to attack the governor. You don't sort of think 'No I didn't' or 'I did'. You just think 'Oh sod them, let them think what they want to think'.[31]

Alice was a woman who told her story to sociologist Mary Eaton for her book, *Women After Prison*. At the time – 1991 – Alice was twenty-four. She had served three prison sentences, all for deception.[32]

There is two and a half times as much violence in women's prisons as in men's, and the number of offences against prison discipline is generally high;[33] women prisoners commit more than twice as many offences against prison rules than men.[34] Yet most of them weren't violent before they went to prison; as I've said repeatedly, only a small proportion of women in prison are there for violent offences. And it seems that even those who had been violent hadn't been as violent, and as often, as the men in prison for violent crimes.

Why are women more aggressive, more difficult to handle, in prison? Two factors contribute to the answer. Women, as women, are under more pressure inside than men if they have children since it is their primary responsibility to bring them up, fulfilling those roles by which they are defined – wives and mothers. A man will miss his children, but he wouldn't have spent as much time or been as intimately connected to them as their mother. They would have been the centre of her life, not of his. Women are closer to their children and are very often solely responsible for them; when you take women from their children, their anguish, anxiety, loss and pain are typically greater than men's.

Also, the man in prison probably has a wife or partner on the outside who continues to look after the children and the home, and he knows that they will very probably still be there when he gets out. The woman in prison, however, is likely to be single, divorced or separated and to have children, whose welfare must be a constant worry.

> The Prison Reform Trust notes that, while 91 per cent of fathers in prison said that their children were being looked after by current or ex-wives or partners, only 23 per cent of mothers in prison said that their children were being looked after by current or ex-husbands or partners.[35]

This 'external' factor, and the greater stigma for women of being inside, plus the added perception of them as bad mothers – they are not 'there' for their children because of wrongdoing – result in impatience, irritation and short tempers which contribute to the higher levels of tension and anxiety. The staff, who are predominantly women, can feel this tense atmosphere and must recognize it, acknowledge it, accept it and work within it, without feeling threatened and fearful, or they could end up compounding the problem by being provoked into overreacting to the slightest breach of discipline. This 'internal' factor can then act as a spark to the smouldering predisposition, producing the higher levels of trouble in women's prisons which give women prisoners the reputation for being harder to handle than men.

The four institutional factors identified by Alexandra Mandaraka-Sheppard in her detailed analysis, *The Dynamics of Aggression in Women's Prisons in England*, are poor staff/inmate relations, staff being young and inexperienced, severe and inconsistent punishments, and lack of incentives for good behaviour.

Mandaraka-Sheppard conducted her research in three open prisons: Askham Grange, Moor Court and Drake Hall; and three closed prisons: Holloway, Cookham Wood and Styal. Her sample of 326 women constituted between 40 and 50 per cent of each prison's total population. She stayed at each prison for about a month, living with the prisoners from eight in the morning to nine in the evening. She points out that punishments which are seen to be too harsh and not consistently and fairly applied are more likely to produce than deter bad behaviour and adds that a regime characterized by frequent reporting and punishments rather than informal means of control has less chance of allowing good relationships to develop between prisoners and staff.

For example, swearing and squabbling, says Mandaraka-Sheppard, have a positive function in that they provide 'an outlet for accumulated aggression.'[36] However, a young and inexperienced officer might put the women involved on report, whereas tolerance of bad language and quarrelling by wiser and more experienced staff, with just a word of reproof, would allow women to let off steam, would serve to diffuse tension and could well help pave the way for the improvement of staff–prisoner relations.

Preoccupation with security matters . . . victimization of some inmates (by delaying their letters, or their visiting orders, searching and incriminating them), concentration on bureaucratic procedure, labelling of inmates and making adverse reports (which presented an obstacle to obtaining parole), jeopardize the staff's work which entails dealing with inmates' problems, and creates a tense atmosphere.

Hence, the relationships between inmates and staff deteriorate and as a consequence there are more violations of rules and more confrontations between inmates and staff.[37]

TWO RULES

Two prison rules help to sum up the catch-22 of the prisoners' position. Rule 7 states that prisoners should have a copy of the prison rules and regulations in their cells. In none of the six prisons in Mandaraka-Sheppard's study did she find this happening. New prisoners had to find out what the rules were from other prisoners. In other words, they could have been breaking the rules, and been punished for that, without having been told what the rules were – because the staff broke the rule that said they had to be told the rules.

Rule 47, which deals with offences against discipline, lists twenty-one such offences and is so loosely phrased as to mean that practically anything can be regarded as a breach of discipline. Mandaraka-Sheppard lists some of the 'offences'; three of them are: having an apple or orange in the locker or dolly bag; walking on certain forbidden parts of the garden; having a wash without permission.[38] As one woman said to me, 'Can you imagine being put on report for walking on the grass in a men's prison? There'd be a riot.'

The institutional regime is another reason for women's greater aggression in prison: there are more petty rules and regulations and closer supervision than in men's prisons [because higher standards are expected of women whom the system is trying to turn into ladies?]. Add this to the women's greater emotional deprivation and anxiety at being separated from their children and you have a highly combustible scenario. In short, if you supervise every movement and moment of people already under pressure by virtue of being in prison, you're looking for and creating the conditions for trouble and will get it.

The most pronounced unexpected finding was that inmates' violent records did not appear to correlate with either minor or serious (i.e. violent) misbehaviour . . .[39]

Those most likely to behave badly in prison were young, single women and women without children.[40] Speculating on why this might be, Mandaraka–Sheppard suggests perhaps it is to do with peer pressure and the need to impress, to conform, to belong to a group. She adds that the young, single and childless have no responsibilities outside,

> and having nothing much to lose, take the risk of the consequences (i.e. being punished in prison for their defiance by losing time). On the other hand, women who are older, married and/or with children, have more at stake and tend to conform to the staff's expectations.[41]

I would speculate that this lack of connection between women prisoners' violent crimes and their violent behaviour in prison shows that the crimes were not committed as an expression of a violent nature or disposition but in response to a particular set of circumstances.

The message that oversupervision, overzealous policing of the rules and inconsistent and unjust punishment lead to trouble has, it seems, been officially taken on board. The booklet *Regimes for Women*, issued by the Home Office for the guidance of staff of women's prisons, acknowledges that while

> the evidence of many years is that women in prison tend to be charged more often under the disciplinary code than men, there is no evidence that they are more disruptive, however, and high levels of disciplinary charging should always cause the Governor to review the establishment's practice in this area.[42]

It also recommends that the use of a direct order should 'always be a last resort in communications between staff and prisoners' and that 'establishments should make every effort also to avoid a proliferation of local rules and regulations'.

The booklet recognizes the crucial part played in staff–prisoner relations when it points out that

> resorting to disciplinary charges of disobedience or disrespect is sometimes an indication that a member of staff lacks the confidence to establish more normal relationships with prisoners – if it becomes standard practice for staff to bring essentially trivial disciplinary charges before a genuine effort of communication has been made, the disciplinary system will rapidly come to undermine prisoners' respect for all staff.[43]

All of which is heartening: but, is there the will to put it into practice and how long will that take?

Chris Tchaikovsky comments that the 'humanity' of the institution reflects the ethos established by the governor and her/his senior staff. 'Some governors are really trying; at other prisons things are not so good. At the beginning of 1994 some regimes seemed to be improving. But now that the female prison population is rising, even faster than the men's, things are getting worse.'[44]

> Women's prisons are full and they are filled with women locked up for minor offences: motoring offences, non-payment of poll tax and TV licences. In one case, the mother of a baby and a two year old was imprisoned for 'stealing' electricity to the value of two hundred pounds and, in another recent case, a woman from a small village was, as an example to others, given a three months' sentence for falsifying qualifications on an employment form![45]

'The prisons are packed, regimes are faltering and governors are despairing. It all seems to be slipping backwards.'[46]

Drugs

As we saw earlier in this chapter, the House of Commons Social Services Committee was concerned, in 1986, about the very high level of the prescription of psychotropic drugs to women in prison, the suspicion being that these very powerful mood-altering drugs were being used to keep women quiet, as a means of social control. Mandaraka-Sheppard, also writing in the mid-eighties, was wary of accepting too easily the arguments for prescribing drugs for 'disturbed' patients . . .

> the result has been to introduce psychiatric methods and psychotropic drugs of therapy in prisons which, under the guise of 'benevolent treatment', have resulted in abuses for the purpose of social control and not for the genuine help of prisoners.[47]

The prescription figures were worrying. They show that between January 1984 and March 1985 more than 145,000 doses of anti-depressants, sedatives and tranquillizers were dispensed to women in prison – proportionately five times as many doses of this type of medication as men in prison received.[48]

The House of Commons Social Services Committee also criticized the figures provided by the Home Office for being misleading. The figures didn't, for instance, distinguish between the different strengths of medication. Largactil in suspension is four times stronger than Largactil in syrup but the figures didn't show that: they were both shown as one dose. The Home Office ceased producing figures in the mid-1980s and so, says Adam Sampson, formerly of The Prison Reform Trust, and now Assistant Ombudsman for Prisons, there are no up-to-date figures to be had. His impression, based on what prisoners and staff have told him, is that the days of the 'liquid cosh' are over. He estimates that dosage levels for women have dropped by two-thirds in recent years.

Chris Tchaikovsky of Women In Prison agrees that the 'liquid cosh and the Largactil shuffle' are largely things of the past for women prisoners. 'There's been a marked improvement in this area.'

One part of the explanation of any excess prescription of drugs for women in prison could be that the women themselves, as well as prison staff, feel it's more natural for women than men to turn to medication for help when stressed. Some women may have been used to having their problems treated by drugs and that may fit with what staff see as appropriate too. As Jill

Matthews of Nacro says, perhaps women in prison want drugs – ask for them – to help them do their time. Women are so accustomed to having their emotional problems medicalized that asking for a tranquillizer inside may be just a reflection of what they do on the outside when they feel they can't cope. Society sanctions this way of women seeking relief: it fits with the perception that women are emotionally a little unstable, a little weak – and need their 'mother's little helpers'.

CONCLUSION

The women in prison are typically petty offenders. Most are young, have children, are single, separated or divorced. As Pat Carlen's research, described earlier, led us to expect, they don't fit the conventional 'married with a husband and 2.4 children living in a nuclear family' set-up. They come from amongst the poorest and most disadvantaged of our society. Many have a background of unhappy family backgrounds and poverty. Black women are overrepresented amongst women in prison.

In the most important ways women have a worse time in prison than men. They are often much further away from home and feel much more keenly the separation from family and loved ones, especially their children. They are also more tightly regulated and more closely supervised than the men. I'd say that's because they are women and better behaviour is expected of women.

Add all this together and you have a large part of the explanation of women's higher aggression levels in prison. However, women in prison for crimes of violence are no more likely to misbehave and/or be violent than other women prisoners. Only in the rare cases where they have been violent out of greed, or where they have harmed children, will they be stigmatized by the other women.

The impression of many working within the prison system is that the use of the 'liquid cosh', i.e. psychotropic drugs, to control women has reduced dramatically over the last ten years. Self-mutilation, mentioned only in passing here, is an appalling problem – it forms the subject matter of Chapter 8. Women suffer more in prison simply because they are women. All of the problems they face within the prison system need to be addressed in the light of the answer to one crucial question: since the overwhelming majority of women in prison pose no danger to the public – there may be only a handful of such women in the entire country – why are so many hundreds of them in prison?

Why do we send women to prison? For punishment, yes – society has a legitimate desire to see wrongdoing punished. But is prison an appropriate punishment for the vast majority of petty offenders? Or do women offenders get sent to prison because men offenders get sent to prison – without any thinking having been done about the differences in the social realities of most women's and men's lives and as to the appropriateness of this form of punishment for most of the women in prison? Fundamental research into women's imprisonment is long overdue. It needs to begin with the question: why do we send women to prison?

CHAPTER 7

Women in Special Hospitals

In the opening scene of *Headrot Holiday*, a play about women in Special Hospitals, a nurse, Jackie, is doling out items of clothing from a huge plastic dustbin. The clothes she chucks towards patients are tatty-looking, crumpled things, often out-of-shape and shrunken.

JACKIE: ... Come on what's the fricking matter with you? For Gawd's sake own up to these bras ... These two are Monica's? ... oh, right, yeah she's in seclusion. Well, she won't be needing them for a couple of days then. Who's is this one? Jesus God, would you look at it? Next size is the scaffolding firm. (*Looks at label*) 38 double 'D'. It's yours isn't it Wanda, sorry I mean Ruth. (*She throws it at* RUTH.) You could make two nice lamp shades out of that in occupational therapy. Ha, ha.

RUTH: (*holds out bra to give it back*) It's not mine.

JACKIE: Never mind. You have it. (*She goes over to* RUTH *and affectionately places the bra on* RUTH's *head*.) I can't think who's it was originally then. You're the only one in this place big enough to fit it apart from Doctor Reed and I hardly think it would flatter him on the Rugby pitch do you?

The playwright based the scene on a description of life in Ashworth Special Hospital provided by psychologist Moira Potier. At the time of their conversation Ms Potier was a principal clinical psychologist at Ashworth, which is in Merseyside. She began work there in 1987, and from then until 1993 she worked as team psychologist on three of the four all-female wards.

In 1992 she gave evidence to the Committee of Inquiry into Complaints about Ashworth Hospital. During the inquiry it emerged that, of 600 complaints made by patients over the last ten years, none had been upheld. Ms Potier told the inquiry:

... women in Ashworth are controlled, suppressed ... their overwhelming experience is that they are treated like children. They are
almost constantly emotionally abused and at times physically abused.
It is my observation that they feel chronically frightened and overwhelmingly powerless, and that they are unable to do anything
substantially to alter their lot.[1]

She was one of the four women and one man employed at
Ashworth who gave evidence to the inquiry, which was chaired
by Louis Blom-Cooper.

When I talked to the women at the time they were giving
evidence to the inquiry, in March 1992, they made jokes about
organizing a rota system amongst themselves so none of them
would have to go on certain wards alone. They were all anxious,
if not frightened, at the thought of the hostility they might have
to face daily following the inquiry. Afterwards, Potier had some
odd phone calls at home. She was, she said, frightened sometimes
and worried about her children.

The inquiry reported in August 1992. In its chapter on women
in Ashworth it said:

The culture at Ashworth seems poignantly anti-therapeutic in the
light of the background of abuse in these women's lives. The culture
is offensively 'macho' in style. Many witnesses spoke of the uni-
formed, key-swinging 'militaristic' approach in Ashworth South
designed to belittle female staff as well as patients. Dr Gravett
described it thus: 'The hospital is male-dominated, and with that
goes the attitudes of the whole of society in the way that males tend
to perceive women conventionally, that women are objects, sexual
objects particularly that can be used, that have definite roles within
society, and if they transgress those roles they are, in fact, more
vilified than if a man did a similar thing.'[2]

The report of the inquiry concluded that

the current regime for women in Ashworth is infantilizing, demean-
ing and anti-therapeutic. Mr Pleming for the MHAC [Mental
Health Act Commission] could have been speaking for us when he

stated: '. . . the Commission's position, I hope is clear, that radical changes . . . are necessary if women in Special Hospitals are to receive the type of care which will improve their situation'.[3]

Moira Potier was awarded an MBE in 1993 for 'services to the NHS'. She had resigned from Ashworth by the time she received it.

I am aware that the inquiry was into complaints about Ashworth Hospital only, not about Special Hospitals as such. However, Mr Pleming said the Mental Health Act Commission's position was that radical changes were necessary *if women in Special Hospitals* were to receive the type of care needed to improve their situation. He saw the need for radical change at Special Hospitals in general. And the ethos evoked by the scene from *Headrot Holiday* is echoed by what women who've been in Specials have told me. They felt degraded, infantilized, powerless and apprehensive about getting out. 'If you're not getting any treatment, how are they going to know when you're better?' Faced as they are with indeterminate stays, this is one of the women's biggest worries. Some, not all, had felt the pressure of being coerced into conforming to stereotyped female behaviour to *prove* they were getting better. And some said that since they'd been out, they'd heard things had begun to improve.

Although there are comments from employees of the Special Hospitals, the focus of this chapter will be on the women themselves since their voices have been so little heard in the past.

WOMEN'S EXPERIENCES OF SPECIAL HOSPITALS

Kim Andrews, who was released from Rampton Hospital in 1985, spent fifteen years in Special Hospitals, mainly at Broadmoor. Here, she looks back on her introduction to the Specials.

I sat in the dock and listened to the experts discuss my future, without their once asking me for my opinion. I was already crippled from the waist down, through overdosing on heroin. Now it seemed my mind was also crippled, for the sentence passed was for me to be sent immediately to Broadmoor Hospital for treatment, for an unlimited time. This seemed somewhat harsh as I had only been charged for possession of dangerous drugs.

Immediately upon my arrival at the hospital, I was divested of my callipers, my only means of mobility. Apparently, they constituted a security risk and could be described as an offensive weapon, so I was left to shuffle around on my posterior. I was offered no physiotherapy or treatment to help strengthen my wasted muscles. It took me several months to regain the full use of my legs; fortunately, I remembered the exercises that the physiotherapist of Holloway Prison had taught me while I was on remand.

Once I became reasonably mobile, I began to take stock of my surroundings. I was aware of the difference between the male side and the female side of the hospital. The women were squashed in one small complex, almost as if we were an afterthought – which I suppose in a way we were, as most institutions were initially built to house men.

All recreational facilities were on the male side – numerous football pitches, cricket pitches and practice nets. We females had one bowling green, which was hallowed ground and nice to look at. All you could do was look at it – you were not allowed to walk on it, unless you were in the team of 50-year-olds.

The total lack of physical activity was one of my biggest problems. Just how was I to cope with my surplus energy and my increasing frustration? I was unable to express myself in an acceptable fashion. I would spend hours each day in rational positive thinking, but by the time I actually gained a staff member's attention, I would be like a powder keg, erupting with anguish and anxiety, my words spewing forth in machine-gun-like bursts, to the chagrin of the poor staff member, whose understandable reaction was to seclude me until I had calmed down. But once quietened down, I would no longer feel inclined to talk, being full of resentment for my seemingly unfair treatment.[4]

In December 1992 Pauline Brown (not her real name) described to me her first few days in Broadmoor.

When I got there the nurses came out to escort me in and I thought 'What have I done wrong, why are there so many people?' They escorted me to the bathroom and I had to strip, be measured, weighed and put into lukewarm disinfectant water. Then I had a whole bucket of lukewarm disinfectant water poured over my head. Then I was 'given the rights'.

Being 'given the rights' means being told you have to do as you're told otherwise you'll find out what the punishment block means. You're told no gangs, no answering back, you're in Broadmoor now. That's the message I got from the nurse while a male nurse stood outside.

I was given one of those funny stiff nightdresses, they're made of pretty awful material – that's so you can't rip them. Then I was locked in a room for three days. They call it seclusion. No light. There was electric light but no natural light, no outside light for three days. I had to ask them to turn the light off at night. I didn't know whether it was night or day. I was shattered. I didn't know what was going on.

That was standard procedure then, in 1984: I hear it's changed now but whether it has changed or not I really don't know. They used to let me out in the mornings to see to my potty, it was so degrading.[5]

Some of the things Moira Potier told the inquiry about Ashworth Hospital in 1992 give a flavour of the atmosphere in which the women live.

There is a common existential experience shared by the women of not being heard and rarely believed, of feeling chronically frightened and overwhelmingly powerless (except in outbursts of impotent rage against property, self or others).[6]

And on some wards, says Potier, women have to ask for every Tampax – free access is withheld for 'security reasons'. Some women talk about the tampons being given 'on a limited basis'.[7]

The inquiry itself, she says, provoked a great deal of ambivalence in the women. There was enormous fear about giving any evidence of their experiences.

They talked with horror of what could happen to them on the inside and the outside – fear of retaliation, of being recalled at some time in the future and being subject to reprisals. There is a fantasy expressed (reality-based?) of the power of the POA [Prison Officers' Association] as all-encompassing. This projected omnipotence resonates with many women's childhood experiences of being terrorized into silence and submission by threats of harm.[8]

Jennifer McCabe of Women in Special Hospitals (WISH) cites Potier as one of those women who, having struggled and struggled to make real changes within the system, eventually have to leave. 'It becomes a matter of self-preservation: they are worn out by battling against institutions whose ethos, practices and habits are so ingrained, so rigid.'[9] She agrees with Potier that the experience of life in the Specials re-creates and reconfirms all the bad early experiences which so many of the women have suffered. So, far from being a therapeutic environment, it's going to make things worse.

It's impossible to treat women in the environment of the Specials.

How can you even begin to treat them when they are living in what you might call a state of shock, a state of fear? And they do live with fear every minute of the day. Fear of being abused or attacked, either by a member of staff or another patient; fear of putting a foot wrong. Most of this fear is managed by unconscious denial on the part of both the staff and the women so that 'happy families' can be played out, masking the underlying reality.

They walk on eggshells all the time. They feel unsafe. I don't think the women in Specials ever experience a moment's peace. Not really. They live with a deep lack of security. And I think the staff live with that as well; and they cope with that by keeping a big barrier between them and the patients. This is not necessarily an obvious physical distance but rather an emotional barrier that is unconsciously maintained, whereby power remains with the staff and the women are thereby unequal, dependent, infantilized. What they need is some healthy loving care, some good experiences for a change, in a supportive environment where they feel safe. In the Specials they get the opposite.[10]

BACKGROUND

Special Hospitals are secure psychiatric hospitals. There are three in England: Broadmoor in Berkshire, Ashworth in Liverpool and Rampton in Nottinghamshire. In late 1993 there were 259 women in the Specials: 90 in Broadmoor, 99 in Rampton and 70 in Ashworth. The comparable figures for men were: 395, 414 and 528, making the total number of men patients 1,337. (Special Hospitals Service Authority figures, as of 31 October 1993, supplied to Women in Special Hospitals (WISH)).

Patients committed to Special Hospitals face an indeterminate stay. Being defined as patients, not prisoners, they are not serving a sentence. They are there until they are deemed to be cured/safe enough to be free. This means, of course, that they don't know how long they are going to be there. As well as being sent to Special Hospitals by the prisons and courts, women may, for instance, have come from Regional Secure Units (RSUs), or from open or locked psychiatric facilities.

Most of the women, and men, in the Special Hospitals are offender patients – they are sent there via the criminal justice system. I am concerned only with the women offender patients, not, for instance, the women there because of learning difficulties or because they are mentally ill.

The women I've met in the Specials are not mad in the sense that they are psychotic (and by psychotic I mean so seriously mentally ill that they are out of touch with reality much, if not all, of the time). However, both Prue Stevenson of WISH and Moira Potier have told me that all of these women know there is something wrong. They are distressed, often deeply, sometimes to the point of hallucinating, often to the point of harming themselves. They all know they need help. They all want help.

But, as Toni, 24, who spent three and a half years in Broadmoor, puts it:

> I didn't need a Special. I didn't need the security of Broadmoor. I didn't need their drugs. I didn't need their so-called treatment. I didn't need their punishments. I didn't need any of it. What I needed was a safe environment and a chance to get my act together.[11]

HOW DO WOMEN GET TO SPECIAL HOSPITALS?

'. . . in 1984 I started a fire − attempted to start a fire. I did £2's worth of damage to an empty house, and £34's criminal damage to a police cell − I just took some wooden boxes from round the pipes − and got remanded in custody and got Section 37/41. Sent to Broadmoor. I was classed as having a psychopathic disorder.

'A 41 is a restriction order − it means you can be detained without limit of time. That was because of the £2's arson damage. But basically I got sent to Broadmoor because of my history. That's all I got sent for: they didn't know what to do so they wanted to lock me up and throw away the key.'[12]

In order to be sent to a Special Hospital you have to be classified under the Mental Health Act as mentally ill, mentally impaired, severely mentally impaired or suffering from psychopathic disorder and, in addition, to be seen as a danger to yourself and others.

Women form 4 per cent of the prison population but make up 16 per cent of the patients in Special Hospitals. However, not all the women patients come via the criminal justice system so you can't make a straightforward comparison with the population of women in prison. But since the majority of women in the Specials are offender patients, i.e. they have come via the criminal justice system, you can say that such women patients are clearly overrepresented in the Specials.

Prisoners can be sent to a Special Hospital without having to go back to the courts, if two doctors agree to the transfer. This means that a woman's relatively short prison term could turn into indeterminate detention. One of the most serious concerns of the campaigners, researchers and ex-patients I've spoken to, is the numbers of women who end up in Specials. They have the clear impression that it is easier for a woman to find herself in a Special via the criminal justice system than it is for a man: that a woman may be much less violent than a man yet find herself in a Special. The very fact of a woman being aggressive renders her odd, freakish, 'unnatural' in a way that it simply doesn't with a man.

According to Dr Adrian Grounds of the Institute of Criminology, Cambridge University, who conducted a study of sentenced prisoners transferred to Broadmoor Special Hospital, proportionately twice as many women were transferred as men.[13]

> ... more and more frequently, women nearing the end of their sentences have their hopes of release dashed by being transferred to Broadmoor.[14]

Dr Gillian Mezey, formerly Senior Registrar at Broadmoor, and now Consultant Psychiatrist at St George's Hospital and Medical School, London:

> If a woman commits an offence which is regarded as incompatible with her female status she has committed a double transgression. She has transgressed against the code of what it is to be feminine – docile, passive and gentle – and she has also transgressed against the criminal law. She may either be regarded as doubly bad, doubly evil, and put in prison for a long time, or, if she is not bad, therefore she must be very, very mad and in need of psychiatric treatment in high security.[15]

Because their aggressive behaviour can and is interpreted quite differently from men's – they need display much less violence than men to be seen as 'abnormal' and as stepping outside the female conventional role – it's far more likely for women than men to find themselves transferred to a Special from prison. Members of WISH tell me they know of women who have self-harmed in prison but were not a danger to anyone other than themselves; nevertheless they were sent to a Special Hospital, categorised as suffering from a psychopathic disorder.

The definition of psychopathy is itself problematic, quite apart from any considerations of gender. 'There does not appear to be any clear distinction between the behaviour of ordinary offenders and those diagnosed as psychopaths,' says Larry Gostin, former Director of MIND. And,

> the World Health Organization does not recognize 'psychopath' as an appropriate diagnosis and has referred to the compulsory admission

of psychopathic patients as one of 'the most serious problems in the British mental health system'.[16]

WISH is particularly concerned about the women who are classified under the Mental Health Act as psychopathic and sent to the Specials from prison. Prue Stevenson says,

The whole concept of psychopathy needs to be looked at, especially in relation to women. About a third of women but less than a quarter of men are admitted into the Specials under this diagnosis. Women are almost one and a half times more likely than men to be classified as suffering from psychopathic disorder.

This suggests that women are judged differently, more specifically – that behaviour which is acceptable in men is not acceptable in women. As a result they are more likely to be seen as in need of treatment. The implications of which, if they are sent to a Special, are especially grave and long term.

Part of the reason why women are proportionately more likely than men to be classified as suffering from psychopathy has to do with how far they fail to conform to society's idea of what it is to be a woman.[17]

During the years since the formation of WISH in 1989 Prue Stevenson has formed the impression that a woman who is aggressive – though not necessarily physically violent – who lives rough and/or abuses drugs is much more likely than an aggressive man doing similar things to be diagnosed as suffering from psychopathic disorder. 'This raises serious concerns,' she says, 'about the use – or misuse – of the Mental Health Act in regard to these women.

'The Mental Health Act defines psychopathy as a persistent disorder or disability of the mind which results in abnormally or seriously irresponsible conduct. This definition is often alarmingly flexible when applied to women and allows subjective values to play a central role.'[18]

And the psychiatrists making the decision about definition, says Dr Mezey, have exactly the same kinds of stereotypes and prejudices [about] – appropriate gender behaviour, etc. [as the majority of society]. Unfortunately although psychiatrists are experts in mental health, they are not experts in social roles and gender.

But what psychiatrists bring into it very often are their own predominantly white, predominantly middle-class, predominantly male expectations, and attitudes about appropriate behaviour for a certain person at a certain time in a certain place.

And I think it's reflected very often in the sort of views that . . . the appropriate feminine role is to be a homemaker, to look after children, to be caring, to be altruistic, to be protective – these are the sort of views, and I think that you must place those sort of attitudes not in a sort of scientific and psychiatric context but in a cultural context.[19]

Dr Mezey told me in May 1991 that she would like to see a 'psychology of gender' incorporated into psychiatric training. 'At the moment it doesn't provide any particular insight into what is normal gender behaviour.'[20]

WHAT SORT OF WOMEN GO TO SPECIAL HOSPITALS VIA THE CRIMINAL JUSTICE SYSTEM?

June Clarke

I was born in 1956 in Birmingham. As a baby I was put into a home with my sister because my mother couldn't cope. She already had thirteen children. When I was four and my sister Mary was five we were taken from the home to foster parents in Chester. The foster parents were very very strict. When other children were playing when it was long light nights in summer we couldn't play. We were put to bed at five o'clock. Mum and dad used to argue, real bad arguments. It was upsetting.

When I was about twelve and Mary was thirteen my dad's dad came to live with us. He was horrible, he wanted to maul us – you know, sexual abuse. It was mostly my sister, I used to try and run away. I think my mum was conscious of it but she was hardly there, she had a job. I didn't realize really it was wrong. My sister used to say it was just a game. And there was another man. He came round with the vegetable van and we would have to go with him. Mum used to get us up about seven o'clock on Sunday to go with him. We took it in turns – he sexually abused both of us. I don't know whether my mum knew about it, we didn't tell her about it. She used to make us go. I thought it was normal. That went on two or three years, until I was sixteen, then we had sex education at school and I realized we didn't have to put up with this kind of thing. We both stopped going with the man.

When I was sixteen I got my first job, and I met my first boyfriend. He was very nice – he wanted to marry me but I thought he was getting a bit serious a bit too soon, so I had to pack him in. He was very upset and I was too. But I didn't want to marry him. That's when my first crimes started. I drank a lot and slashed some tyres. I don't know why I did it. I was upset about packing him in. I was out of control.

It wasn't long before I found this other man. He was twice my age, in his early thirties. And it was the same situation again: he wanted to leave his wife and get married but he had four sons and the eldest one was fifteen, which was not far off my age. I was pretty upset again, but I knew I couldn't get married to him. Then I went to his works and set his works on fire. I'd been drinking and thinking about it and I don't really know why I did it. The police came. I was mixed up. I was paying him back for what he had done to me. He knew it wouldn't work. The police interviewed me. I told them I did it so they drove me down to the station and said I would be out, I would be OK, if I signed a statement, which I did. But after being put in a cell I was taken to Risley remand centre the next day. It was ten to eleven weeks before I got to court. I was actually put on the hospital side and they just injected me with paraldehyde. It knocks you out and you don't know where you are. Actually you sweat, it comes through the skin and you can smell it. Everybody else knows that you've had that injection because they can smell it. It's meant to sort of knock you out, just keep you like a zombie.

I was locked in a special cell. I was terrified. There were two doors: one to lock you up and the second door to put you in darkness. You couldn't see anybody, you couldn't hear anybody. They'd close the first door and then the other door on top of it so there was not even light coming round the door. You were in total darkness unless you screamed and shouted for the light to be on. But even then they didn't put the light on. I don't know why they did it to me – it was my first time there. I was working in the workshop when something went missing and I ended up in that cell again. I stayed there for five or six days. They just chucked paper plates at me with food on and if I didn't eat it it was just left there.

When I got to Crown Court they sent me to a psychiatric hospital in Cheshire. They gave me ECT there. I did six months in that hospital then I was released again. They said they didn't have any more treatment for me.

Three months and I was back in trouble with the police. I set a bin on fire, a waste paper bin, in the middle of town – Chester. I was drunk and I'd nowhere to go. I didn't want to go back home. My dad's father was still there. My sister was married by this time. I didn't want to go to her. She only had a flat and it was dirty, she never looked after it. Her husband used to batter her all the time. Anyway, after I'd lit the fire the police stopped me and gave me a beating – as usual. I think I was shouting in the cells and they told me to shut up. Somebody beat me to shut me up. There was about five of them, three men and two women. I was charged and got three months. I spent three months locked up. You're usually allowed out of your cell during the day but they said I was a danger to staff.

Then I was released back on to the streets. They gave me some money, it's not much, and a train warrant to get back to Chester. So I got back to Chester and spent all the money on drink and then I was back living on the streets again. There was a day centre where I could have a shower and a meal. I had to pay £1 but I used to get that back off Social. So I was still on the streets when I was nineteen, just hanging around, just waiting for my next drink. I slashed some tyres but they didn't know it was me. Then, I broke some car windows. I was walking down the street and this car knocked down a dog and instead of stopping it just drove off. The dog died in my arms. That made me hate cars; I just wanted to destroy all the cars in the world. I started to get my revenge by smashing up all the cars I could. Now I see that every car I was actually destroying was somebody's property, but I didn't see that then.

In the end I turned myself in because I knew I was actually getting dangerous. I felt I might do something more than damage to cars, that I might hit somebody. I said: 'Look, I've done all these things, smashed things – I even blew one up . . .' I told them I couldn't live with the worry of getting somebody else into trouble. All through my life if I've done something wrong I've always owned up to it. I never let anybody else get into trouble for me. So they just charged me; I didn't mind being charged for TICs (taken into consideration) for other things which I hadn't done. The court sent me to Risley again and the same things happened. I got injected. I was locked up all the time. They let me have a bath, that was one good thing – once a week. I was sent to Crown Court again. This was where Ashworth came in. A doctor came to see me with a nurse. He asked me a load of questions, like why I did what I'd done, how did I feel. I said I just felt awful. In the end they said I was going to come here (Ashworth Special Hospital). It was terrible the things they did to you . . . they used to put you in straitjackets because some people would bang their heads. It was horrible. They used to make you sit in the day-room with a straightjacket on and you'd have everybody walking past and laughing at you. I wouldn't speak to the doctor who'd brought me here because I'd been told it was so nice here. I was in for an unlimited time. I seemed to spend most of my time in solitary because I misbehaved. When you were quiet, they said you were depressed, when you were loud, they said you were disturbed. You couldn't win. Anyway, one day they said I was better – but I felt worse. When I say I was misbehaving I don't mean to them. I was hurting myself, cutting up, things like that. I was still doing it when they said I was better.

When I got out again I made contact with my foster parents, they had me for a while but it was too much for them. I was still drinking but now I was on tablets from here and I took an overdose. When my foster parents said they couldn't cope with me I was back on the streets. I tried a couple of bedsits but I never kept up with my rent. By this stage I was in my early twenties and I'd been raped a couple of times. I thought it was my fault for sleeping rough. That's when I got pregnant and the foster parents took me back in. I went out one day when I was four or five months pregnant; this was my first assault on anyone. I went into a shop and I could feel people watching me. So I picked up a knife out of the store and walked out with it and this woman store detective grabbed me by the shoulder and I stabbed her in the arm.

I was lucky, I got nine months. I went to Styal Prison. I was there when I had the baby, a little girl, Margaret. After a while I got into trouble in prison. There was this girl who was having an affair with one of the male officers. But when I came in he thought I was the bee's knees and this other girl was jealous and so she told all the girls I was doing things with him. I wasn't though, I wasn't interested. In the end I had a fight with her and I was taken down to the punishment block and she was left in the hospital. Then I couldn't look after my little girl so I rang my foster parents and asked them if they'd take her, foster her. And they said they would.

When I came out of prison I spent a lot of time at my foster parents' house with my daughter but it didn't work out. My mum had taken her over. She'd slotted in as Margaret's mum. I didn't do anything at all for her, mum was always doing things for her. I didn't even change her nappy without mum telling me how to do it. I wrote to my MP that I needed a flat because of my baby, that I had nowhere else to go. He directed the council to give me a flat. But Margaret was still at my mum's because at that time she was still a ward of court to my foster parents so I couldn't legally remove her.

I was by myself every night in the flat and I took an overdose. It was nearly lethal. I didn't wake up for five or six days. I was lucky to be alive. After that I didn't want to go back to the flat. My dad and sister were waiting for me when I came out of hospital after the overdose. I said I'd never go back to the flat so my dad beat me up in the street because he said I was being stupid. Maybe I was being stupid, but I was frightened of the dark, frightened of the nights. I couldn't go back. I walked into another town, I think it was Fleet, and it was cold, it was winter. Snow was covering everything. I smashed a window and told the police. So I was back inside again. They gave me three months' imprisonment.

I came out of there (Styal) once again. I came out in winter, my second time in a year. I was in a pub and this man wanted me to have a drink with him and I said no, I didn't want to have a drink with him. He kept pestering me all evening and so I said leave me alone and he wouldn't leave me alone and I'd got a glass in my hand and I'd forgotten I had the glass and I went to punch him and I split his face open with the glass. I ran away and then I saw him being brought out of the pub by the ambulanceman. I waited until all his mates had stopped looking for me and then I gave myself in to the police and told them I was the one that did it. So I came back to Risley and then a doctor from Broadmoor came to see me. He wanted to take me there. But they couldn't fund me. I was very glad because of what I'd heard about Broadmoor. Then Peter Gravett came and he brought me back here. The place had changed a bit, there were no more straitjackets. But they broke my arm, the assistant nurses, they were men; they broke my arm getting me into seclusion. They didn't have any qualifications for being nurses. I made up my mind I was going to make this place work for me this time. I used all of my therapy, did all the schooling I could. And it took eighteen months to get out that time. And I felt a bit better.

I went back to my parents' house and spent six months looking for a job. My daughter was around four or five by this time. I was looking for a job to help my mum with money for my daughter because my mum insisted that she have most of my money. They let me go out once every two or three weeks, the rest of the time I was just doing housework, the washing and ironing and things like that and I really got fed up with it. Then I met this nice guy, he was very nice to me and he wanted to see me the next week but I wasn't allowed out of the house. Anyway, I walked out of the house and left them. I went with this lad. My parents wouldn't let me go back into the house so I actually slept rough two nights. I went to my social worker and he got me a place in a home for the homeless; that was nice, it was clean. They had an all-night caretaker. I spent about three months there but one night when I went back I was locked out. I banged on the door and they wouldn't let me in. I asked why and they said I'd set a fire and rung for the Fire Brigade and so I lost my place there. But I hadn't either set the fire or rung for the Fire Brigade. Then I was placed in a hotel. But I couldn't cope there with the thought of them blaming me for that fire so I actually set fire to two shops, about two o'clock one morning. The Fire Brigade came and the police and when I said I'd set the fires I was taken to the police station and they said if I signed a statement saying I did the fires they would send me to a psychiatric hospital. So I actually signed the papers and the next day I was sent to Risley. So I was being locked up, being injected, being beaten. So Crown Court came along again . . .

I've been here in Ashworth just over three years this time. And this time I've learnt a lot. They say they can't do anything more for me, that I shouldn't be in here any longer, I should be in a halfway house. I don't know. I don't know what to think. I know it's my last chance if I do get out. If I get upset again and set a fire or hit somebody I'll be back in here for a very long time. I've seen it happen to other people. It makes me worry about getting out. I'm afraid that if I go out something will upset me and I'll go out of control and then the next time instead of two or three years I'll be here for a long time, a very long time.

At present June Clarke is still in Ashworth.

I'd talked to June Clarke during the lunch break of a conference at Ashworth Special Hospital in January 1993. After the conference, in the minibus on the way to Liverpool station, I happened to sit next to a participant whom I hadn't met during the course of the day. We got chatting and I told her how appalled I'd been by what June had to say. Her 'Um?' invited me to say more. I began to tell her the story. She nodded her head repeatedly and almost as soon as I'd begun took over the narrative.

I stared. I hadn't mentioned a name . . . but maybe she knew June? She sighed and replied that sadly she didn't need to know the woman I was talking about in order to fill in the bones of her biography. As a Mental Health Act Commissioner she'd heard the same story so many times before that she could anticipate – as she had, by finishing off June's story – what was coming next. Of course she hadn't known the minutiae but she had identified the core elements: rejection, abuse, institutional- ized care, running away, drugs, booze, bad company, brushes with the cops, violence, prison, more violence, more prison, Special Hospital.

The Ashworth Inquiry's report on women in Ashworth quotes Peter Gravett's evidence:

> The vast percentage of the female patients have been seriously sexually abused and been subject to violence by men in their past. Most of them have been neglected, they have been in and out of care. They have gradually become criminalized, in and out of penal institutions and hospitals and have eventually ended up in Ashworth Hospital having offended.[21]

A consultant psychiatrist at Rampton Special Hospital echoes what Dr Gravett has to say:

> These girls, when you look at their past history, you could absolutely cry about it, because they've all had very deprived backgrounds . . . a high proportion of these women have been abused in childhood, physically and sexually.[22]

> Many women in Special Hospitals have life histories which involve not just sexual but physical abuse. Often a downward spiral of events precedes their incarceration in a Special Hospital (e.g. poor and abusive home life, taken into care or living rough, possible involvement in petty crime, prostitution, begging, drug and alcohol addiction, current indictable offence).[23]

As a psychologist who worked with women in Ashworth for six years, Moira Potier is familiar with the history of many of the women who live there. They have all, she says, experienced disrupted family lives.

> Their security has been shattered at an early age by the intrusive acts of powerful others, including physical, emotional and, most notably, sexual abuse (often in the context of generational abuse). The subsequent devastating sequelae include a very poor or non-existent sense of self, shattered trust, non-existent or poorly defined boundaries between self and others underlying a tendency under stress to regress to psychotic-like states, consequent very low self-esteem and the experience at times of overwhelming guilt, anger, hopelessness and despair leading to all forms of self-abuse including para-suicidal behaviour.[24]

Feminization as Proof of Normalization

. . . I was called into the office by Dr L who said he'd heard that I'd not been going over the male side. I said I wasn't interested and of course it was men that put me in there, so I wasn't interested. But going over the male side is supposed to mean you're normal. He said I'd have to try and be interested because if I didn't go over the male side, the next time he did his ward rounds he'd have to write to the Home Office and tell them I wasn't co-operating. 'Get dressed up, put on some make-up and go over the male side,' he said. I had no choice.

So the next time there was a disco I went over the male side. I was crying my eyes out but one of the nurses I got on with said she'd come with me and she did. And I sat there and all these men are coming at me, asking me to dance and I kept saying 'No'. I thought, 'This is good enough isn't it, I've come, haven't I?' Then the nurse came up to me and said she had to do a report when she got back, so could I at least have one dance then she could put it in her report.

So I danced and I said 'You touch me where you're not supposed to and I'll . . .' but then I thought, even if he did do something I couldn't do anything. They could whip me away into the punishment block if I objected, tell me this was just the way they were. I was in a no-win situation. I just prayed and hoped that the record finished quick because I felt I didn't care what they did to me I wasn't dancing anymore. I just said to the nurse that I wasn't doing it anymore. I didn't care what she said. When we were going back over the female side she said: 'Good girl'. I thought: 'You bitch'. It was just the way she said it, you know, 'Good girl' . . .[25]

Pauline Brown (not her real name) has now been out of Broadmoor five years. She is married, has a little girl and works for a charity.

The notion that feminization is proof of normalization, i.e. of getting better, came up mainly in connection with Broadmoor, where I was told that on the women's side the tension level was much higher, the atmosphere much more oppressive, than on the male side.

Dr Chandra Ghosh, consultant psychiatrist at Broadmoor Hospital, sums up what other staff and visitors have told me: 'The difference in the atmosphere, between the women's and the men's sides, is palpable. Walking from one to the other is like going from one world to another.' She goes on to say that on the male side you can see the therapy working as the male staff interact with the male patients, teaching them and showing them how to live without the need to be aggressively macho; how to be a man without being violent; how to relate towards women as equals, instead of fearing and hating and attacking them.

The reason why women spend longer than men in Broadmoor, an average nine years for women, eight years for men, is not because the offence which brought them there was more dangerous – often it was much less so – it is because the whole therapy with which they are involved is anti-therapeutic.

Look at the therapy of a woman who has been sexually abused, a therapy which is geared towards making her more feminine. The therapy does not look at the reason why the woman still gets involved in relationships where she uses sexual favours to hold on to power. What the therapy is actually doing is teaching her how to do it better, it is reinforcing the bargaining and her using of herself as an object and therefore the therapy itself is actually continuing the abusive process.

Obviously this creates very big problems for many of the women in here who have been sexually abused. Rather than helping them to be who they are as individuals this feminizing therapy is anti-therapeutic and delays their leaving the hospital.[26]

Dr Ghosh stressed that she was speaking personally and that her views did not represent those of the management of Broadmoor Hospital. She no longer works on the women's side at Broadmoor.

WISH's annual report contains an account by an ex-patient of her time in Rampton Special Hospital. The extract quoted reflects the sorts of things other ex-patients describe: the petty restrictions, the boredom, the enormous power of the staff, for good or ill, the lack of help, the powerlessness of the patients. This woman wrote up her account in October 1993, the year she left Rampton.

Looking back at Rampton, there were some hard times. I don't think things could ever be as terrible. They say if you can survive Rampton, you can survive anything. It wasn't all bad: there were some good things. In some ways it did me good. I was sentenced to eight years but was transferred to a Special Hospital and ended up doing ten years. Two in Ashworth and eight in Rampton.

My problem was drugs but I never got any help for that in Rampton and it was only when WISH published an article in *Open Mind* about my not being able to leave Rampton until I had seen a psychologist and my having to wait over a year to see one that I got to talk with anyone, properly, about my offence.

The bad ones [staff] dominated my life there. If anyone stepped out of line they didn't do it again. I've seen acts of brutality; there was no need for it . . . My RMO (Responsible Medical Officer) was a lovely man; he wanted me to go sooner but he left and then I had various RMOs. Each one has to get to know you, which puts you back.

My daily life was better than most because I worked in the print shop; very few women get to work there. The man who ran it was brilliant. In there you weren't a patient, you were a person, a friend. I don't think I would have survived without the print shop . . . My salvation was going to work, otherwise you'd be stuck on the yard, you couldn't go to your rooms, the cigarette lighter was turned off at nine o'clock so you couldn't smoke again until dinner time. At weekends your rooms were closed, apart from an hour on Saturday morning whilst you cleaned them just before dinner and tea time. If you wanted anything you had to wait until then. Everything fitted round the needs of the staff, what was convenient for them.

Nothing ever seems to happen to the staff: they can humiliate you, make your life a misery but nothing ever happens to them. You can complain to the Mental Health Act Commission but after they'd talked to you they'd go into the office and as soon as they'd gone the staff would really go to town on you.

I think the Specials should close. I saw and mixed with a lot of different patients from all the wards. There was not one patient I would have been afraid to be in a room with. I think people need smaller units where you can gradually go out into the community. People need help, but they don't need that (the Specials), they don't need locking up 24 hours a day and the key thrown away. You don't get the help you need.[27]

Treatment

'The judge said he was sending me to a Special Hospital for "understanding, care and treatment",' one ex-patient told me. 'Well, I could have done him under the Trade Descriptions Act, because I didn't get any understanding, care or treatment.'

The same patient went on to say that towards the end of her 10-year stay in Broadmoor she had met a psychiatrist who had helped her a lot, 'she really tried to understand me – wow!' And she added that from what she'd learned since getting out, things were improving. 'There's still a long way to go but there have been changes in the last five years.'[28]

Kim Andrews was told by her psychiatrist when she left Broadmoor that she'd been there for 15 years 'and all we've ever offered you is containment – you've had no treatment.'

Another ex-patient, Ricky, was asked by a psychiatrist what she thought they could do for her. 'I said, "I dunno, you're the doctor" and he said, "Well, I tell you, all we're doing is containing you until you burn out."'[29]

Terri Simpson, ex-patient (see Chapter 1):

Lancs House is classed as the intensive care unit in Broadmoor. But for people like me it's the punishment block. There's no treatment there, that's a load of crap. I got out of there despite, not because of, them [staff]. I had lots of people on the outside who were friends who came every weekend to see me. I never had any therapy there, nothing. But I started talking to my friends on visits.

I was made from an illegal junkie to a legal one. I was given injections every week, Clopixol. When I had it in tablet form I was on twenty-three tablets a day of all different kinds: Largactil, Tofranil – you know, anti-depressants, the lot, they just give them to you to control you. If you didn't take them you got 'em in the arse. I was given ECT. Everybody was shoved in the same boat. They had anorexics there. They didn't give a damn if you had eaten on the ward or whatever, if you missed a meal in the dining hall you were classed as depressed. And, of course, ECT was one of the main treatments for anorexics.

I'd been there about five weeks when I had ECT. I was terrified because when you went for ECT they just bundled you in a room with a shutter across the window. Now to me, I'd been in prison, and to be locked up like that in prison was because you'd done something wrong.

The consensus among the women I spoke to was that they didn't get any treatment, just drugs, lots of them, which they saw not as treatment but as a means of control. ECT and seclusion they saw as punishment for unacceptable behaviour, not treatment. Hardly anyone mentioned the use of 'talking therapies' unless it was to say there was a need for something of that sort.

Milieu therapy After being in Rampton for six months, one woman asked about treatment and was told that living in 'a structured environment – or maybe it was constructive environment –' was the treatment. This is milieu therapy: the theory that you get better by virtue of being in that environment or milieu 'until you burn out'.

They want to get you there, but when you're there, they don't want to know. They (the doctors) never come and see how you are. I was lucky if I saw the RMO twice a year. When I used to work in the sewing room on the machines, they used to say that was treatment – going to that room every day and sewing. Women used to come in from outside, like domestics, to make curtains and stuff for the hospitals – same work as us – but to us it was treatment, to them it was just work.[30]

Drugs In the view of the women and those seeking to support them these are widely overused. However, Prue Stevenson of WISH says she has noticed a decrease recently at Ashworth, where the doses were incredibly high. She's now able to have lucid conversations with some women whom she hasn't been able to talk to for years. She adds that though it's absolutely right that such a decrease in the prescription of psychotropic drugs should happen, if they are stopped too fast it can leave women feeling very vulnerable because they've become so used to them.

ECT This is a controversial treatment, and whether or not it has any long-term effect is debatable. June Clarke had ECT in a psychiatric hospital before she ever got into a Special Hospital. They didn't ask her permission, they just did it. 'The thing was I was laid on the bed and there were other people having their ECT before you got your injection and you could see all the bodies jump. They just worked their way round the ward.'

It's shocking to realize that this totally inhumane way of giving ECT, without asking for consent, was apparently standard in at least one psychiatric hospital somewhere around the late seventies/early eighties.

Kim Andrews told me she was given ECT when she cried, 'sometimes without anaesthetic'. Officially, when a patient doesn't consent a second opinion is required from a mental health commission doctor. But talking to women who've been in the Specials the impression gained is that the question of consent didn't come up.

The occasional use of ECT – where a patient is severely depressed and suicidal, everything else has been tried, and the patient has given permission – is seen as a last resort by some professionals. It's the picture of non-consensual ECT being too easily used, i.e. misused, that is the cause for concern. I was told by hospital staff that ECT is used at Rampton and occasionally at Broadmoor. Lona Roberts, senior clinical psychologist at Broadmoor, said, however, that psychotherapy or anti-depressives were the preferred therapy there. She added that it was normally given with the patient's informed consent; where a patient didn't consent, a second opinion was required from a mental health commission doctor. Moira Potier said she never knew of any patient being given ECT at Ashworth during her time there. However, there is a feeling amongst campaigners at present that in some areas the use of ECT is on the increase.

Talking therapies

There was no treatment, there was nothing. I asked what was happening with me. They asked me what I meant and I said that when I went for my tribunal (to assess whether it is safe to release a patient) if they saw that I'd been there three months with nothing happening, no treatment, they were obviously going to say, 'Well, she's not had any treatment, so she can't be better, so she can't be released.'

The staff asked if I wanted to go on medication. I said of course I didn't but asked if I could have some sort of therapy because I needed it. I wanted individual therapy but they wouldn't give me that. They said we have group therapy here or nothing. So I had group therapy but it took me a long time to talk because I didn't trust anybody. There was always a nurse present in group therapy, which I didn't like because they write about what you say in their reports. I had group therapy for four years.

But for the four or five months before I left I had individual therapy with a priest. He was very good. I told him things I could never say in the group. Like about how when I stabbed that woman it was my Mum and Dad's faces I saw. And especially that guy's face [the man who had been sexually abusing her]. I couldn't say that in the group because I thought if I did the nurses would be off into the office to report that I was mad.

The work I did with the priest in those four or five months was more than I did in four years of group therapy. At first I was a bit wary because he was a man, but I decided to try it. And it just flowed out. I didn't see him at first, I just saw the collar and I knew that collar meant that unless I said I was going to kill myself or somebody else he wouldn't tell anyone what I said. I could trust him. I knew if I told him what I felt and what I'd really been thinking and feeling for years then it would get it out of my system. It was a real breakthrough. I knew I could really open up without it being used against me, to keep me in for longer.[31]

Pauline Brown's story pinpoints one fundamental problem for talking therapies within Special Hospitals: how can you trust the person you're talking to/being treated by when part of their job is to report on you and to be your jailer. Say the wrong thing and you might be condemning yourself to more months, maybe even more years, inside. That's assuming there is a member of staff available and willing to listen. Undoubtedly there are some very good staff around who are doing their best but, judging by what the women themselves say, these are in the minority.

What you hear over and over from the women, as Jennifer McCabe has said, is that no one ever listens to them, ever asks them what they think is wrong, what they think they need. But there are signs of improvement here. There is, it seems, an increasing awareness of the need for and the value of talking therapies as provided by psychologists:

Ashworth – changes are underway, although there's a long way to go still;

Broadmoor – I was told there has been a 'dramatic' increase in the psychological input over the last three years, with people being trained in how to counsel the sexually abused, nurses being involved in counselling patients and nurses also being encouraged to take training courses which included counselling and psychotherapy courses;

Rampton – a psychiatrist/psychotherapist with a special interest in self-injurious behaviour has been appointed. The locked ward for psychopathic women patients has been designated a nursing development unit. It's a King's Fund operation for the development of care for difficult-to-manage women patients

However, Jennifer McCabe of WISH is not overly optimistic.

'Some very good senior people have left out of self-preservation. It seems that the very best and most innovative of the staff have the hardest time grappling with the system to get it to change.' She does acknowledge, however, that there are some good staff trying hard to do their best for the women and that there may well be a few managers, a few good people, who want to produce a therapeutic environment.

> But the idea of punishment is embedded in Specials. We, society, want those people dumped there, out of sight, and punished. Specials do that job of punishment for us. And until that wider, fundamental issue is confronted there won't be any real change.
>
> As things stand the true atmosphere in the Specials is one of fear and I would seriously question the value of any attempt at counselling or psychotherapy in such an atmosphere, and where the whole thrust of the underlying culture is towards punishment rather than rehabilitation.

She believes that with the way the Specials are at the moment even talking therapies are 'some way down the road', with the women needing above all to be in a caring environment where they feel safe and where they can have some good experiences and learn to feel good about themselves, perhaps for the first time.

> These women are amongst the most severely damaged and the most vulnerable in our society. They need the most skilled, the most qualified, the most experienced staff to work with them in an environment of caring and trust. All of that needs to come before the intensity of individual therapy. And far from Special Hospitals enhancing this, they actually make it impossible.[32]

Seclusion Typically, a woman in seclusion wears only an untearable dress, no underwear. While conditions vary between the three hospitals the overriding characteristic is that the room is as bare as possible. There is always a cardboard chamber pot and a mattress. The blankets and the mattress are made of rough, untearable material. All of this is designed so that the woman cannot harm herself. Seclusion is supposed to be used for patients who harm or attempt to harm themselves or others.

However, women say they are put in seclusion for such things as swearing, abusive language, refusing to go to work or disobeying orders. And also, says Prue Stevenson, more women than men, proportionately, are put into seclusion. 'This suggests that higher standards of behaviour are set for women than men and that women are more likely to be punished if they don't conform.'[33]

Moira Potier, writing in 1993, described the use of seclusion at Ashworth Hospital as one of the commonplace abuses of power experienced by women who lived there and as a technique of oppression. 'Techniques of oppression' she defined as 'sanctions available to staff if patients infringe rules (i.e. express emotions in any but a narrow range of ways) . . .'[34] It was used, she said, inappropriately and too readily and had no known therapeutic value.

However, as I said, there are real signs of hope here. Prue Stevenson, speaking to me in February 1994, said there had been a dramatic decrease in the use of seclusion. 'It's partly to do with the report of the Ashworth inquiry, which recommended that the use of seclusion be phased out completely. And we've been involved in campaigning for that too.' At Rampton, says Dr Mary McMurran, Director of Psychological Services, seclusion is not typically used.

Lona Roberts, senior clinical psychologist at Broadmoor, says:

Seclusion is used only when it is essential and mainly for the prevention of harm to others. A small group of female patients occasionally become especially disturbed and engage in self-harm which is common among women. In such cases where the self-harm becomes life-threatening or there is a risk of serious injury normal clothing and bedding is replaced with protective clothing and bedding. This, however, is not routine.[35]

In October 1993 the Special Hospitals Service Authority issued a booklet on the use of seclusion in the Special Hospitals. It stated that its objective was 'to promote alternative approaches to the care and treatment of disturbed behaviour and to limit the use of seclusion to exceptional circumstances'.[36] It quoted the Ashworth inquiry report and said the circumstances of seclusion would therefore be:

- a rare event
- only used in response to disturbed behaviour
- a medical emergency
- only used for the shortest possible period
- in accordance with guidance in the Code of Practice, Mental Health Act

The booklet also focuses on the partnership between staff and patients and says that the process of this partnership 'includes recognition of rights and personal dignity and the importance of maintenance of human interaction'.[37] It further warns that 'incorrect assumptions regarding issues of dangerousness, gender, creed and ethnicity may have a profound effect on practice'.[38] The booklet points out that, amongst other things, the SHSA is committed to continual monitoring of the levels of use of seclusion.[39]

Leaving the Specials

> Having been visiting Broadmoor for a year and a half there are plenty of aspects which are quite disturbing. The general atmosphere is more like a prison than a hospital and J. appears to be quite institutionalized. She is treated like a child, has no privacy and is very passive and accepting of the treatment she is given to control her 'illness'. There seems to be hardly anything in the stultifying daily routine that offers any mental stimulation; all that J has to do is make furry animals in OT. That just gives her loads of time to think about her unhappiness and dwell on her problems. She is given a lot of medication and the drugs have made her put on a lot of weight, they also make it very hard for her to concentrate. Sometimes when she is feeling particularly low she will hurt herself which is really upsetting. All I can do is try and boost her almost total lack of self-esteem and try to encourage her to concentrate on today and tomorrow as she has a huge fear of leaving Broadmoor. This shocked me as I expected everyone to be desperate to get out of the place![40]

And other women too have told me of their fears of leaving the hospital. They didn't cope before, they said, and when they got out it was going to be worse. All the campaigners I have spoken to stressed the need for more preparation for women before they leave and for better and longer-term support afterwards.

Speaking about these needs, Prue Stevenson says that women in the Specials need more contact with the outside world through trips out to exhibitions and conferences, for instance,

> and they would also benefit from more people coming into the Specials from outside.
>
> While in the Specials they need to be given more responsibility for running their daily lives – cooking their own meals, for example. And they need to be involved in decisions about treatment. That's absolutely essential if they are to build up confidence and self-esteem. Treating them as adults and not as children would make a great difference to how they eventually coped outside.[41]

The women themselves view the Specials as the end of the line; their fear of not coping arises out of the fear of the penalty: finding themselves back in a Special, facing once again a sentence without a release date.

Practical Problems

Many patients who are ready to leave the Specials face delays once they've been recommended for release. This is because of a combination of factors: there aren't enough suitable halfway houses and hostels, and Regional Secure Units and local psychiatric hospitals or wards may well be reluctant to take them because of fears that they'll be difficult to handle.

Jenny, an ex-patient, recalls that she actually got transferred to another hospital three years after her psychiatrist said that she could leave. A couple of hospitals had turned her down, after which, Jenny said, Broadmoor stopped looking. In the end, with the help of her old doctor, she managed to get a place in the Maudsley Hospital.

Research by Susanne Dell in 1980 showed that, although hospital authorities were worried about accepting patients they thought might be difficult and/or dangerous, only 10 out of 105 patients transferred from Specials caused difficulties which led to them being prosecuted or returned to a Special Hospital.

> These problems lead to patients being detained when they no longer require maximum security. Patients are continuing to be contained in Special Hospitals when it has been acknowledged that they no longer meet the admission criteria of 'requiring the highest level of security'. It must obviously be questioned, Dell concludes, whether or not such a practice is even legal.[42]

Restricted patients, who are detained until they receive permission from the Home Secretary to leave, can also face delays caused by the time it takes for that permission to come through.

More hostels, designed and staffed to serve as halfway houses for women released from the Specials – many of whom have neither homes nor families to go to – are badly needed. The hostels and supportive staff to run them are made all the more necessary by the almost inevitable institutionalization the women suffer – a result of having their lives run for them for years, in matters large and small, by a maximum-security system.

However, some women do get out, and not only survive but go on to make use of what they've been through for the benefit of other women, as Kim Andrews did, one of the founder members – along with Terri Simpson and Prue Stevenson – of WISH.

Since she was freed in 1985, Kim Andrews has helped a lot of women to adjust to life on the outside. This is how she describes her feelings about her own release.

> . . . [after fifteen years in Rampton and Broadmoor] society did not exactly greet me with open arms. The very mention of Broadmoor seemed to conjure up such diabolical images in people's minds, that I found most of my day was spent in educating the public. I had to frequently reassure them that what you see is what you get. I didn't change into a werewolf every full moon. I was viewed and handled with kid gloves, given my daily dose of patronization and awe.
>
> My resettlement officer, meanwhile, thought it unrealistic of me

to be looking for work, when so many ordinary folks were out of work and through no fault of their own. How could I imagine that I was employable? He found my request ludicrous; I found his attitude beneath contempt.

On the whole, though, life was exciting and I felt young at heart. My body had aged, but my mind seemed to have been in limbo all the time that I was locked up. It was a bit of a culture shock for me to think of disco and dancing, to find that now I really ought to be my age and go to the granny nights. Life had passed me by, but I wasn't going to be put off easily.

Little things would send me into raptures, like a bath full of water – not the designated three inches allowed in the hospital. Riding on a train again, having my own front door key, turning on the light when I required. Oh, such utter joy in the simplest of tasks! I am still overdosing on freedom.[43]

CHAPTER 8

Self-Harm: the Silent Scream

MIRIAM SMITH (not her real name)

I was sexually abused by my father from the age of two. I had a semi-breakdown at the age of thirteen. The abuse went on until I was around fourteen. I started self-harming when I was thirteen, at puberty. I think what triggered it was anger and it was wanting help, desperately wanting someone to ask me why I was doing it. It was around the time when I was realizing something was not quite right. I didn't really know what; I was just starting to understand that my family wasn't the same as everybody else's.

When it first started I'd sit at school in a classroom and I'd get a compass and dig it into my hand and just sit there doing it. And they were concerned at school: they said I need psychiatric help. My parents thought the school was recommending psychiatric help because I was difficult. At the beginning I never really made any marks that lasted, so they didn't know about that.

My mother knew about elements of the abuse, such as my father used to tie me up with ropes, because my grandmother told her. But I didn't really acknowledge the abuse until a few years ago. It took me a long time to come to terms with it; I repressed the memory.

I went into hospital for the first time when I was fifteen and a half, into an adolescent unit. I stayed there for a year and a half. It didn't help much. They put me on behavioural modification which basically meant being locked up for what was supposed to be half an hour if I showed any sort of emotions that they thought were inappropriate. But half an hour could turn into days for which they would give me a mattress and sort of left me to it. It's what they like to call behavioural modification without the reward.

I remember the first night I was in there my mum had put a load of Mars bars in my case and when they opened my case they decided I was going to make myself sick with them and so they force-fed me. There were four nurses, one of them pushing food down my throat. And when I asked them why they'd done it they said it was to let me know who was in charge. That would be about twenty years ago. It's probably changed a bit. The particular hospital I was in actually has an eating facilities unit now which it didn't have before.

I was in there about a year and half until I was about sixteen then I moved to an adolescent hostel in South London where I stayed until I was eighteen and a half. I actually went back to college and got two O-levels on the Youth Opportunities Programme. I worked for a year and a half in a geriatric hospital.

I was self-harming all this time still. It was getting worse. By the time I was eighteen I was cutting my arms; using solvents; drinking too much. I did actually have a period around that time when I got out of all that. For about a year and a half things were really good. And then it went wrong again when I left the adolescent hostel – it was the first time I'd lived on my own. I started taking overdoses again and went back to all the same things again, only over the years it got worse. It's like an addiction you have to do more and more to get the same effect. When you cut yourself you release endorphins so you do get a high, you shut off the pain. It's like going beyond the pain barrier really.

I saw various doctors and social workers but they basically didn't want to know, couldn't cope with it. I had one doctor who had me taken off her books. I had a social worker who basically didn't want to know. I felt as though I was on my own. I think at that point I was the lowest I had ever been and that's when I got anorexic and bulimic. Nobody in the system, in the medical profession, asked me why and I didn't feel safe enough to say anything. I think people only volunteer information when they feel safe, when they trust the person they're talking to. And people in the system don't tend to make you feel safe – they can't cope with it so they all ignore the situation. If you bring it up, if you try to mention it, they say, 'Oh don't say things like that'; they discourage you from talking about it.

I don't think it has changed much from my experience with psychiatric hospitals in the last few years. People can't cope with emotions and certainly not situations where people are talking about abuse. One time, though, there was a nurse who decided that he knew so much about it he actually got me to the point where I was having flashbacks, without being able to cope with them, and he couldn't cope with them either. He couldn't cope with what he was doing, he didn't have the experience, and that was quite dangerous really. In my experience anyone who wants to understand or does understand doesn't stay in the system for very long.

When I came out of hospital I went to live in a hostel. I was anorexic, self-harming and using solvents again and in the end I left there because basically they said if you lose too much weight we will put you in hospital. They didn't want to know. I left there and went to live with someone but we had problems, we split up and I was homeless. I registered as homeless and they decided that I was ill enough to need a roof over my head so I was living in a bed and breakfast place. I was anorexic, I tried to kill myself.

So I was back in hospital again and this time they did treat the anorexia. They took all my clothes away, put me on drugs that were too strong so I kept fainting, weighed me three times a week and joked about my weight. I got angry and they called me stupid and said I would be like that the rest of my life. In the end I phoned up the person who used to counsel me at the hostel and said, 'I don't want to be like this for the rest of my life.' And that was the start of getting over it, the start of me getting myself together.

That was about ten years ago, when I came to live in this flat. I carried on seeing my therapist. I got a place on a full-time training course – a design course – I got through the course. I had problems every so often but I got through it. It was quite a stressful time, I was still self-harming some of the time. It was the first time I'd actually tried to do anything like that. I got through but I cracked up at the end of it. I finished the course but then I couldn't cope with the anticlimax at the end of it and went to pieces. I was self-harming, I think I took an overdose and ended up in hospital.

When you self-harm it's not like you want to die, you just can't imagine how you're going to get through the next five minutes. You do it because you can't imagine doing anything else, you can't see how you're going to get through. To me it's like drowning. The rest of the time you swim but when you get to this point you just don't swim anymore, you just feel like – it's just like going under water and not being able to breathe. It feels like you're totally unable to control what's going on and you just can't stand it any longer.

I managed to get a job while I was in hospital. I'm still doing it. I work in education. I don't want to be more specific. I think in some ways the self-harm got worse. I think it's to do with me having therapy because when you start to deal with things it's very difficult and the urge to do it is very strong. Other people have told me they have stopped having therapy because it makes them worse. But I feel I have to go through that and persist with therapy if I'm going to get better. I see my therapist once a week.

I stopped self-harming for a year and a half, until Easter this year, 1994. That's the longest I've ever stopped for since the year and a half, two years, when I was in the hostel, when I was eighteen. I started at Easter, this year, because the relationship that I was in broke up. At the moment I'm finding it very hard. I've actually been in hospital again recently and they basically said, again, that being in this sort of hospital was no good to me at all, they couldn't do anything to help me. It's true that it's very difficult to help people who self-harm, because if they want to do it they will do it. And also there's the stress of being in hospital, listening to other people's problems, it's sometimes worse than being outside. And I'm very lucky because I've got lots of friends, so I've got a lot of support outside, which a lot of people don't have. This time in hospital I was lucky. There were people who actually understood it wasn't doing any good but they didn't get angry. They just decided it wasn't doing me any good being in there so they would get me out. But they didn't get angry with me and that's an improvement. It's the only, only time I've ever been in hospital and they've had that attitude to it. Obviously they get frustrated but there's a difference between being frustrated because they feel helpless and can't do anything and being angry with you.

I think the only way that people are going to be able to do anything about women who self-harm – and men – is for the attitude of the people who work in the system to change. For a start there should be more training about self-harm for nurses and doctors. Horrific things have happened to people I know in casualty departments: people who have been sewn up without an anaesthetic. Basically their attitude is 'you've done this yourself'. It's the same when people take overdoses: you've done this yourself so you're wasting our time and our money. Which is a stupid attitude because that person is then going to go off and do something else and end up back there, or they're going to do something and not want to go for treatment and they're actually going to end up killing themselves.

What needs to happen is for people in the system to talk to people who do self-harm rather than going along in their own way and thinking they know better. There need to be more units, special units for people who self-harm. There need to be groups of people who self-harm. Unfortunately it's difficult for people who self-harm to run them because of the nature of self-harm. Perhaps there could be groups led by people who have stopped for five years, but it does need to be at least five years because one of the problems is that if you're trying not to self-harm it's very difficult to be around people who are doing it. If you're around people who are doing it you tend to want to do it. It's like being an alcoholic: you can't ever say that you've given up, you're cured. You just fight one day at a time. It's a matter of sheer determination: other people can help through sympathetic listening; therapy can help. Also the system needs to start looking at the problem earlier, they need to look at children who have been abused and deal with it at that stage, before it starts. Somebody I know actually started self-harming at seven. It's definitely got its roots in what's happened to a person as a child.

Sometimes I hide my scars, sometimes I don't. I've a terrible dilemma about that. I hide them at work but around my friends sometimes I will, sometimes I won't. Obviously if I've just done something then I wouldn't inflict that on someone, it's got to heal a bit . . . It's a way of saying, 'Look how much I'm hurting.' It's also about being disconnected from yourself. When you're abused, and I mean most people who self-harm have been abused, your body is taken control of, it's like it belongs to someone else so to a certain extent what you do to it doesn't matter because it's not yours. I can remember feeling really strongly that I've got my brain and my mind, but I'm not actually connected to anything, I'm totally disconnected to anything. To the extent that one of the things I've done when it's been really bad – because having been abused I hate my sexual organs – I actually shoved glass inside myself. It actually frightens me that I've got to that point but I just hope that I'm going to get past it. It was the day I was discharged from hospital. The day before I had actually felt really strong. Then I had a major nightmare about the abuse. I got up the next morning and some woman was wearing some of my personal things. I was so angry that I hit her. And I couldn't cope with the fact that I'd hit her and I did it.

When you've been abused it's like the person who abused you is inside you and I'm constantly trying to get him out of the inside of me. After the nightmare I felt I was never going to get rid of him. It felt like he was fighting back; like he was saying, 'I'm still inside you, I've still got control.' I think if I hadn't had my therapist there when I needed her I would have ended up somewhere like one of the specialist hospitals or in prison or I would have died. I don't know how I would have survived without her. It has taken me a long time to trust and it's the trust that you have to have. It's also important that my therapy is open-ended. My therapist has known me since I was about sixteen. Having said that I suppose I shouldn't still be doing the things I do but I think she understands that I do them under stress, when it gets really really bad. I'm really trying to go out and do things. I have this list of things I want to do in my life. I went on a retreat and I went on an archaeological dig and I went to learn to ride a horse. The latest thing is I'm learning how to ride a motorbike. It's one day at a time. It's all you can do.

Miriam (who comes from London, and is now thirty-five years old) is a typical case. It's a story of abuse and/or poor parenting as part of an unhappy childhood, followed by self-harm which began in adolescence and which was little understood and hardly treated at all by staff who found it altogether too frightening and repelling to deal with. The result: for years Miriam felt more punished than comforted by those who were meant to be helping and treating her, an experience which re-created her lonely and desperate childhood and probably perpetuated and deepened her distress, thus aggravating her tendency to self-harm rather than helping her to do it less.

Self-harming, a form of violence against one's own body that is much more common amongst women than men, is a problem which is only now beginning to emerge into the public consciousness. Though alcohol addiction, drug abuse and eating disorders can all be considered as forms of self-harm, what I'm concerned with is self-harm which takes the form of intentionally cutting, burning, scratching or swallowing harmful things, e.g. razor blades. In its extreme form it can involve putting out an eye, but the most common manifestation of this type of self-harm is cutting.

The extent of the problem isn't known. However, we do know that over a hundred thousand people a year present at hospital accident and emergency units as a result of self-injury of one form or another, which may include overdoses.

Workers at the Bristol Crisis Service for Women, which runs a help-line for women who self-harm, regard this as a very conservative estimate. It has been estimated that more than 1 in every 200 of the general population self-harms[1] – an almost unbelievable figure – and the consensus is that the highest rates of self-harm occur in institutions and that women are much more likely to self-harm than men.

Diane Harrison self-harmed for many years. Today she helps other women who self-harm and runs training workshops for professionals in how best to help women who self-harm. She sees self-injury as a way of trying to survive overwhelming feelings of helplessness and despair, a way of trying to carry on. This is completely different from a suicide attempt, where there is a wish to destroy the self totally. Self-harm is about getting through each moment. It's a symbolic language from the unconscious, where you are trying to tell yourself what's going on inside even though you can't make the conscious links. It can be a way of trying to rid yourself of dirty feelings inside that seem to be taking over, like a poison.[2]

Diane began cutting herself at around the age of seven or younger; it lasted until her thirties. She had no memories of sexual abuse and in fact couldn't remember much of her childhood at all,

so I just thought I was mad ... I reached a crisis when my marriage broke up and I was knocked over and had my leg in plaster, so I couldn't run away any more. I was seeing a social worker and I started to tell her about the abuse, even though I couldn't believe what was coming out of my mouth. Then at least I could begin to understand why I was cutting myself, although it got worse temporarily. You can't stop until you've got some understanding of what's gone on in the past and no longer feel guilt.[3]

Abuse, either physical or sexual, together with a generally unhappy childhood because of poor parenting, seems almost always to be in the background of women who self-harm. A study of 74 subjects with psychiatric problems (personality disorders or 'bipolar II disorder') monitored them for self-destructive behaviour such as suicide attempts, self-harm and eating disorders. The researchers found that of the 28 people who reported self-cutting when they entered the study, 22 (79 per cent) had histories of significant childhood trauma and 25 (89 per cent) reported major disruptions in parental care. 'Only one did not give a history of either childhood trauma or disrupted care.'[4] The same study found that those who self-harmed and who attempted suicide were highly likely to have suffered sexual and physical abuse as children.[5]

Women at the Bristol Crisis Service for Women say that over

half the women who phone them about self-harm say they were sexually abused as children. They believe that a much higher rate of sexual abuse would be revealed if they were to ask callers directly if they had been sexually abused as children.

Discussing the causes of self-harm, Lois Arnold, Self-Injury Training and Information Project Worker at the Bristol Crisis Service for Women, refers to recent research which shows that the huge majority of child abusers were men and the majority of abused children were girls. While she is certain that the causes of self-harm are many and complex this could be one clue as to why more women than men do self-harm.

Why Do More Women Than Men Self-Harm?

It's not clear in the population at large how many more women self-harm than men but it has been estimated that 1 in 7 of women prisoners[6] will self-harm or self-mutilate. The comparable figure for male prisoners I've seen given is 1 in 33.[7] Eaton quotes Benn and Tchaikovsky as showing that 'while less than 1 out of every 100 men mutilate themselves in prison, the same figure for women is *1 in 6* [emphasis in original]'.[8] Estimates of the figure for women in Special Hospitals is much higher. In research on Section 3[9] (of the Mental Health Act 1983) patients in Broadmoor, it was found that 88 per cent of the women, compared with 15 per cent of the men, self-harmed.[10]

And, in 1993, Moira Potier reported that of 79 women resident in Ashworth, 40 had been diagnosed as having psychopathic disorder, 34 of whom had been sexually abused in their childhood and teenage years. All 40 of the women had been, or still were, self-harming.[11]

Could the high rate of women's self-harming both within Special Hospitals and the population in general have something to do with the way women are expected to be and behave in our society? Could it be in part at least a reflection of how women are socialized – of what it is to be a woman in our society? In a paper entitled 'The Ultimate Violence: A Study of Self-Mutilation in Women's Prisons', Susan Apps hypothesizes that, while the experience of imprisonment itself may make women more vulnerable to self-injury, the way women are socialized into being acceptable women is a major contributory factor to their higher rate of self-harming in prison than that of male prisoners.

While her work focuses on women in prison, it nevertheless has great relevance, insofar as it relates to the construction of femininity, for all women who self-harm, whether they do so in prison, in Special Hospitals or in the community. Apps is very well aware that her research was limited and that, self-injury being such a complex issue, it is 'vital to be able to record and analyse the phenomenon in relation to many variables'.[12] However, she does believe that 'the notion of a theory of femininity ... open[s] the way to an alternative understanding of the phenomenon' and that that theory, together with the 'prison as a cause of self-injury' theory, helps us to understand why self-mutilation rates are so high in women's prisons.

The notions of femininity Apps is talking about have already been discussed in some depth in Chapter 3. To re-cap briefly, women are brought up to: cope and care for others; be good in the home; be attractive to men; be passive, and not show anger.

They learn that their bodies are the most important asset they have, more important than anything else, including intelligence, on the path to achieving the rewards of 'normal' womanhood. Beauty becomes a passport to happiness, which results in women becoming preoccupied with their looks and gaining obsessions about their physical appearance, to such an extent that attitudes about themselves are tied up with perceptions about how they look.[13]

All of this is so deeply internalized that women themselves are unaware of it.

Lois Arnold of the Bristol Crisis Service for Women agrees.

The whole focus is on our bodies. Our bodies are there for men's pleasure, not ours, and they never measure up. And women are supposed to pluck their eyebrows, shave their legs, slim themselves, wear high heels. It doesn't seem to me to be a very large step from the woman who sits there, you know, bashing her thighs with her fists, saying 'I'm so fat, I shouldn't have eaten that cream cake' to a woman cutting herself.[14]

For Arnold, it's a continuum with societal encouragement at one end, and condemnation at the other.

In her hypothesis Apps outlines five ways in which concepts of femininity may contribute to self-injury. Two of the points – the first two listed – relate specifically to women in prison, the rest to women in general.

Women's separation from their children Since they are socialized to believe they are the only ones who can really bring up their children properly, what use are they if you take away their primary role? Depression because of the loss of this role, which *told* a woman who she was and brought self-esteem, together with anxiety about what's happening to her children and her lack of control over her life in prison, can combine to lead a woman to self-harm. She's a worthless woman, her body must be worthless – why not 'brand' it as such?

Women's defining of themselves in the context of how they relate to others Women tend to define themselves not in terms of themselves, as autonomous individuals, but in the context of relationships, for instance, as 'friendly' or 'sympathetic'. However, in prison, 'close friendships or physical contact to any degree' between women are not allowed, thus closing off another outlet for sharing feelings. 'This makes women feel inadequate personally, as their need to be wanted is denied. They lose identity and this may lead to self-injury.'[15]

Appearance The face and body are the centres of attention/attraction; perfection is the goal. Apps speculates that when women need help desperately, harming their bodies, which are so precious to them, may occur to them more often than to men 'because they are always aware of them'.[16]

Attention Apps points out that a woman who disfigures her body is 'guaranteed immediate attention', because people don't ruin 'their most important asset unless they are desperate'.[17] While I accept that the appearance of a woman's body is seen as being more important to her than the appearance of a man's body is to him, I am very wary of emphasizing in any way the attention-seeking aspect of self-harming. In institutions it can so often be interpreted by staff as *just* attention-seeking, treated as merely manipulative and punitively dismissed.

Even where there is an element of wanting attention, surely any woman – anybody – who goes to the lengths of cutting or burning her body to get some attention is desperately in need of real attention, i.e. someone willing to listen sympathetically, to hold her, and to help? Most people have the attention they need, or feel sufficiently confident of getting it, to not have to resort to such appalling measures. Self-harming has been described as 'the silent scream' for help – if so, it's a cry for help that should not be ignored as *mere* attention-seeking.

Hearing what a woman who has self-harmed for twenty-five years has to say on the subjects of self-harm and attention-seeking helps put them in perspective:

> . . . nor is it attention-seeking. We would rather endure the pain of badly infected cuts or burns than be found out. It's degrading asking someone to fix something you've done on purpose. Nevertheless, the urge is often overwhelming – the longer you resist, the worse the outcome. I never thought of the consequences at the time, although afterwards I'd feel stupid and embarrassed. Luckily, the pain usually stopped me from going too far – some people can't stop cutting until they see bone.[18]

Women not being allowed to display anger Women are brought up and learn from everything around them that, in order to care for others, they must repress their own anger and frustrations: their anger must be turned inwards, upon themselves. Any harm they do must be to themselves, not to others. Self-harming is literally a physical manifestation of that anger.

The experience of the Bristol Crisis Service for Women supports this. They say that women tell them that often before harming themselves they experience 'a build-up of tension and angry feelings, and that when they harm themselves they may feel as though they have "left their body" and are "watching from outside". After expressing or releasing the feelings in this way there can be a dramatic alleviation of tension'.[19]

Obviously much more research is needed into the causes of self-harming – not all women who've been abused self-harm, not all women in institutions self-harm. However, the links with abuse, poor parenting, and lonely and unhappy child-hoods, and the more recently described link with women's socialisation would provide excellent starting points for such research.

Self-Harm amongst Women in Institutions

We've seen that an estimate of 1 in 200 of the population self-harm and that the consensus is that more of these will be women:[20] that 1 in 7[21] women in prisons self-harms and that the number of women who self-harm in Special Hospitals could be somewhere between 1 in 2[22] and nearly 9 out of 10.[23]

It's difficult to do research on women in the general population when most of them choose to hide their self-harm and/or are not treated sympathetically when they appear at casualty: most of what research there is concentrates on populations in Specials or prisons. At least some of what has been learned about these specific groups of women, given that they are influenced very much by the surroundings in which they are forcibly held, would apply to women in the general population who self-harm.

It is arguable that the women who end up in Specials via the criminal justice system are amongst those whose lives have been the most cruel, the most empty, the most chaotic from when they were tiny. Put that together with the high rate of sexual abuse amongst women diagnosed as having psychopathic disorder and it comes as no suprise to learn that all of the women in Ashworth Hospital in 1993 with that diagnosis had self-harmed or were still doing so.

Writing about women who self-harm in prison, Apps points out that uncertainty about what is happening in a woman's life can lead to self-harm and also to despair. Here she is speaking of the high proportion of women who self-harm while on remand or early in their sentence: 'Unable to contact and assure them-selves as to the well-being of loved ones, not knowing when their court case is due, or whether they will have a life worth returning to when they are released, also causes despair.'

A woman she interviewed, Julie, told her:

They don't let you know anything inside. I was told the night before: 'By the way you're up in court tomorrow.' I was scared, I cut up, they don't give you time to think about it properly, just enough time to get frightened . . . It's not natural for women to mutilate. The psychiatrists and doctors don't get down to the deep-rooted problem of why they are doing it. Deep down, women are depressed about their family, kids, where they're going to from prison.

Apps goes on to speculate that maybe one of the reasons there's less self-injury in men's prisons is that 'when a man is inside, he knows his wife is keeping the family together and that the children are being looked after in his absence'.[24]

Helen Liebling, a psychologist at Ashworth Special Hospital, who is continuing to research self-harm, has drawn up a list of factors which may contribute 'to so many women harming themselves in often horrendous ways'.

1 How women are brought up and socialized.

2 The distress and pain these women have experienced in their lives.

3 The way women's wards of Special Hospitals are run, with more emphasis on security and routine rather than on understanding, caring and treatment.

4 The lack of control women have over their lives.

5 The traditional stereotypic way in which women are perceived results in women who deviate from the expected 'norm' being treated as mad and the behaviour is not tolerated as it may be for men.

6 Expression of angry feelings.[25]

Only one of these six factors relates specifically to women in Specials: all the others could equally well apply to women who self-harm in general. Speaking specifically about women in Specials and referring to the work of Wendy Jackson, Liebling says: 'If a woman internalizes her anger, it may reinforce the diagnosis of mental illness. If she is verbally or physically aggressive, that too is likely to be viewed as further evidence of mental instability. If she self-harms, "it is likely to result in long hours in solitary confinement". Thus women in Special Hospitals are "trapped in a no-win situation".[26]

H. M. Cookson, who studied self-harm amongst women in Holloway prison in the late 1970s, noted that it had two positive effects for them: it distracted them from mental suffering such as depression and anxiety and by 'provoking a response from her environment she will gain some control over it and feelings of helplessness and depersonalization will be reduced'.[27]

In 1989 Kate Williams, a psychologist at Ashworth Hospital, who has since left, studied women who self-harmed in the community. She found an association between social anxiety and self-harming. The women who self-harmed were dissatisfied with their bodies and with themselves.

> This resulted in the woman feeling that her self, her life and her body, were out of control. Hence, gaining control was considered to be an important factor in the development and maintenance of self-injurious behaviour as it enabled the individual to gain at least temporary control over the self, and in particular, over the body.[28]

Thus, the factor of control, the need to assert control, and to do so by harming one's own body, is an area which would repay intensive research.

In fact, following on from their pilot study, Liebling and Chipchase are continuing their research at Ashworth, using a large sample of women patients and staff. They hope to compare their findings with data from women in a psychiatric hospital, a Regional Secure Unit (RSU) and a women's prison. They also plan to interview a sample of male patients at Ashworth who self-harm and to compare these groups.

Their research includes structured interviews with staff who work with women who self-harm to determine any differences in perception of the reasons for this behaviour and the implications of these. The interviews are looking at how self-harm is perceived and managed and the support and training needs of staff who work in this area.

My own view is that so many common factors keep occurring when talking about self-harm by women in institutions and in the community – abuse, poor parenting, a lonely and unhappy childhood, the emphasis on the appearance and the body itself, the repressed anger, feelings of worthlessness and self-hatred, the desperate need to feel in control of something, the need to relieve the unbearable tension – that future research will show a continuum rather than a sharply differentiated split between the women who self-harm in institutions and those who self-harm in the community.

Attitudes and Treatment

... people, even family and friends, rarely understand. After Dee Cox ... 'came out' publicly [about her self-harming], local people reacted cruelly.

One former friend [says Cox] now crosses the road and shouts abuse, and someone told social services I was a danger to children. That's ridiculous; the only person I harm is me, and I never do it when children are around.[29]

The following is an extract from an official censored prison letter:

'You made me feel really embarrassed telling me to pull up my sleeves and show you the cuts I'd done. I hate looking at them. I feel ashamed for doing it now, but at the time it's the only way to let out the way I feel. I just slash them without thinking. I don't feel the pain at the time. It's later when I can't stand it. The cuts start to swell after a while so by the time the doctor gets here they're really sore and tender. They didn't use an anaesthetic, so it's agony. The last time I had them stitched I went all dizzy, my ears were buzzing and I couldn't see. I felt terrible. I know it's stupid to do it in the first place, but I'd rather leave it open than get it stitched and go through all that pain over again.'

Following this incident, the woman was prescribed large doses of Largactil and kept in solitary confinement. Classic prison 'treatment'![30]

Within a hospital setting, self-mutilating patients rapidly assume an 'identity' which is equated with their symptomatic acts. They become known to both patients and staff as 'cutters', 'slashers', 'slicers' and 'scratchers' – labels which confine the patient to the level of his symptom, yet confirm for him a distinctive and functional role in the hospital.[31]

Anybody working within custodial environments where this has become a regular feature of life knows that the above remains as relevant today as it was over 20 years ago. Institutional wisdom perceives these 'performances' as the maladaptive, attention-seeking, malignancy of 'untreatable psychopaths'.[32]

People are appalled by self-harm whether they are friends and relatives or the staff whose job it is to treat the women who do it in prisons and Special Hospitals. And there is no denying that it is difficult to look at the evidence of such wounding and not be shocked. Not morally shocked, just simply as in having the breath punched out of you at the realization that what you are seeing has been done by that woman to herself. We all need help in understanding but none more so than the staff of prisons and Special Hospitals, because they have so much power either to help the women or to make matters worse.

For the time being, though, it seems that the tendency is for staff to distance themselves from women who self-harm; their response is either to ignore it, if it is minor, or to be punitive – at the very least unsympathetic – when it is more serious.

Nursing staff in Specials may well interpret self-harm by women patients as further evidence of the non-conforming perversity of female psychopaths

who do not comply with conventional stereotypes of womanhood – femininity, domesticity and motherhood. On the contrary, this particular group of women had accumulated such an assortment of 'master statuses' such as 'personality disordered', 'offenders', 'failed women' and 'self-abusers' that tremendous ambivalence, if not hostility, was felt toward them.[33]

The routine response to such self-harming, says Burrow, is seclusion and medication.[34]

Seclusion means being put into a 'strip' cell with only a dress of some tough material to wear and no furniture. Mary Eaton describes the 'institutional response' as punitive, the pain is denied and the perpetrator is further punished. By solitary confinement she is further denied control over her own person. The response of the prison is a further negation of the self. For some women this may mean a removal from prison to a Special Hospital, with no release date.[35]

(However, in a letter to Miss Apps, the Principal Medical Officer of Holloway Prison said: 'I know of no patient "sectioned" to a Special Hospital through being a danger to themselves.')[36]

And once in a Special, as has been said, a woman who self-harms is similarly likely to find herself spending long hours in solitary confinement.[37]

Women who self-harm in the community and who go to casualty seeking medical attention may well find themselves misunderstood and treated by staff who are angry and impatient with them. You don't have to be institutionalized to have your wounds sewn up without anaesthetic: it has happened to women who've gone to hospital for help. Diane Harrison says:

> Women often have a lot of anger about their visits to casualty, where they may be dismissed as time-wasters. Doctors tend to ask, 'Were you trying to kill yourself?' because they can't distinguish between suicide and self-harm. It makes me angry, but as an ex-nurse I know that when you've got very little time it's easier to label someone than to give proper thought to what to do.[38]

What Can be Done to Help

There's evidence to show that where there is too much control in an institution there's likely to be more self-harming.[39] There's also research to show that where there's a therapeutic regime in which both staff and patients regard the most important aspects of the environment as 'support, expression, involvement and personal problem-orientation'[40] there's likely to be a very much lower rate of self-harm.

Women who self-harm talk about the importance of being listened to; Miriam Smith emphasizes the importance of open-ended therapy; the women at the Bristol Crisis Service for

Women say that above all they listen to and believe what the women who call tell them. Diane Harrison agrees with Miriam Smith about the need for talking therapies which are not short term. She herself, she says, had 'seven years of therapy and I needed all of it'.[41] Support groups, such as the ones she's been running for some years, can also help. And, she says, there's a need for crisis centres as well, 'somewhere to just sit and talk'.[42]

When it comes to training professionals, she says she and her co-worker always start their training workshops with a brain-storming exercise about misconceptions:

> for example, that self-injury is to do with attention-seeking or game-playing . . . What the professionals always ask is, 'What do we do about it?', but we tend to focus on their own feelings about self-harm, raising awareness and looking at support and supervision, and other things follow from that.[43]

To sum up then, what would help is: training for professionals who work in the system; more self-help groups; crisis centres; more open-ended therapy with therapists who know about self-harm; more helplines like the one in Bristol. And underpinning all of that is the need for attitudes to be informed by the sort of understanding and compassion which inspires the Bristol Crisis Service for Women's booklet, *Women and Self-Injury*. On a page designed to help those who are considering offering to help on the telephone crisis line, and in answer to the two questions: how do you help women who call you? and, how can I help women who self-injure?, they say:

> . . . we have found we can best help by giving our attention to what is happening for the woman. Above all, we listen to and believe what she tells us.
>
> We do not judge the extent of her crisis. Instead we concentrate on how she sees her situation and the feelings which make her want to self-injure. There are limits to what we can offer by phone but we can encourage feelings of safety by letting her know we are with her and will not judge her.

Although we might encourage the woman to outwardly express her feelings by hitting something or shouting, we would not try to stop a woman who is cutting or injuring herself. We accept that she is in control and that it is her way of coping at this time.

Many women do not trust anyone and fear rejection or punishment. If a woman chooses to come to us, we believe we should respect that trust, however fragile, and the risk she takes in calling us . . .

. . . identifying and looking at all the feelings will take time, especially for the woman who has never spoken about this before. It takes time for enough trust to build up and we can only share this stage with her, not let our impatience take over. We try to build on the woman's feelings of safety by being there with her and giving reassurance.[44]

CHAPTER 9

Conclusion

This is a book about violent women. It has also proved to be a book about women in general because violent women are not qualitatively different from other women, whatever the myths would have us believe about 'deadlier than the male' evil monsters. Before I began I was a little apprehensive. What would these violent women be like? I had met violent men during research into attitudes towards rape, some of which was conducted in men's prisons (in New Zealand). And I had been frightened by some of those men whose violence seemed to be with them all the time.

None of the women I've met had been frightening, which doesn't *prove* anything of course. Lenore Walker, the psychologist responsible for the formulation of the Battered Woman Syndrome, has told me that she has met women who've frightened her. My point is: very few women are violent, and of those it seems highly likely that only a handful will be violent in a random or continuous way as part of who they are.

This is one of the important things that has emerged while I've been working on this book: women's violence comes from a place different from men's. A 'violent' woman is not the female equivalent of a violent man, as language would suggest. Most of the women I've met ended up in Special Hospitals, and they had had typically appalling lives, characterized by rejection, abuse, confusion, drugs, booze and a deep distrust of authority. I have spoken to only one battered woman who killed: Sara Thornton, whose single act of violence against her battering, alcoholic husband, Malcolm, left her serving a life sentence for murder.

It's impossible to understand why these women did what they did without an awareness of how much the realities of all women's lives are influenced, not to say dominated, by their relations to men, by the way they are defined as good or bad women in reference to how they interact with men. It is because that awareness is lacking and they are seen and judged as other, in terms of stereotypes based on their gender, in relation to men, that so many of the problems arise. That fundamental lack of acknowledgement of the male-powered society in which women live their lives is the root problem that needs to be tackled, if women who are violent are to receive justice and all women are to live in a just society.

For that to happen the 'understanding' of men as naturally aggressive and women as naturally passive because of their different biology needs to be shown up for the reductionist sham that it is. We are much more complicated, primarily social, creatures than such simplistic theories would suggest. If we are programmed at all, our own individual capacity to make choices – that random element of choice – is part of the programme that makes it open-ended, not determined – either by genes or socialization.

The logical conclusion of such a determinist view of human nature rules out justice because, if you held such a view, no one can help herself, no one is responsible for her own actions. A recent manifestation of these biological interpretations of female behaviour has been the seemingly easy acceptance by the courts of PMT as an excuse for violence. This reduces women: it says they can't help themselves because of their female hormones, i.e. because they are women. That is the case writ large but that implication is there in the use of biology and psychiatry to explain and even to excuse some female crimes of violence.

We do not see any parallel hormonal theory evolving to explain male violence: men are the rational norm and able to control their hormones and emotions, or at least they are expected to. Nor are males likely to be psychiatrized by the criminal justice system in the way that women are.

Two points need to be made here; both concern justice. First, it is clear to me from Hilary Allen's work that some men, by being refused psychiatric help, are suffering injustice and this needs to be looked at and studied very carefully. They are suffering as a result of the power of the male equalling the norm equalling the rational stereotype: the fear of admitting any kind of weakness and therefore risking loss of control is so great that unless a man is positively raving he's going to be seen as rational and responsible.

The second point is that women who commit violent crimes should be punished. Sara Thornton, Jackie Child, other women I have talked to, didn't deny they'd done wrong and deserved punishment. Jackie Child was found guilty of manslaughter and accepts the fairness of the verdict. But I was in court the day the prosecution and the defence summed up. After the prosecution's speech it seemed certain to me she would be found guilty of murder. Her defence counsel, Helena Kennedy QC, had to work extremely hard to offset jury prejudices to do with a woman whose lifestyle had been shown to involve heavy drinking. The case seemed to turn on what sort of woman she was, rather than the actual crime. She was at very real risk of a life sentence, at least in part because of being perceived as a woman who drank regularly. Her gender performance was in the dock with her: how she measured up as a proper woman was on trial as well.

Battered women who kill their violent husbands are subject to the same scrutiny. While the courts are generally sympathetic to a woman who has finally snapped and responded by killing her abuser, especially if in all other respects she comes across as a good, conventional wife and mother, there are very real problems for any woman who does not kill in immediate response to an attack and/or doesn't fit the approved stereotype.

Sara Thornton failed on both counts and got life for murder. The male-made law has no notion of the realities of women's lives in general and of the circumstances of battered women in particular. It is itself a 'male-equals-objective' law. As we saw in Chapter 5, it wasn't until 1891 that it became illegal for a husband to beat or imprison his wife. Ingrained attitudes take longer to die than laws do to change – and it takes a lot to get laws changed.

Once in prison women suffer more from the worry about, and separation from, their children than men offenders. Women who have committed violent crimes behave no differently than those women imprisoned for non-violent crimes.

Although levels of aggression are higher in women's prisons than men's, women imprisoned for violent crimes are no more likely to misbehave than other women prisoners. Nor are they treated any differently by their fellow prisoners, unless they have killed for greed or harmed children. If the former, they tend to be shunned; if the latter, they are at risk of being abused and harmed by other inmates.

It's easier for women offenders to go from prison to a Special Hospital than men. Campaigners are alarmed at the way the label 'psychopath' can be attached to a woman who is aggressive; she can find herself in a Special facing an indeterminate stay. Much less aggressive behaviour on the part of a woman, it seems, warrants transfer to a Special Hospital since an aggressive woman is deviant and abnormal in acting against her natural role.

And some women in Specials suffer even more because they are under pressure to behave in a proper, feminine way to prove they are getting better, i.e. returning to normal.

THE WAY FORWARD

Violent women who cannot show they conform to approved stereotypes are at greater risk of harsh treatment from the criminal justice system than those women who commit such a crime but otherwise fit the approved societal mould.

But this is not because of some sexist conspiracy on the part of the people who run and are employed in this system. The Scottish sheriffs who sent bad mothers to jail were not lying when they said they didn't discriminate against women. However, as Pat Carlen's research showed, they weren't speaking the truth either. The truth is, the system operates against such deviant women because the system itself is deeply embedded in a very traditional and conservative part of the society on whose behalf it operates.

Violence is primarily a male problem. Overwhelmingly it is men who are violent, not women. This needs to be clearly seen and understood. Research needs to be conducted into why men commit violent acts. If we are to have a chance of decreasing male violence we must understand from where it springs.

Part of the solution will lie in changing the way masculinity is constructed in our society – with a very much smaller tolerance of aggressive behaviour. If and when that happens, along with an increasing awareness of the restrictions and limitations and sometimes downright brutality that some women suffer as a result of the tolerance of male aggression, so I would expect women's lives to improve and there to be even less violence on the part of women than there is now.

Those who endorse the view that 'feminism increases female violence' may well be falling foul of the androcentric fallacy that men provide the norm for behaviour and standards for humanity. Women's liberation does *not* mean liberating women from restrictions so that, once these are removed, women will revert to the norm and behave like men – men being the norm. Women are not 'deviant' men. Men are not the norm – the belief that they are constitutes the androcentric fallacy which underlies and underpins women's treatment as 'other', as second class.

And it's on the basis of that misunderstanding that the second step of the argument follows: since men are aggressive, when women are liberated they will be just as aggressive. The truth is that each of us has the potential to be aggressive, but society encourages this in men and discourages in women.

Certainly as women move out of the home into the workplace they will have the same potential and opportunity for wrong-doing as men. But women, especially working-class women, have been going out to work for years and we've seen no upsurge in female crime – the numbers follow pretty well the same patterns as for male crime. Women are still, by and large, petty, non-violent offenders – in much smaller numbers than men.

To say that 'feminism winning means women will rule' is to talk in a masculinist way. If people become persuaded of the truth of the feminist message – that women have less power and control over their own lives because they are women and that this is unjust – what will follow will be a redistribution of opportunities and power: a sharing which will mean that all of us have a better chance, as individuals with all our different shortcomings and gifts, to live our lives as fully as possible. That's the utopian view. In practical terms, what needs to be fought for now – apart from changing attitudes towards women in general and women who commit violent crimes in particular – are changes in the law, prisons and Special Hospitals.

Changes in the Law

As far as women who commit violent crimes are concerned, there needs to be raised awareness of, and debate about, the extent to which their conformity to approved stereotypes influences how they are perceived and treated. Mezey suggested gender training for psychiatrists. Why not also for police, lawyers, magistrates, judges – all those involved in the criminal justice system? An acknowledgement of the need for such training would be a start.

The crucial question concerns battered women who kill, on whom I've focused particularly: is it just that a woman who finally responds with a single act of violence against her abuser when she can take no more, following perhaps years of abuse, should receive the same life sentence as someone who kills in cold blood, for example for gain?

This may well be the outcome if she doesn't respond straight away. But, given that women are usually less physically strong than men, that they are socialized to be caring not aggressive, that these women have often been beaten over a long period of time and are afraid of provoking a worse, maybe lethal beating, it's all too likely they will respond using a weapon and after a delay.

Then they face the problem of fitting into the acceptable legal categories for self-defence and for the partial defence of provocation which would reduce their crime from murder to manslaughter. They could plead temporary insanity under the heading of diminished responsibility; while this may sometimes be the case, in the majority of cases the response is entirely reasonable, given what the woman has gone through. There's also the objection that this defence avoids the question of justification, locates the cause of the crime in the woman and not the abuser whose behaviour provoked the woman, and fits suspiciously neatly into the tradition of explaining women's behaviour in terms of mental instability. I have a similar feeling of unease to do with the potential overreliance on the use of Battered Woman's Syndrome.

My own view is that the best way to remedy the injustice faced by some battered women who kill is to get rid of the mandatory life sentence and the law on provocation and diminished responsibility. I would also like to see a thorough investigation done of the way the law on self-defence works with a view to widening it, along US lines. The work on that could start now but, given the conservatism of our legal system, I feel that any change to the law on self-defence is in the future.

However, I do sense the beginnings of a real groundswell of support for the dropping of the mandatory life sentence. This should be the immediate target for change, with changes to the law on self-defence as a longer-term objective. If the mandatory life sentence were dropped the jury could decide on the degree of culpability and the judge on the sentence. It's to be hoped that the gender training mentioned earlier, about the real position of women in our society, could be provided for judges fairly quickly. I believe that the dropping of the mandatory life sentence is currently the best available option for battered women who kill: it would at least allow the criminal justice system greater flexibility to respond to the complex circumstances of events and personalities than at present.

Changes in Prisons

Organizations such as The Howard League for Penal Reform, the Prison Reform Trust and the National Association for the Care and Resettlement of Offenders (Nacro) all work to improve the lot of women in prison. However, in March 1983, the first funded ex-prisoner group set up specifically for women prisoners, Women in Prison, was set up.

The deaths of two women prisoners, both by burning, separated by a gap of ten years, were the catalyst. The first woman died in 1973 while Chris Tchaikovsky, now director of WIP, was herself in prison. Tchaikovsky believes she died because officers had tampered with a bell so that the emergency bell didn't ring.

Ten years later, and Tchaikovsky, having put her criminal past behind her, discovered feminism and attended university, bumped into a woman on the Holloway Road who told her that another woman had set fire to herself in Holloway – and had later died from her burns. Tchaikovsky investigated and spoke to a senior officer who confirmed to her satisfaction that the second woman had been seen burning by an officer and had been left on fire while that officer went off to ask someone what to do.

She visited a woman she knew in Holloway – a prison rebuilt since her time – and found it was filthy, and that there was 23-hour lockup and the tension levels were alarming. At the time she was an advisory member of the GLC Women's Committee. She wrote a report, stressing the need for a campaigning and welfare group. This led to the founding of WIP.

By listening to, and gathering evidence directly from, prisoners and ex-prisoners, and by making their experiences known, WIP hope to change people's attitudes towards imprisonment. The group is both radical and reforming. In the long term they want the dismantling and total abolition of the present prison system. In the short term they work to do everything they can to ameliorate the damage done by prison. Says Tchaikovsky,

> Prisons are unintelligent, destructive and counter-productive. If we want to create criminals then we couldn't do better than have prisons. Prisons feed their own future and create the very people they claim to protect us from.
>
> If, for instance, when I was seventeen there'd been some intelligent person around who had helped me sort out my confused head it could have saved the community – and me – a lot of grief.
>
> How ridiculous it is to keep women in prison who are not a danger to society, a percentage of whom are fine defaulters, at a cost of over £600 a week. What we need is a specific policy developed for *women* prisoners based on why we are sending women to prison and what it is meant to achieve. That's long overdue.[1]

In the meantime, WIP is campaigning for increased funding for non-custodial alternatives to prisons, e.g. sheltered housing, drug dependency centres, alcohol recovery units. These would make it possible to remove from prison all those women who are there primarily because of alcohol or drug dependency, mental or emotional problems, homelessness, poverty or their inability to pay a fine.

What workers at WIP want in the long term is reflected in what they do now. For instance, they help women to find hostel accommodation and, whenever possible, arrange bail for women on remand. They also try to find alternatives to custody, e.g. drug rehabilitation unit, hospital bed, education/training project, etc. They attend crown and magistrates' courts and make representations to the bench.

WIP members visit isolated women in prison and women in Special Hospitals, and do what they can to help with the practical problems that beset imprisoned women, their children and families.

> Women prisoners are in a catch-22 situation. There are so few women in prison that people think you must be really bad, a real hard case to get sent there. And people think that if you weren't a hard case before, once you've been to prison, you're bound to be.
>
> It's just not true. Women do change, straighten out. We employ ex-prisoners at WIP. Women can and do change. They can turn around and go on to lead productive lives. But prison doesn't help them to do that; it makes it harder.[2]

Lyn Barlow, an ex-prisoner, now at University of East Anglia reading Politics and Women's Studies, puts it like this:

> I, as were many girls brought up in care and classed as rebellious, was groomed to expect prison as being almost an inevitable consequence of being who I am. When I found myself in East Sutton Park Prison, scrubbing floors alongside Elaine, who I had met in a remand assessment centre when we were both twelve, I realized what a good job they'd done of making us accept their vision of what we would

become. It also made me realise that I, and every other concerned woman, have the power to change their prophecies forever.[3]

Changes in Special Hospitals

Prue Stevenson, Terri Simpson and Kim Andrews founded Women in Special Hospitals (WISH) in 1990. Simpson and Andrews were both ex-patients, Stevenson had been a teacher in the psychiatric unit, C1, at Holloway Prison. She resigned in 1985, breaking the Official Secrets Act to speak out about conditions on the wing and her concern at the high numbers of women, especially young women, being transferred from Holloway to Special Hospitals. Between 1986 and 1991 one in six of the women transferred to Specials were aged 20 or under.

Until WISH was set up there was no organization working on behalf of women in Specials. The two leading mental health organizations, MIND and Mencap, acknowledged that they were unable to offer women in the Special Hospitals the support they badly needed, nor were they able to take up the many issues which concerned these women. Since 1990 there has been a big increase in the awareness of issues surrounding women in Specials and in secure psychiatric units. The work of WISH has been central in raising that awareness. Above all, says Stevenson, what needs to be acknowledged, before real progress can be made, is that women in Special Hospitals have special needs.

> We must listen to what they are saying and give them the help they are asking for. In particular, the women who are labelled psychopathic have been categorized as failures, yet they have been failed right down the line. Society has labelled them psychopaths and continues to punish them by putting them into long-term psychiatric hospitals. Even now, their needs are not being met.[4]

Women in Special Hospitals feel powerless, infantilized, degraded. They are afraid of getting out after an average stay of nine years. And, facing what they regard as an indeterminate sentence they are afraid they might never get out.

Proportionately more women than men find themselves in

Specials via the criminal justice system. There's an alarming tendency to use the suspect term 'psychopathy' to describe women who, because they are aggressive and/or have committed violent crimes, are perceived as unnatural, abnormal, freakish. The women who go there (I am talking about offender patients who form the majority of patients in Specials) have had lives characterized by: rejection as children, physical and/or sexual abuse, institutionalized care, drugs, booze, brushes with the police, prison.

Once in a Special, the women feel they are given no treatment since they regard drugs as being used for control, and ECT and seclusion as punishment. They don't talk much about psychological forms of help such as psychotherapy and counselling – but when they get this they are usually appreciative. Changes have taken and are taking place: the use of seclusion has decreased and the Special Hospitals Services Authority is seeking to limit its use to exceptional circumstances.

The importance of what kind of staff look after the women cannot be overemphasized. Bad staff, who feel it is their job to punish those in their care for whom they feel only contempt, can make life hell on earth – how one woman at least has described her time in Specials. However, the women are full of praise for those who are kind and treat them as people.

Some women feel the pressure to conform to stereotyped feminine behaviour to 'prove' they are getting better, i.e. becoming normal, which adds to their problems, and is particularly hard upon lesbian women. One of the women's biggest fears has to do with their 'sentence' in a Special being indeterminate. They worry about how they can prove they are better, and thus be allowed to leave, if they are not getting any treatment. They worry that they might never get out. And they worry about whether they'll be able to cope on the outside if and when they do get out.

Various suggestions have been made as to how things could be improved for women in Specials. Since the safety of the public doesn't require most of the women to be contained in conditions of maximum security, there is no need for them to be. More and varied facilities are needed, says Prue Stevenson, offering differing degrees of security, as appropriate for an individual at a particular time.

> There's a need for smaller units which, though small, nevertheless have access to a wide range of educational and training programmes. It's important that the women use their time, instead of sitting around all day bored. Maybe the smaller units could be attached to the larger hospitals so that facilities could be shared.[5]

There could be a maximum security unit for such women as are deemed dangerous to the public but the vast majority of women at present in the Specials could be better treated in smaller units, as described above, run by well-trained and well-motivated staff with the emphasis on care, not containment.

A radical alternative to the Specials for women is provided by an NHS in-patient unit, the Henderson Hospital at Sutton in Surrey. The Henderson is a therapeutic community. It specializes in treating people with anti-social and borderline personality disorders in a non-secure setting. Dr Bridget Dolan, a research psychologist at the Henderson, points out that borderline personality disorder is a diagnosis often applied to women who: harm themselves or others; have an inappropriate, or lack of, control of anger; act impulsively; experience extreme mood disturbances, and often have a pattern of unstable interpersonal relationships. Self-mutilation and histories of severe sexual abuse and physical abuse are common. She says,

> These symptoms are present in many of the women labelled 'psychopaths' in Special Hospitals. Psychiatrists are extremely pessimistic about treating personality disorder. Often the view taken is that patients in Special Hospitals will grow out of their disorder, or mature over time. However, personality disorders are treatable.[6]

At the Henderson they use no drugs for psychological symptoms and all treatment is voluntary, with the complete consent of the patient. Patients live and work together and examine the issues that led to their problems and their ways of interacting with people.

> The unit uses a democratic model to empower the patients who take an active role in the day-to-day running of the unit. All therapy is group-based, with the patients receiving both active support and confrontation from their peers. We find these methods extremely successful and many of these therapeutic community principles could be applied in Special Hospitals with little resource implications.[7]

Such a model with its atmosphere of consultation – shared decision-making with patients as to the running of the place (including which new patients to accept into the community) – would certainly foster independence and co-operation rather than dependency and resentment. And the atmosphere in such a community, along with properly trained staff, would probably lead to less self-harming amongst the women and would provide a much more caring environment in which to begin to look at their problems.

> Such a setting would be the opposite to the environment of Ashworth, as described by Moira Potier. The maximum-secure Ashworth with its emphasis on authority and control, with its acceptance of conformity as 'cure' and with many nurses regarding the patients as being there because they have done something wrong and therefore deserve to be punished, is a highly ambivalent place in which to nurture real personality development as the outcome of 'treatment'.[8]

She herself endorses the therapeutic community model. However, that might be a long time coming and in the meantime she has drawn up a list of 'pointers' for reforming the system, which could apply not only to Ashworth, but also to the other Specials.

• Women should be given responsibility for making choices and decisions based on clear information. The women themselves have asked to have clear information about treatment plans and goals.
• Training in advocacy skills should be given to patients.
• Staff should be trained to see themselves as patient advocates and to act accordingly. 'If all staff saw their role as supporting patients to achieve their potential and overcome the mistakes

and failures of the past, being "on the patients' side" would no longer be seen as aberrant.'[9]

Add to this the introduction of a perhaps anonymous complaints procedure which was seen to work and to get results without rebounding on the patients and here is a practical framework for reform.

Taking the longer-term and wider view there is a desperate need for properly funded research to look at such questions as: why do we send women to Special Hospitals? what is the purpose of Special Hospitals in regard to women? how is the term 'psychopathic disorder' being used? what is the role of staff? how can they be best helped to fulfil that role?

A conference entitled 'A Research Agenda for Women and Special Hospitals' was held at Ashworth Hospital in January 1993. Women patients participated in it. One single message that emerged most clearly was that any future research must include listening to the women themselves. They are the people such research is designed to benefit; their views, they themselves, are crucial to its fundamental validity and must be part of any successful process of reform.

A good part of the inspiration for this book came from Terri Simpson, whose story begins it, and Kim Andrews. Both had been perceived as violent and unmanageable; both had ended up in a Special Hospital, which they describe as the lowest you can go and as bad as it gets. Neither of them was mad – whatever that means – and neither of them should have been there. Between them they spent eighteen and a half years in Specials. Not only did they survive, they reclaimed their lives and went on to help other women who, like them, had been dumped and forgotten in the Specials. Together with Prue Stevenson, they went on to form WISH. Women in Prison was formed by ex-prisoners. Both WISH and WIP, along with other groups such as Southall Black Sisters, Rights of Women, Justice for Women and the Bristol Crisis Service for Women, now provide practical help and emotional support for women and campaign for reforms.

Some of the women who've suffered the most under the system, working with other women, are changing the system.

They are doing this doggedly and consistently, day in, day out, at a time when the consensus views on law and order seem to range from bring back the birch/the rope to lock the bastards up and throw away the key. In this climate they are making progress: their voices are being heard by at least some of those running the system.

The women who inspired this book have survived hard and cruel experiences. When I think of them, of what they have endured and what they have achieved, a picture comes to my mind from my convent-school days of a man in a prison cell. From his barred window he can see only the mud which stretches from the foot of the prison wall to the horizon, and the sky above. His only choice is at which to look.

These women have chosen to look at the sky. They have chosen to produce from their own terrors, suffering and desperation, help and compassion for others. They are an inspiration to all of us. It is largely by their efforts and those of the women who work with them, backed up by other reformers, that greater understanding, justice and compassion will come for women who are perceived by society to be violent, and judged to be evil, vilified as less than natural women and seen to be deserving only of condemnation and contempt – as Terri, Kim and other women like them were.

Notes

INTRODUCTION

1 Term used by Simone de Beauvoir in *The Second Sex*.

CHAPTER 2 Men, Women and Aggression

1 Jones, *Women Who Kill*, p. 4.
2 Rose, Lewontin and Kamin, *Not in Our Genes*, p. 6.
3 Rose, Lewontin and Kamin, *Not in Our Genes*, p. 5.
4 Rose, Lewontin and Kamin, *Not in Our Genes*, p. 25.
5 Miedzian, *Boys Will be Boys*, p. 74, referring to Peggy Sanday's *Female Power and Male Dominance: On the Origins of Sexual Inequality*, and on unpublished pages by Robert R. Holt entitled 'Correcting the War System to a Peace System'.
6 Rose, Lewontin and Kamin, *Not in Our Genes*, p. 253, with quotes from E.O. Wilson, *On Human Nature*, Cambridge, Massachusetts, Harvard University Press, 1978, pp. 99 and 105.
7 Rose, Lewontin and Kamin, *Not in Our Genes*, p. 236.
8 Fausto-Sterling, *Myths of Gender*, p. 132.
9 Personal interview with author.
10 Fausto-Sterling, *Myths of Gender*, p. 142.
11 Fausto-Sterling, *Myths of Gender*, p. 141.
12 Fausto-Sterling, *Myths of Gender*, p. 137.
13 Rose, Lewontin and Kamin, *Not in Our Genes*, p. 145.
14 Rose, Lewontin and Kamin, *Not in Our Genes*, pp. 144–5.
15 Formaini, *Men: the Darker Continent*, p. 8.
16 Formaini, *Men: the Darker Continent*, p. 18.
17 Nicholson, *Men and Women*, p. 170.
18 Miller, *For Your Own Good*, p. 65.
19 Oakley, *Sex, Gender and Society*, p. 186.
20 Rose, Lewontin and Kamin, *Not in Our Genes*, pp. 289–90.

CHAPTER 3 Stereotypes, Biology and Female Crime

1 Mills, *Womanwords*, p. 79.
2 Naylor, 'Women Who Kill', p. 5. Naylor is here referring to J. Walkowitz, *Prostitution and Victorian Society*, Cambridge University Press, 1980.
3 BBC Television, *Crime and Punishment*, press pack.
4 White, 'Blair Waves the Flag for Family Value: Attack on Poverty Linked to "Individual Responsibility"' in the *Guardian*, 26 June 1993.
5 Heidensohn, *Women and Crime*, p. 114, quoting from Cesare Lombroso and Guglielmo Ferrero, *The Female Offender*, 1895.
6 Miedzian, *Boys Will be Boys*, p. 8.
7 C. Bennett, 'In the Blood or in the Head?' quoting Dr Dalton in the *Guardian*, 1 June 1993.
8 Ussher, *Women's Madness*, p. 250.
9 Ussher, *Women's Madness*, p. 250.
10 Ussher, *Women's Madness*, p. 251.
11 Kennedy, *Eve Was Framed*, p. 104.
12 S. Lees, 'Lawyers' Work as Constitutive of Gender Relations' in M. Cain and C. Harrington (eds.), *Lawyers in a Postmodern World*, p. 149, quoting from *The Standard Edition of the Complete Psychological Works of Sigmund Freud*, vol. 19: *The Ego and the Id*, London, Hogarth Press and The Institute of Psycho-Analysis, 1961, pp. 257, 258.
13 Morris, *Women, Crime and Criminal Justice*, p. 54. See also Brovermann *et al*, 'Sex Role Stereotypes: A Current Appraisal', *Journal of Social Issues*, 1972, 28, 2: p. 59.
14 Psychiatric report, case 41 – female charged with robbery, taken from *Justice Unbalanced* by Hilary Allen.
15 Psychiatric report, case 123 – male charged with robbery, taken from *Justice Unbalanced* by Hilary Allen.
16 Allen, *Justice Unbalanced*, pp. 1–2.
17 Allen, *Justice Unbalanced*, p. xi.
18 Kennedy, *Eve Was Framed*, p. 87.
19 Naylor, 'Women Who Kill', p. 10. Naylor is here referring to A. Sampson, 'Witchcraft: a Criminal Activity?', MPhil thesis, University of Cambridge, 1984.
20 Morris, *Women, Crime and Criminal Justice*, pp. 70, 73.
21 Morris, *Women, Crime and Criminal Justice*, p. 71.
22 Adler, *Sisters in Crime*, pp. 7–8.

23 Jones, *Women Who Kill*, pp. 2–3.
24 Jones, *Women Who Kill*, p. 3.
25 Gelsthorpe, *Sexism and the Female Offender*, pp. 155–6.

CHAPTER 4 What Kind of Crimes Do Women Commit and Do They Get Off Lightly?

1 Home Office, *Gender and the Criminal Justice System*, p. 7.
2 Mandaraka-Sheppard, *The Dynamics of Aggression in Women's Prisons in England*, pp. 5–6.
3 Letter to the author from the Home Office, 7 January 1993.
4 Letter to the author from P.H. White of the Home Office, 16 December 1993, who supplied these figures. Mr White pointed out that 'these figures relate to the position as at 27 August 1993, subsequent court decisions and other information received may cause differences at a later date'.
5 Humphries, 'The Referral of Women to Special Hospitals – Causes and Consequences', p. 50 quoting Dr. Mezey.
6 Home Office, *Gender and the Criminal Justice System*, pp. 14–15.
7 Home Office, *Gender and the Criminal Justice System*, p. 16.
8 Heidensohn, *Women and Crime*, p. 3, which discusses the Home Office *Criminal Statistics*, 1983a, p. 218.
9 Farrington and Morris, 'Sex, Sentencing and Reconviction', p. 229.
10 Farrington and Morris, 'Sex, Sentencing and Reconviction', p. 247.
11 Morris, *Women, Crime and Criminal Justice*, p. 90.
12 Kruttschnitt, 'Respectable Women and the Law', p. 221.
13 Kruttschnitt, 'Women, Crime and Dependency', p. 495; also Morris, *Women, Crime and Criminal Justice*, p. 90.
14 Personal interview with author.
15 Kennedy, Conference on Perspectives on Female Violence, 7–8 March 1991.
16 Carlen, *Women's Imprisonment*, p. 59.
17 Carlen, *Women's Imprisonment*, p. 60.
18 Carlen, *Women's Imprisonment*, p. 63.
19 Carlen, *Women's Imprisonment*, p. 67.
20 Allen, *Justice Unbalanced*, p. 87.
21 Allen, *Justice Unbalanced*, pp. 102–3.
22 Allen, *Justice Unbalanced*, p. 104.
23 Marks and Kumar, 'Infanticide in England and Wales', pp. 329–39.

24 Letter to the author from the Home Office, 2 March 1993.

25 Wilczynski, 'A socio-legal study of parents who kill their children in England and Wales'.

26 Morris and Wilczynski, 'Rocking the Cradle' in H. Birch (ed.), *Moving Targets*, p. 207.

27 Wilczynski, 'A socio-legal study of parents who kill their children in England and Wales'.

28 Letter to the author from the Home Office, 2 March 1993.

29 Wilczynski, 'Child-killing by parents: social, legal and gender issues', p. 10.

30 Morris and Wilczynski, 'Rocking the Cradle' in H. Birch (ed.), *Moving Targets*, p. 143.

31 Morris and Wilczynski, 'Rocking the Cradle' in H. Birch (ed.), *Moving Targets*, p. 143.

32 Morris and Wilczynksi, 'Rocking the Cradle' in H. Birch (ed.), *Moving Targets*, p. 144.

33 Morris and Wilczynski, 'Rocking the Cradle' in H. Birch (ed.), *Moving Targets*, pp. 144–5.

34 Morris and Wilczynski, 'Rocking the Cradle' in H. Birch (ed.), *Moving Targets*, p. 145.

35 Morris and Wilczynski, 'Rocking the Cradle' in H. Birch (ed.), *Moving Targets*, p. 146.

36 Morris, *Women, Crime and Criminal Justice*, pp. 102–3.

CHAPTER 5 Battered Women Who Kill

1 J. Nadel, 'Sexual Provocation with a Twist' in the *Observer*, 25 April 1993.

2 P. Ghazi and S. Lonsdale, 'Women Beaten by the Law', in the *Observer*, 4 August 1991.

3 Browne, *When Battered Women Kill*, p. 164. Browne is referring to J. O'Faolain and L. Martines, *Not in God's Image: Women in History from the Greeks to the Victorians*, New York, NY, Harper and Row, 1973, as cited by M. D. Pagelow, *Family Violence*, New York, NY, Praeger, 1984, p. 281.

4 O'Donovan, 'Defences for Battered Women Who Kill', p. 221.

5 O'Donovan, 'Defences for Battered Women Who Kill', p. 226. O'Donovan is referring to L.J. Taylor, 'Provoked Reason in Men and Women: Heat of Passion Manslaughter and Imperfect Self-Defence', 1986, 33 *UCLA Law Review*, p. 1694, citing *Holmes* v. *D.P.P.* [1946] 2 All ER 124.

6 O'Donovan, 'Defences for Battered Women Who Kill', p. 226. O'Donovan is referring to L.J. Taylor, 'Provoked Reason in Men and Women: Heat of Passion Manslaughter and Imperfect Self-Defence', 1986, 33 *UCLA Law Review*, p. 1694, citing *Holmes* v. *D.P.P.* [1946] 2 All ER 124.

7 Wilson and Daly, 'Till Death Us Do Part', in Radford and Russell (eds), *Femicide*, p. 84.

8 P. Ghazi and S. Lonsdale, 'Women Beaten by the Law', in the *Observer*, 4 August 1991.

9 Dobash and Dobash, *Violence against Wives*, p. 136.

10 Campbell, *Men, Women and Aggression*, p. 116.

11 Campbell, *Men, Women and Aggression*, p. 108.

12 Home Office, *Gender and the Criminal Justice System*, p. 14.

13 This was said to me during a telephone conversation with the Home Office, 24 May 1993.

14 Browne, *When Battered Women Kill*, p. 145.

15 Horder, *Provocation and Responsibility*, p. 187.

16 Edwards, *Women on Trial*, p. 176. Edwards is referring to W. Bacon and R. Lansdowne, 'Women Who Kill Husbands: the Battered Wife on Trial', in *Family Violence in Australia* by C. O'Donnell and J. Craney (eds), Melbourne, 1982, pp. 67–93.

17 Edwards, *Policing 'Domestic' Violence*, p. 171.

18 Dobash and Dobash, *Violence against Wives*, p. 135.

19 Wilson and Daly, 'Till Death Us Do Part', in Radford and Russell (eds), *Femicide*, p. 88. They are referring to C.R. Showalter, R.J. Bonnie and V. Roddy, 'The Spousal-Homicide Syndrome', *International Journal of Law and Psychiatry* 3: pp. 117–41.

20 Browne, *When Battered Women Kill*, p. 144. Browne is referring to Barnard, Vera, Vera and Newman, 1982. She adds that 'all the respondents in this study were interviewed as a part of psychiatric evaluations required by the courts, either to determine their competency to stand trial or their legal sanity at the time of the alleged crime; obviously, a very non-random sample. However, all but one male defendant were judged competent to stand trial at the time they were evaluated.'

21 Browne, *When Battered Women Kill*, p. 181.

22 Browne, *When Battered Women Kill*, p. 12.

23 Browne, *When Battered Women Kill*, p. 182.

24 Campbell, *Men, Women and Aggression*, pp. 114–15.

25 Browne, *When Battered Women Kill*, p. 183.

26 Campbell, *Men, Women and Aggression*, p. 121.

27 Home Office, *Gender and the Criminal Justice System*, p. 21.

28 Southall Black Sisters was started in 1979 to meet the needs of Asian and Afro-Caribbean women. Over the last sixteen years they have helped thousands of women facing violence and abuse at home. Apart from providing welfare services and support, they have also run campaigns to highlight and bring about changes in the social, political, economic and cultural constraints that have led women to seek their help. They were involved in the successful campaign to free Kiranjit Ahluwahlia.

29 Personal interview with author.

30 Mama, *The Hidden Struggle*, pp. 320–21.

31 O'Donovan, 'Defences for Battered Women Who Kill', p. 240. Letter from Sara Thornton to O'Donovan, 5 October 1990.

32 Campbell, *Men, Women and Aggression*, p. 121.

33 Campbell, *Men, Women and Aggression*, p. 121.

34 R. Miller, 'Murderers . . . or Victims', in the *Sunday Times*, 2 May 1992.

35 R. Miller, 'Murderers . . . or Victims?', in the *Sunday Times*, 2 May 1992.

36 A. Lloyd, 'Victims or Villains', in the *Guardian*, 12 March 1991.

37 Letter to the author from S.M. Edwards, 19 July 1993.

38 Edwards, 'Battered Women Who Kill', pp. 1381, 1392.

39 Letter to the author from S.M. Edwards, 19 July 1993.

40 I shall use 'husbands' and 'wives' to cover female and male partners in a relationship.

41 C. Nuttall, 'Courts Regard Female Killers as No Deadlier Than the Male', in the *Sunday Times*, 9 May 1992.

42 This was said to me during a telephone conversation with the Home Office, 24 May 1993.

43 Personal interview with author.

44 S. Lees, 'Naggers, Whores and Libbers: Provoking Men to Kill', in Radford and Russell (eds), *Femicide*, pp. 270–71.

45 Personal interview with the author.

46 L. Radford, 'Pleading for Time', in Birch (ed.), *Moving Targets*, p. 186. Radford was commenting on the 1991 Home Office figures but her point stands.

47 Kennedy, *Eve Was Framed*, p. 219. She was quoting from a *Daily Express* article, 14 February 1976.

48 Kennedy, *Eve Was Framed*, p. 216.

49 Kennedy, *Eve Was Framed*, p. 217.

50 J. Nadel, 'Sexual Provocation with a Twist', in the *Observer*, 25 April 1993.

51 D. Campbell, 'Nagged Killer Goes Free', in the *Guardian*, 30 January 1992.

52 R. Miller, 'Murderers . . . or Victims?', in the *Sunday Times*, 2 May 1993, and A. Johnson, 'Woman Who Stabbed Husband 28 Times Goes Free After Retrial', in the *Guardian*, 21 December 1994. In Deember 1994, Carol Peters was cleared of murder, convicted of manslaughter, given a 4-year sentence and freed, because of the time she had already spent in prison.

53 Edwards, 'Neither Bad nor Mad: the Female Violent Offender', p. 85.

54 Kennedy, *Eve Was Framed*, p. 205.

55 Kennedy, *Eve Was Framed*, p. 215.

56 Defendants will be charged with murder rather than manslaughter where it is clear there was an intention to kill or to cause grievous bodily harm.

57 O'Donovan, 'Defences for Battered Women Who Kill', p. 221.

58 O'Donovan, 'Defences for Battered Women Who Kill', p. 222.

59 O'Donovan, 'Defences for Battered Women Who Kill', p. 222.

60 Browne, *When Battered Women Kill*, p. 167. Browne is referring to *State* v. *Rhodes*, 61 Phil. L. [N.C.] 453 (1866). See also Maeve Doggett, *Marriage, Wife-Beating and the Law in Victorian England*, Butterworth: Weidenfeld & Nicolson, 1992, p. ix and pp. 4–15 on the right of a man to beat his wife, which includes discussion of the 'ancient doctrine' that it was lawful for 'a husband to beat a wife, provided that the stick were no thicker than his thumb'.

61 Personal interview with author.

62 O'Donovan, 'Defences for Battered Women Who Kill', p. 223. O'Donovan is quoting Devlin, J., *R.* v. *Duffy* [1949] 1 All ER 932.

63 L. Radford, 'Pleading for Time', in Birch (ed.), *Moving Targets*, pp. 175–6.

64 Edwards, *Policing 'Domestic' Violence*, p. 181.

65 Edwards, *Policing 'Domestic' Violence*, p. 182.

66 O'Donovan, 'Defences for Battered Women Who Kill', p. 223.

67 Edwards, *Policing 'Domestic' Violence*, p. 184.

68 Personal interview with author.

69 Personal interview with author.

70 Horder, 'The Doctrine of Provocation: Should Parliament Intervene?', pp. 218–19.

71 Horder, 'The Doctrine of Provocation: Should Parliament Intervene?', p. 217.

72 Horder, 'The Doctrine of Provocation: Should Parliament Intervene?', p. 218.

73 Horder, 'The Doctrine of Provocation: Should Parliament Intervene?', p. 219.

74 Horder, *Provocation and Responsibility*, p. 197.

75 Radford, 'Self-Preservation', p. 9.

76 Radford, 'Self-Preservation', pp. 9–10. The Rights of Women (ROW) is a feminist organization, formed in 1975, which aims to inform women of their rights and to promote the interests of women in relation to the law. ROW has been part of several successful policy initiatives, including defending child benefits and existing rights on abortion, promoting progressive amendments to the Sex Discrimination Act, and the criminalization of rape in marriage.

77 O'Donovan, 'Defences for Battered Women Who Kill', p. 229.

78 Personal interview with author.

79 Radford, L., 'Pleading for Time', in Birch (ed.), *Moving Targets*, pp. 185–6.

80 Jones, *Women Who Kill*, p. 305.

81 Jones, *Women Who Kill*, p. 304.

82 Radford, L., 'Pleading for Time', in Birch (ed.), *Moving Targets*, pp. 186–7.

83 Radford, 'Self-Preservation', p. 8.

84 O'Donovan, 'Defences for Battered Women Who Kill', pp. 234, 235.

85 Kennedy, *Eve Was Framed*, p. 220.

86 Radford, L., 'Pleading for Time', in Birch (ed.), *Moving Targets*, p. 187.

87 Kennedy, *Eve Was Framed*, pp. 94–5.

88 Radford and Mavolwane, 'We'll be Freeing All the Women', p. 11.

89 Radford, 'Self-Preservation', p. 11.

90 Radford, 'Self-Preservation', p. 11.

91 'Continuing' would need to be defined, our suggestion being 'several assaults on different occasions'.

92 Radford, J., 'Self-Preservation', p. 12.

93 Personal interview with author.

94 Personal interview with author.

95 *The Lane Report*, press release, p. 3.

96 *The Lane Report*, p. 24.

97 *The Lane Report*, pp. 17–18.

98 *The Lane Report*, p. 19.

99 *The Lane Report*, p. 20.

100 Kennedy, Conference on Perspectives on Female Violence, 7–8 March 1991.

CHAPTER 6 Women in Prison

1 Carlen, *Women's Imprisonment*, p. 13.
2 Nacro, Briefing No 33: *Women in Prison*, p. 2.
3 Hedderman and Hough, *Does the Criminal Justice System Treat Men and Women Differently?*, p. 3.
4 Fax from Carol Hedderman to author, 16 January 1995.
5 Cavadino, (letter) 'One law for men, another for women', in the *Guardian*, 25 March 1994.
6 Sampson, (letter) 'One law for men, another for women', in the *Guardian*, 25 March 1994.
7 Hedderman and Hough, *Does the Criminal Justice System Treat Men and Women Differently?*, p. 3.
8 Personal interview with author.
9 Personal interview with author.
10 Personal interview with author.
11 Personal interview with author.
12 According to the Holloway Reception Survey done by Ingrid Posen in 1987.
13 Personal interview with author.
14 R. Spencer, '£7m Downfall of Drug Addict Marquess', in the *Daily Telegraph*, 7 December 1993.
15 Mandaraka-Sheppard, *The Dynamics of Aggression in Women's Prisons in England*, pp. 57–8.
16 Genders and Player, 'Women in Prison: the Treatment, the Control and the Experience', in Carlen and Worrall (eds), *Gender, Crime and Justice*, p. 166.
17 Mandaraka-Sheppard, *The Dynamics of Aggression in Women's Prisons in England*, pp. 4–5.
18 Mandaraka-Sheppard, *The Dynamics of Aggression in Women's Prisons in England*, p. 5.
19 Kennedy, *Eve Was Framed*, p. 161.
20 Kennedy, *Eve Was Framed*, p. 165.
21 Kennedy, *Eve Was Framed*, p. 167.
22 Personal interview with author.
23 Carlen and Worrall (eds), *Gender, Crime and Justice*, p. 160.
24 Personal interview with author.
25 J. Bower, 'When Prison is a Death Sentence', interview with Alison Liebling in the *Yorkshire Post*, 6 July 1994.
26 Personal interview with author.
27 Personal interview with author.

28   Nacro, *Fresh Start for Women Prisoners*, p. 5.
29   Personal interview with author.
30   Nacro, *Fresh Start for Women Prisoners*, p. 4.
31   Eaton, *Women after Prison*, p. 5.
32   Eaton, *Women after Prison*, p. 1.
33   Morris, *Women, Crime and Criminal Justice*, p. 121.
34   Nacro, Briefing No 91, *Women and Criminal Justice*, p. 5.
35   Nacro, Briefing No 33, *Women in Prison*, p. 3.
36   Mandaraka-Sheppard, *The Dynamics of Aggression in Women's Prisons in England*, p. 101.
37   Mandaraka-Sheppard, *The Dynamics of Aggression in Women's Prisons in England*, p. 200.
38   Mandaraka-Sheppard, *The Dynamics of Aggression in Women's Prisons in England*, p. 81–2.
39   Mandaraka-Sheppard, *The Dynamics of Aggression in Women's Prisons in England*, p. 195.
40   Mandaraka-Sheppard, *The Dynamics of Aggression in Women's Prisons in England*, p. 105.
41   Mandaraka-Sheppard, *The Dynamics of Aggression in Women's Prisons in England*, pp. 196–7.
42   HM Prison Service, *Regimes for Women*, p. 27.
43   HM Prison Service, *Regimes for Women*, p. 27.
44   Personal interview with author.
45   WIP, Director's Report, December 1994.
46   Personal interview with author.
47   Mandaraka-Sheppard, *The Dynamics of Aggression in Women's Prisons in England*, p. 208.
48   Carlen and Worrall (eds), *Gender, Crime and Justice*, p. 165.

CHAPTER 7   Women in Special Hospitals

1   Home Office, *Report of the Committee of Inquiry into Complaints about Ashworth Hospital*, p. 229.
2   Home Office, *Report of the Committee of Inquiry into Complaints about Ashworth Hospital*, p. 230.
3   Home Office, *Report of the Committee of Inquiry into Complaints about Ashworth Hospital*, p. 232.
4   Andrews, 'Overdosing on Freedom', p. 10.
5   Personal interview with author.
6   Potier, 'Patient care at Ashworth Hospital', p. 4.
7   Potier, 'Patient care at Ashworth Hospital', p. 7.

8 Potier, 'Patient care at Ashworth Hospital', p. 16.

9 Personal interview with author.

10 Personal interview with author.

11 Personal interview with author.

12 Terri Simpson's story is told in full in Chapter 1, 'A Tale of Two Women'.

13 Grounds, 'The Transfer of Sentenced Prisoners to Hospital', pp. 54–71.

14 Collier and Dibblin, 'Justice Weighted against Women', in the *Observer*, 28 October 1990, referring to Dr Adrian Grounds.

15 Collier and Dibblin, 'Justice Weighted against Women', in the *Observer*, 28 October 1990, referring to Dr Gillian Mezey.

16 Stevenson, 'Women in Special Hospitals', p. 14.

17 Personal interview with author.

18 Lloyd, 'Altered States', in the *Guardian*, June 1991, referring to Prue Stevenson.

19 Humphries, 'The Referral of Women to Special Hospitals – Causes and Consequences', pp. 59–60.

20 Lloyd, 'Altered States', in the *Guardian*, June 1991, referring to Dr Gillian Mezey.

21 Home Office, *Report of the Committee of Inquiry into Complaints about Ashworth Hospital*, p. 229.

22 Humphries, 'The Referral of Women to Special Hospitals – Causes and Consequences', p. 42.

23 Jackson, 'The Influence of Social Factors on the Definition and Subsequent Treatment of Women Diagnosed as Mentally Ill', p. 58.

24 Potier, 'Giving Evidence: Women's Lives in Ashworth Maximum Security Psychiatric Hospital', p. 337.

25 Personal interview with author.

26 Personal interview with author.

27 WISH Annual Report 1992–3, pp. 15–17.

28 Personal interview with author.

29 Humphries, 'The Referral of Women to Special Hospitals – Causes and Consequences', pp. 74–5.

30 Stevenson, 'Women in Special Hospitals', p. 16.

31 Personal interview with author.

32 Personal interview with author.

33 Stevenson, 'Women in Special Hospitals', p. 16.

34 Potier, 'Giving Evidence: Women's Lives in Ashworth Maximum Security Psychiatric Hospital', p. 340.

35 Fax to author.
36 SHSA, *The Use of Seclusion*, introductory page.
37 SHSA, *The Use of Seclusion*, p. 2.
38 SHSA, *The Use of Seclusion*, p. 3.
39 SHSA, *The Use of Seclusion*, introductory page.
40 WISH Annual Report 1992–3, pp. 21–2, reporting Anne Parisio, WISH Visitor to Broadmoor.
41 Personal interview with author.
42 Humphries, 'The Referral of Women to Special Hospitals – Causes and Consequences', p. 95.
43 Andrews, 'Overdosing on Freedom', pp. 10–11.

CHAPTER 8 Self-Harm: the Silent Scream

1 Favazza, 'Why Patients Mutilate Themselves', p. 137.
2 Johnstone, 'Self-Harm', p. 20.
3 Johnstone, 'Self-Harm', p. 20.
4 van der Kolk *et al*, 'Childhood Origins of Self-Destructive Behavior', p. 1667.
5 van der Kolk *et al*, 'Childhood Origins of Self-Destructive Behavior', p. 1665.
6 Apps, 'The Ultimate Violence', p. 2.
7 Apps, 'The Ultimate Violence', p. 2.
8 Eaton, *Women after Prison*, p. 52. Eaton is referring to M. Benn and C. Tchaikovsky, 'Dangers of Being a Woman', *The Abolitionist* 23, 1987.
9 'Section 3 patients are those transferred to Special Hospitals under the Mental Health Act 1983 without having been convicted by the courts of committing an offence. The Act states that they must be suffering from Mental Disorder which requires medical treatment in hospital or, if 'suffering from Psychopathic Disorder or Mental Impairment . . . treatment must be likely to alleviate or prevent deterioration'. In addition there is a condition specified that the patient requires detention for his/her own health or safety, or for the protection of others. The conditions of detention must be reviewed after six months, and thereafter annually.' (Sellars, C. and Liebling, H., 'Section 3 Patients: the "Non-Offenders"?', *Division of Criminological and Legal Psychology Newsletter*, 1988, pp. 30–35)
10 Liebling and Chipchase, 'A Pilot Study on the Problem of Self-Injurious Behaviour in Women in Ashworth Hospital', p. 19. They

are referring to C. Sellars and H. Liebling, 'Section 3 Patients: the "Non-Offenders"?', *Division of Criminological and Legal Psychology Newsletter*, 1988, pp. 30–35.

11 Potier, 'Giving Evidence: Women's Lives in Ashworth Maximum Security Psychiatric Hospital', p. 336.

12 Apps, 'The Ultimate Violence', p. 27.

13 Apps, 'The Ultimate Violence', p. 15.

14 Personal interview with author.

15 Apps, 'The Ultimate Violence', pp. 28–9.

16 Apps, 'The Ultimate Violence', p. 28.

17 Apps, 'The Ultimate Violence', p. 28.

18 Jones, 'Women Who Cut Themselves Up', p. 72.

19 Bristol Crisis Service for Women, *Women and Self-Injury*, p. 4.

20 Favazza, 'Why Patients Mutilate Themselves', p. 137.

21 Apps, 'The Ultimate Violence', p. 2.

22 Potier, 'Giving Evidence: Women's Lives in Ashworth Maximum Security Psychiatric Hospital', p. 336.

23 Liebling and Chipchase, 'A Pilot Study on the Problem of Self-Injurious Behaviour in Women in Ashworth Hospital', p. 19. They are referring to C. Sellars and H. Liebling, 'Section 3 Patients: the "Non-Offenders"?', *Division of Criminological and Legal Psychology Newsletter*, 1988, pp. 30–35.

24 Apps, 'The Ultimate Violence', p. 21.

25 Fax to author.

26 Fax to author. Liebling is referring to Jackson, 'The Influence of Social Factors on the Definition and Subsequent Treatment of Women Diagnosed as Mentally Ill', pp. 60–61.

27 Liebling and Chipchase, 'A Pilot Study on the Problem of Self-Injurious Behaviour in Women in Ashworth Hospital', p. 19. They are referring to H.M. Cookson, 'A Study of Self-Injury in a Closed Prison for Women', *British Journal of Criminology*, 1977, 17, 4: pp. 332–47.

28 Liebling and Chipchase, 'A Pilot Study on the Problem of Self-Injurious Behaviour in Women in Ashworth Hospital', p. 20. They are referring to K. Williams, 'Factors Associated with Self-Mutilation'. Unpublished thesis for M. Clin. Psychol.

29 Jones, 'Women Who Cut Themselves Up', p. 71.

30 Carlen and Worrall (eds), *Gender, Crime and Justice*, p. 182.

31 Podvoll, 'Self-Mutilation within a Hospital Setting', p. 213.

32 Burrow, 'The Deliberate Self-Harming Behaviour of Patients within a British Special Hospital', p. 145, quoting E.M. Podvoll.

33 Burrow, 'The Deliberate Self-Harming Behaviour of Patients within a British Special Hospital', p. 145.

34 Burrow, 'The Deliberate Self-Harming Behaviour of Patients within a British Special Hospital', p. 143.

35 Eaton, *Women after Prison*, p. 53. Eaton is referring to Benn, M. and Tchaikovksy, C., 'Dangers of being a Woman', *The Abolitionist*, 23, 1987.

36 Apps, 'The Ultimate Violence', appendix two.

37 Jackson, 'The Influence of Social Factors on the Definition and Subsequent Treatment of Women Diagnosed as Mentally Ill', pp. 60–61.

38 Johnstone, 'Self-Harm', p. 20.

39 Apps, 'The Ultimate Violence', p. 22. Apps refers here to the work of Cookson, H., 'A Survey of Self-Injury in a Closed Prison for Women', *British Journal of Criminology*, 1977, 17, 4: pp. 332–47. Cookson, she says, 'found that on days of high numbers of self-injuring there were more staff on duty than usual and fewer prisoners'.

40 Burrow, 'The Deliberate Self-Harming Behaviour of Patients within a British Special Hospital', p. 146. Burrow is quoting Cullen, J.E., 'Prediction and Treatment of Self-Injury by Female Young Offenders', in D.P. Tarrington and R. Tarling (eds), *Predictions in Criminology*, Albany, State University of New York Press, 1985.

41 Johnstone, 'Self-Harm', p. 21.

42 Johnstone, 'Self-Harm', p. 21.

43 Johnstone, 'Self-Harm', pp. 20–21.

44 Bristol Crisis Service for Women, *Women and Self-Injury*, p. 7 (and see Useful Addresses).

CHAPTER 9 Conclusion

1 Personal interview with author.

2 Personal interview with author.

3 Personal interview with author.

4 Lloyd, 'Altered States', in the *Guardian*, 25 June 1991.

5 Personal interview with author.

6 Personal interview with author.

7 Personal interview with author.

8 Potier, 'Giving Evidence: Women's Lives in Ashworth Maximum Security Hospital', p. 346.

9 Personal interview with author.

Bibliography

All the publishers are based in the UK unless otherwise indicated.

TELEVISION AND NEWSPAPERS

BBC Television, *Crime and Punishment*, press pack, April 1993.

Daily Telegraph
Spencer, R., '£7m Downfall of Drug Addict Marquess', 7 December 1993.

Guardian
Bennett, C., 'In the Blood or in the Head?', 1 June 1993.
Campbell, D., 'Nagged Killer Goes Free', 30 January 1992.
Cavadino, P., 'One law for men, another for women' (letter), 25 March 1994.
Johnson, A., 'Woman Who Stabbed Husband 28 Times Goes Free after Trial', 21 December 1994.
Lloyd, A., 'Altered States', 25 June 1991.
– 'Victims or Villains', 12 March 1991.
Sampson, A., 'One Law for Men, Another for Women' (letter), 25 March 1994.
White, M., 'Blair Waves the Flag for Family Value: Attack on Poverty Linked to "Individual Responsibility"', 26 June 1993.

Observer
Collier, S. and Dibblin, J., 'Justice Weighted against Women', 28 October 1990.
Ghazi, P. and Lonsdale, S. 'Women Beaten by the Law', 4 August 1991.
Nadel, J., 'Sexual Provocation with a Twist', 25 April 1993.

Sunday Times
Miller, R., 'Murderers . . . or Victims', 2 May 1992.
Nuttall, C., 'Courts Regard Female Killers as No Deadlier Than the Male', 9 May 1992.

Yorkshire Post
Bower, J., 'When Prison is a Death Sentence', 6 July 1994.

BOOKS, JOURNALS AND REPORTS

Adler, F., *Sisters in Crime*, Prospect Heights, Illinois, Waveland Press Inc., 1985.
Allen, H., *Justice Unbalanced*, Open University Press, 1987.
Andrews, K., 'Overdosing on Freedom', *Openmind*, December 1991/January 1992.
Apps, S., 'The Ultimate Violence. A Study in Self-Mutilation in Women's Prisons', dissertation, 1988.
Benn, M. and Tchaikovsky, C., 'Dangers of Being a Woman', *The Abolitionist*, 23, 1987.
Birch, H. (ed.), *Moving Targets*, Virago Press, 1993.
Bristol Crisis Service for Women, *Women and Self-Injury*, 1992.
Brovermann, I. *et al*, 'Sex Role Stereotypes: a Current Appraisal, *Journal of Social Issues*, 28, 2, 1972.
Browne, A., *When Battered Women Kill*, New York, The Free Press, 1987.
Burrow, S., 'The Deliberate Self-Harming Behaviour of Patients within a British Special Hospital', *Journal of Advanced Nursing* 17, 1992.
Cain, M. and Harrington, C. (eds), *Lawyers in a Postmodern World*, Open University Press, 1994.
Campbell, A., *Men, Women and Aggression*, New York, Basic Books, 1993.
Carlen, P., *Women's Imprisonment: a Study in Social Control*, Routledge and Kegan Paul, 1983.
Carlen, P. and Worrall, A. (eds), *Gender, Crime and Justice*, Open University Press, 1987.
Daniels, S., *Headrot Holiday*, Methuen Drama, 1992.
Dobash, R.E. and Dobash, R., *Violence against Wives: a Case against the Patriarchy*, Open Books, 1980.
Eaton, M., *Women after Prison*, Open University Press, 1992.
Edwards, S.M., *Policing 'Domestic' Violence. Women, the Law and the State*, Sage, 1989.
– *Women on Trial*, Manchester University Press, 1984.

– 'Battered Women Who Kill', *New Law Journal*, 5 October 1990.
– 'Neither Bad nor Mad: the Female Violent Offender Reassessed', *Women's Studies International Forum*, 1986.
Eichenbaum, L. and Orbach, S., *Outside In*, Penguin, 1982.
Farrington, David P. and Morris, A., 'Sex, Sentencing and Reconviction', *British Journal of Criminology*, 23, 3, July 1983.
Fausto-Sterling, A., *Myths of Gender: Biological Theories about Women and Men*, revised edition, New York, Basic Books, 1992.
Favazza, A.R., 'Why Patients Mutilate Themselves', *Hospital and Community Psychiatry*, 1989.
Formaini, H., *Men: the Darker Continent*, Mandarin, 1991.
Gelsthorpe, L., *Sexism and the Female Offender*, Gower, 1989.
Genders, E. and Player, E., 'Women in Prison: the Treatment, the Control and the Experience' in Carlen and Worrall (eds), *Gender, Crime and Justice*, 1987.
Grounds, A.T., 'The Transfer of Sentenced Prisoners to Hospital, 1960–83: a Study in One Special Hospital', *British Journal of Criminology*, 1991.
Hedderman, C. and Hough, M., *Does the Criminal Justice System Treat Men and Women Differently?*, Home Office Research and Statistics Department, Research Findings No. 10, May 1994.
Heidensohn, F., *Women and Crime*, Macmillan Inc., 1985.
HM Prison Service, *Regimes for Women*.
Home Office, *Gender and the Criminal Justice System*, HMSO, 1992.
– *Report of the Committee of Inquiry into Complaints about Ashworth Hospital*, (Cm 2028–1), HMSO, 1992.
Horder, J., *Provocation and Responsibility* Oxford University Press, 1992.
Humphries, J., 'The Referral of Women to Specialist Hospitals – Causes and Consequences', MSc dissertation, University of Surrey, 1991.
Jackson, W., 'The Influence of Social Factors on the Definition and Subsequent Treatment of Women Diagnosed as Mentally Ill', BA dissertation, Manchester Polytechnic, 1992.
Johnstone, L., 'Self-Harm', *Openmind*, April/May 1994.
Jones, M., 'Women Who Cut Themselves Up', *New Woman*, June 1993.
Jones, A., *Women Who Kill*, New York, Fawcett Crest, 1980.
Kennedy, H., *Eve Was Framed*, Chatto and Windus, 1992.
– Conference on Perspectives on Female Violence, St George's Medical School, 7–8 March 1991.

Kruttschnitt, C., 'Respectable Women and the Law', *The Sociological Quarterly*, 1982a.

– 'Women, Crime and Dependency', *British Journal of Criminology*, 1982b.

Lees, S., 'Lawyers' Work as Constitutive of Gender Relations', in Cain and Harrington (eds), *Lawyers in a Postmodern World*, 1994.

– 'Naggers, Whores and Libbers: Provoking Men to Kill', in Radford and Russell (eds), *Femicide*, 1992.

Liebling, H. and Chipchase, H., 'A Pilot Study on the Problem of Self-Injurious Behaviour in Women in Ashworth Hospital', *Division of Criminological and Legal Psychology Newsletter*, No. 35, October 1993.

Mama, A., *The Hidden Struggle. Statutory and Voluntary Sector Responses to Violence against Black Women in the Home*, London Race and Housing Research Unit, c/o The Runnymede Trust, 1989.

Mandaraka-Sheppard, A., *The Dynamics of Aggression in Women's Prisons in England*, Gower, 1986.

Marks, M.N. and Kumar, R., 'Infanticide in England and Wales', *Medicine, Science and the Law*, 33, 4, 1993.

Miedzian, M., *Boys Will be Boys: Breaking the Link between Masculinity and Violence*, Virago Press, 1992.

Miller, A., *For Your Own Good: the Roots of Violence in Child-Rearing*, Virago Press, 1987.

Mills, J., *Womanwords*, Virago Press, 1991.

Morris, A., *Women, Crime and Criminal Justice*, Basil Blackwell Ltd., 1987.

Morris, A. and Wilczynski, A., 'Rocking the Cradle', in Birch (ed.), *Moving Targets*, 1993.

National Association for the Care and Resettlement of Offenders (Nacro), *Fresh Start for Women Prisoners: the Implications of the Woolf Report for Women*, 1991.

– Briefing No. 33, *Women in Prison*.

– Briefing No. 91, *Women and Criminal Justice*.

Naylor, B., 'Women Who Kill. Images of Deviant Women: A Case Study', thesis submitted for MPhil in Criminology at Cambridge University, 1986–7.

Nicholson, J. *Men and Women: How Different are They?*, Oxford University Press, 1984.

Oakley, A., *Sex, Gender and Society*, Aldershot, Gower, 1985.

O'Donovan, K., 'Defences for Battered Women Who Kill', *Journal of Law and Society*, 18, 2, 1991.

Podvoll, E.M., 'Self-Mutilation within a Hospital Setting: a Study of

Identity and Social Compliance', *British Journal of Medical Psychology*, 1969, 42.

Potier, M., 'Giving Evidence: Women's Lives in Ashworth Maximum Security Psychiatric Hospital', *Feminism and Psychology*, Vol. 3(3), Sage, 1993.

— 'Patient care at Ashworth Hospital: Focusing on the Experiences of Women in the Institution', submission to the Committee of Inquiry into Complaints about Ashworth Hospital, 1992.

— 'A Preliminary Analysis, in Terms of Power, of the Issues Arising from the Treatment of Women in Conditions of Maximum Security', unpublished article, 1991.

Radford, J., 'Self-Preservation', *Rights of Women Bulletin*, Summer 1992.

Radford, J. and Mavolwane, S., 'We'll be Freeing All the Women', *Rights of Women Bulletin*, Spring 1993.

Radford, J. and Russell, D.E.H. (eds), *Femicide*, Open University Press, 1992.

Radford, L., 'Pleading for Time', in Birch (ed.), *Moving Targets*, 1993.

Rose, S., Lewontin, R.C. and Kamin L.J., *Not in Our Genes*, Penguin, 1990.

Sellars, C. and Liebling, H., 'Section 3 Patients: the "Non-Offenders"?', *Division of Criminological and Legal Psychology Newsletter*, 1988.

Special Hospitals Service Authority, *The Use of Seclusion and the Alternative Management of Disturbed Behaviour within the Special Hospitals*, SHSA, 1993.

Stevenson, P., 'Women in Special Hospitals', *Openmind*, October/November 1989.

Ussher, Jane M., *Women's Madness: Misogyny or Mental Illness?*, University of Massachusetts, 1992.

van der Kolk, B.A., Perry, J.C. and Herman, J.L., 'Childhood Origins of Self-Destructive Behavior', *American Journal of Psychiatry*, December 1991.

Wilczynski, A., 'Child-killing by parents: social, legal and gender issues', paper presented at the British Criminology conference at the University of Wales, Cardiff, 28–31 July 1993.

— 'A socio-legal study of parents who kill their children in England and Wales', PhD dissertation, University of Cambridge, 1993.

Williams, K., 'Factors Associated with Self-Mutilation', thesis submitted for M.Clin.Psychol., University of Liverpool, 1989.

Wilson, M. and Daly, M., 'Till Death Us Do Part', in Radford and Russell (eds), *Femicide*, 1992.

Useful Addresses

BRISTOL CRISIS SERVICE FOR WOMEN
PO Box 654
Bristol BS99 1XH
Tel: 0117 925 1119

HOWARD LEAGUE FOR PENAL REFORM
708 Holloway Road
London N19 3NL
Tel: 0171 281 7722

JUSTICE FOR WOMEN
The London Justice for Women Collective
55 Rathcoole Gardens
London N8 9NE

NATIONAL ASSOCIATION FOR THE CARE AND RESETTLEMENT
OF OFFENDERS (NACRO)
169 Clapham Road
London SW9 0PU
Tel: 0171 582 6500

PRISON REFORM TRUST
59 Caledonian Road
London N1 9BU
Tel: 0171 278 9815

RIGHTS OF WOMEN
52–54 Featherstone Street
London EC1Y 8RT
Tel: 0171 251 6575/6/7

SOUTHALL BLACK SISTERS
  52 Norwood Road
  Southall
  Middlesex UB2 4DW
  Tel: 0181 571 9595

WOMEN IN PRISON (WIP)
  36 Aberdeen Studios
  22 Highbury Grove
  London N5 2EA
  Tel: 0171 226 5879

WOMEN IN SPECIAL HOSPITALS (WISH)
  25 Horsell Road
  London N5 1XL
  Tel: 0171 700 6684

Index